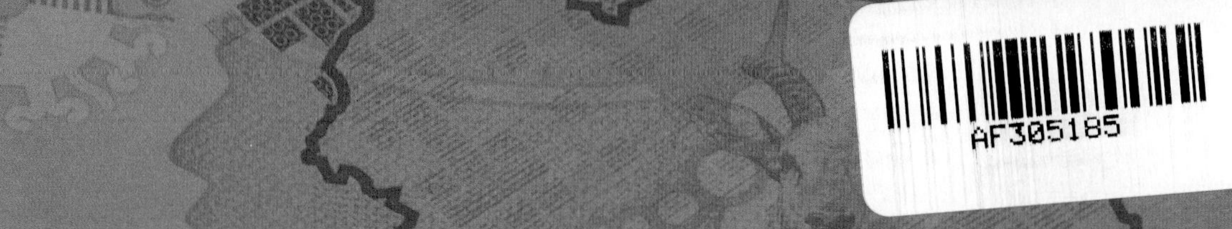
BANK OF UGANDA
AN 7965988
LEGAL TENDER FOR ONE THOUSAND SHILLINGS
FOR BANK OF UGANDA
GOVERNOR
0° Latitude EQUATOR

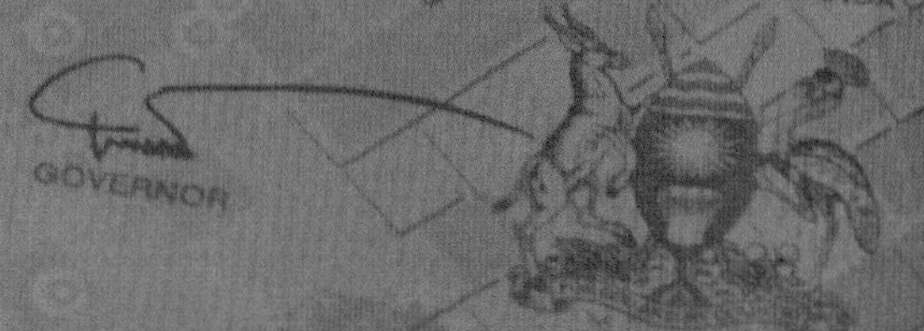
1000
ONE THOUSAND

K OF UGANDA

Acaye Kerunen

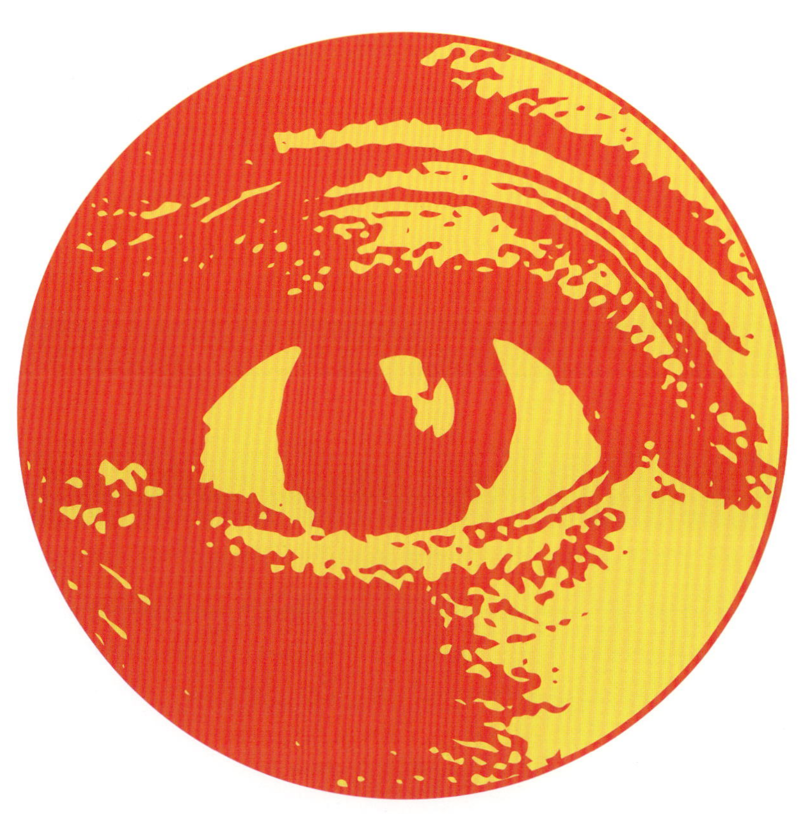

Collin Sekajugo

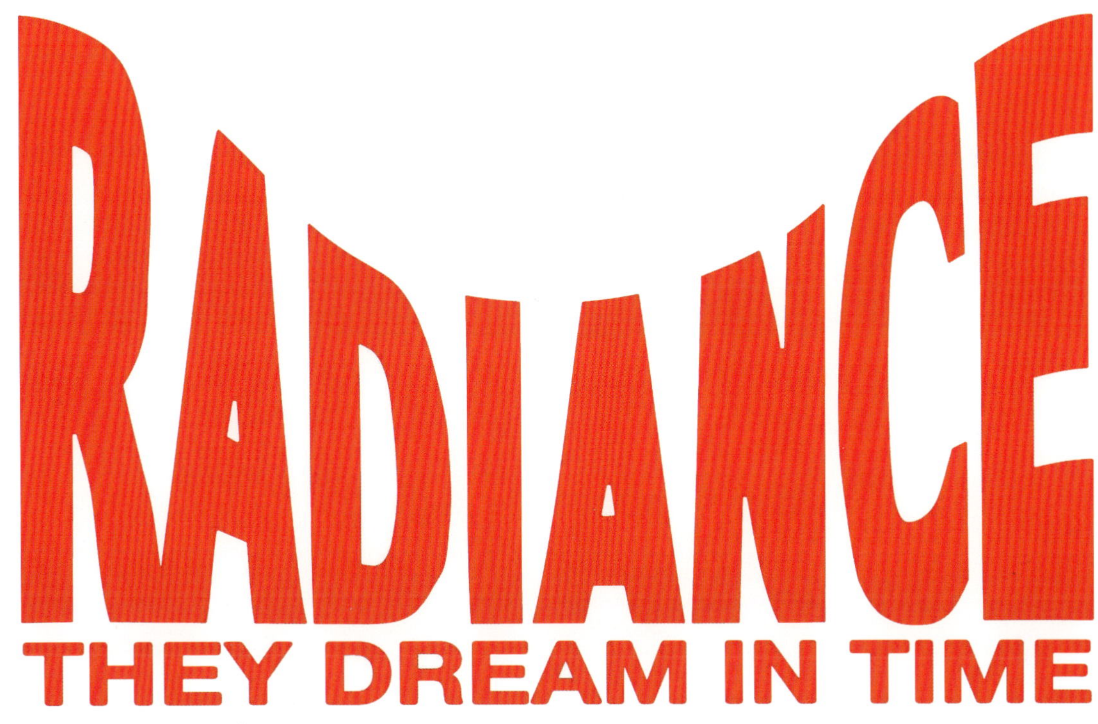

RADIANCE
THEY DREAM IN TIME

edited by
Shaheen Merali

Uganda National Pavilion
at the 59th International
Art Exhibition
La Biennale di Venezia 2022

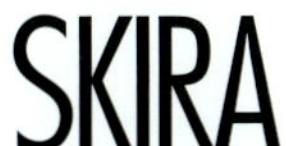

Catalogue design
Alexander Palmestål

Editorial contribution
Shaheen Merali
Acaye Kerunen
Collin Sekajugo

Editorial coordination
Bjorn Stern

Translations
Anna Artale
Fabio Scrivanti

First published in Italy in 2022
by Skira editore S.p.A.
Palazzo Casati Stampa
via Torino 61
20123 Milano
Italy
www.skira.net

Printed and bound in Italy.
First edition

ISBN: 978-88-572-4818-9

Distributed in the world by
Thames and Hudson Ltd., 181A
High Holborn, London WC1V 7QX,
United Kingdom.

Note to the Reader
No linguistic or editorial changes
have been made to the text out
of respect to the author's stylistic
choices. Typesetting, spelling and
punctuation conform to the style of
this book except where the author's
use is intentional.

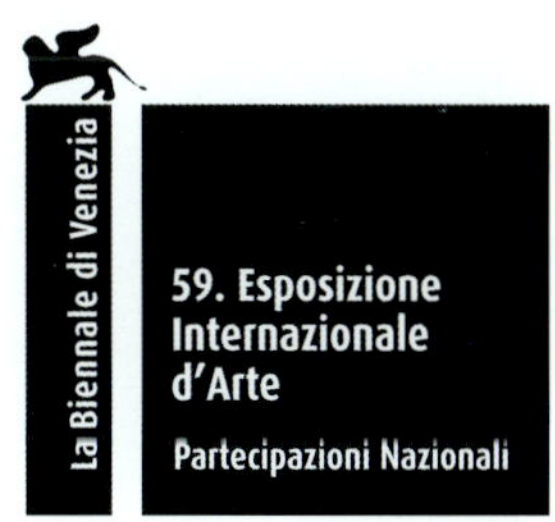

Sponsored by

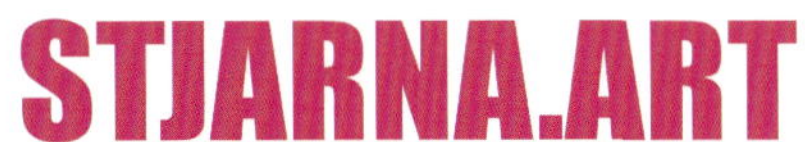

Supported by

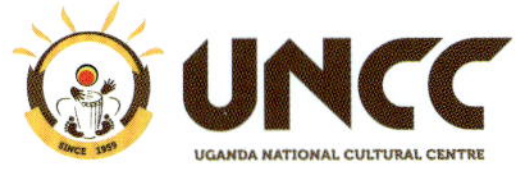

ARTLAND

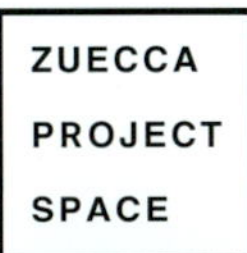

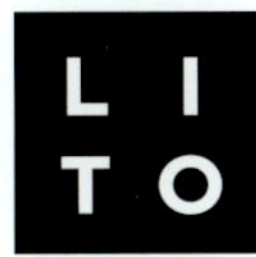

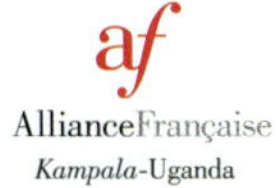

VENICE
ART FACTORY

Uganda National Pavilion
at the 59th International
Art Exhibition
La Biennale di Venezia 2022

Commissioner
Mme Juliana Akoryo Naumo,
Uganda Ministry of Gender, Labour and
Social Development

Curator
Shaheen Merali

Artists
Acaye Kerunen
Collin Sekajugo

Palazzo Palumbo Fossati
San Marco 2597, Venezia

23 April – 27 November 2022

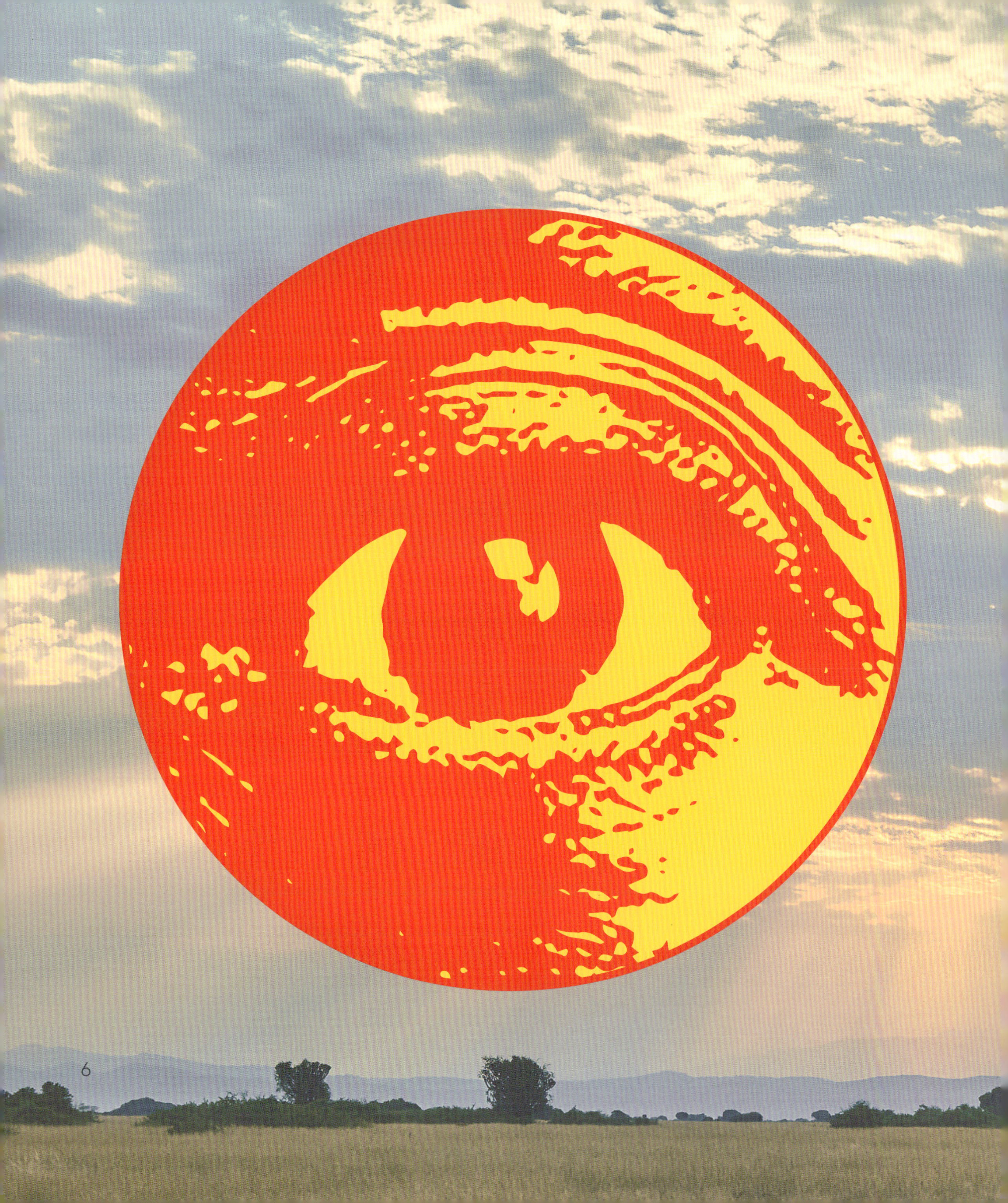

We are thrilled to inaugurate the Uganda Pavilion at the 59th Venice Biennale with Acaye Kerunen and Collin Sekajugo. Their paintings and installation work, steeped in social activism, are placing Ugandan contemporary art into the international spotlight. Uganda's unique cultures and talents will be showcased through their works as emblems of the rich diversity of the country, which consists of over sixty-five indigenous communities.

As the mother Ministry of Gender, Labour and Social Development (MGLSD), Uganda National Cultural Centre (UNCC), and the arts and creative industry at large, we applaud the artists and Stjarna.art for this timely collaboration. I look forward to seeing the enormous networking, collaborations and transformations that this initiative will bring about for Uganda.

I therefore invite you to visit the Uganda National Pavilion in Venice, as well as our beautiful Uganda as a tourism and arts destination of the world.

Juliana Akoryo Naumo
Uganda Ministry of Gender, Labour and Social Development
For God and My Country

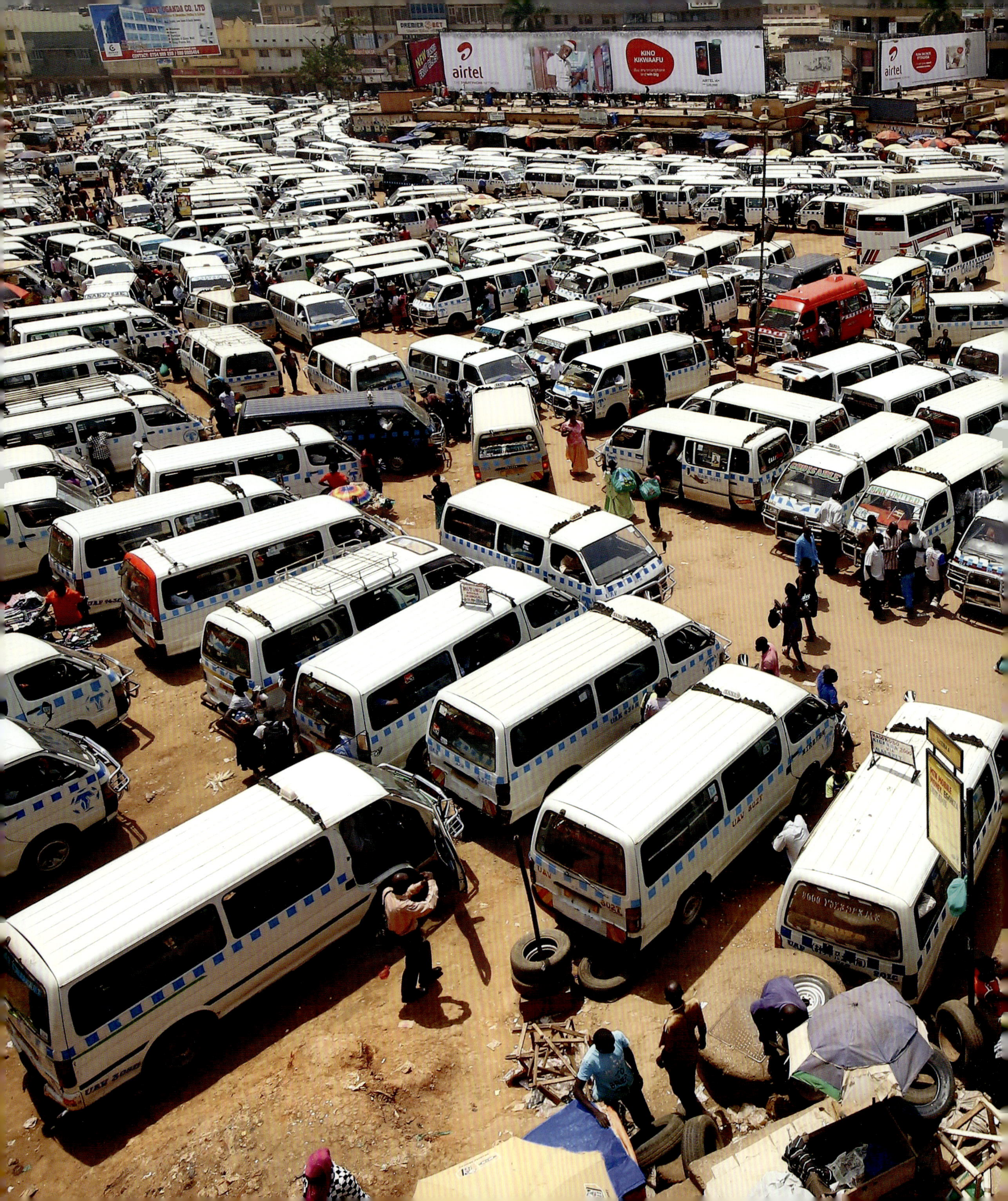
PREMIER BET
airtel
KINO
KIKWAAFU
airtel

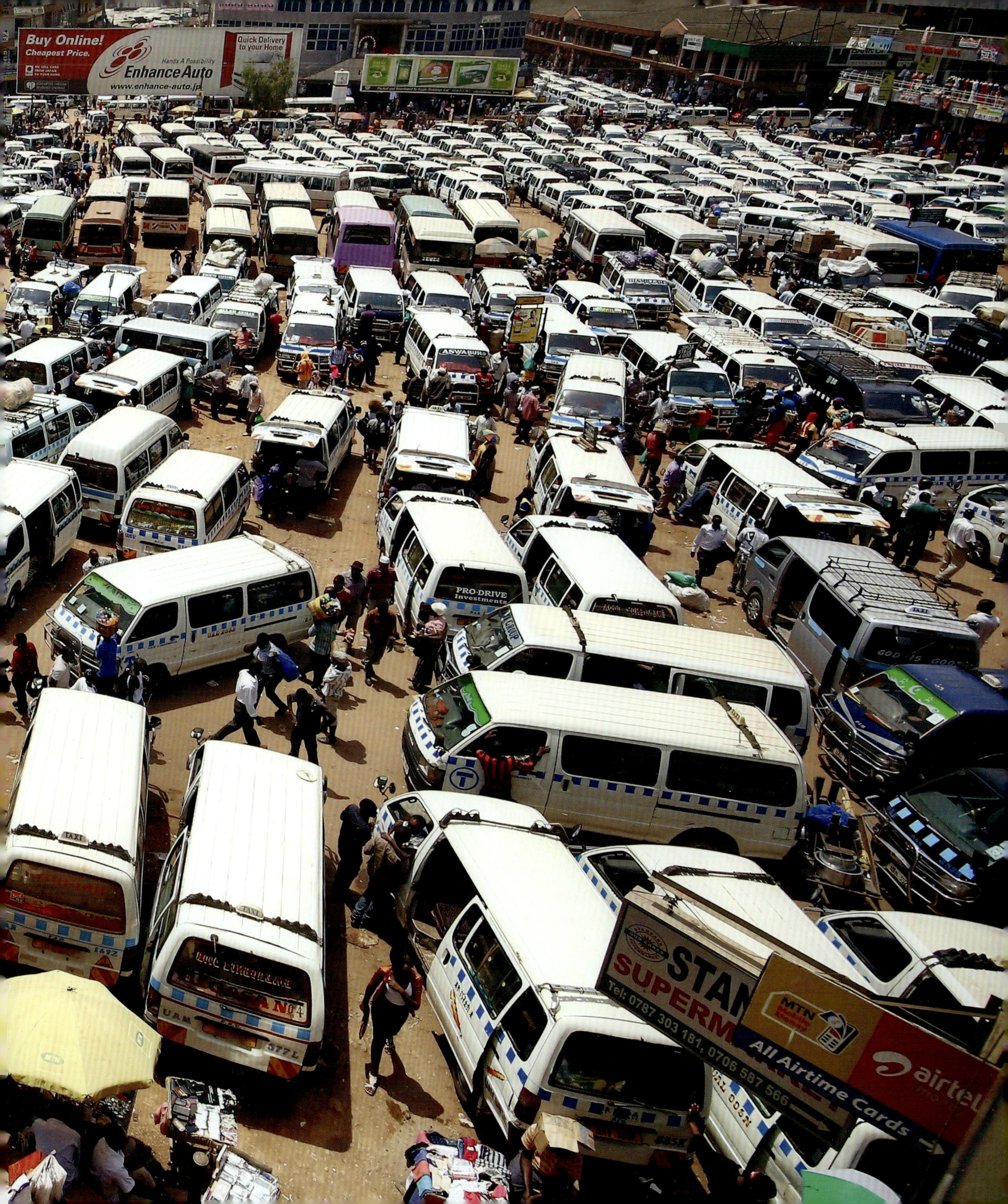

Buy Online!
Cheapest Price.
Enhance Auto
Hands A Possibility
www.enhance-auto.jp
Quick Delivery
to your Home
PRO-DRIVE
Investments
STAN
SUPERM
Tel: 0787 303 181, 0706 587 566
MTN
All Airtime Cards
airtel
GOD IS GOOD

Radiance, They Dream in Time (Rearranged)

Shaheen Merali

Introduction

In the whirlwind of the Venice Biennale, two artists from Uganda and based in Kampala, Acaye Kerunen and Collin Sekajugo, present their work in an exhibition entitled *Radiance, They Dream in Time* at the Palazzo Palumbo Fossati. For every nation presenting for the first time in this global gathering, this is a historic moment and Uganda's inaugural pavilion at the Venice Biennale is a fertile ground in which to present the artists' ideas to further understand the semantic intelligence of Ugandan traditions and its modernity.

The plethora of exhibitions in the various sections of the Venice Biennale, often emerging from within its axis, set in the Giardini and the Arsenale, extends its mission into Venice's celebrated narrow lanes and the canals. Here exhibitions, curators and artists summon narratives that continue in the evolving life of Venetians whose own heritage to the Silk Route and immersion in the human dilemma of the Black plague led to European enlightenment. The sinking city yields tremendously, often with triangulated relationships to this past and, in this puzzling time of human history, the convenors of the Venice Biennale are requesting its artists and curators to embrace the city and allow visitors to experience the world's diverse forms as somewhere between a mirror, a document and the return to enchantment.

The Uganda Pavilion in the city on the waters

The Biennale's celebrated collateral section and the National Pavilions outside of the Giardini and Arsenale independently occupy vestiges of Venetian public space for the duration of the biennale. These events are charged to present critical positionality based on conceptual precepts set by the artistic director. Often these unique events and exhibitions combine the vertiginous influences of the famous city on the waters, mapping and tracing around the Adriatic laguna. Being outside of the high walls and gated entrances of the Giardini and the Arsenale allows curators to define exhibition-making differently. Often everything melds into its extramundane vicinity and offers a point of double attraction, one that comes to define being in Venice to showcase the world as an important part of its cultural history. The prosaic presentation within the city further contends with the reality and rhythms of neighbourhoods allowing for a completely different inflexion to those who exhibit in the structural coherence and stability of its main two venues, the Giardini and Arsenale. The Uganda National Pavilion is presented in the understated splendour of Palazzo Palumbo Fossati, an unassuming building in the path of the

millions of tourists who roam unsystematically and unregulated in a postmodern path between culture and consumption. It is these very heterogeneities and multiplicities inside the city that makes the Uganda National Pavilion in the Palazzo Palumbo Fossati a suitable place to celebrate the earliest model of a global art event for a country's inaugural pavilion. The exhibition *Radiance, They Dream in Time* will mark the moment 'We are here' within the city, as have many African and Asian countries. The curator and artistic director of the 56th Venice International Art Exhibition, Okwui Enwezor, called one of his sections the Garden of Disorder. To have remained outside the realm of disorder, the Giardini, the central section which remains marked by European nations, and increasingly crammed by Eurospheric privilege, has a demographic linked to capitalist expansion, or those who enjoy proximity to it including settler colonialists. Coming out of Venice centrism, the Ugandan pavilion is another witness that has come to occupy this 'global' iterative process known for its expansion of hemispheric perspectives that the 59th Venice International Art Exhibition
is further embracing.

Venice and freedoms beyond ourselves

Uganda is a territory where human life had been compromised and governed by Germany (1885–1916) and the British (1916–61) administrations; a persecution over eight decades that haunts its very geopolitical psyche. The flight towards independence involved walking back to humanity, a route only accessible by walking on multiple tightropes, clearing previous ideological constraints and imagining a national movement that would lead to national liberation.

The ever-growing library of resources, critical analyses, scholarship, varied approaches and interpretive or creative responses, has benefited the world and Ugandans. The variety of humanitarian, educational and 'development projects' reach their 60th anniversary in 2024, comprising a veritable library of experts and expertise whose idiosyncratic voices remain in an unconscious assimilation of ideas and knowledge. Still 'development' remains somewhere between a goal and an inquiry, caught between many philosophical perspectives, and yet everything, including truth, remains according to Oscar Wilde "rarely pure and never simple". The tendency to perceive nation and race (Fanon 1961)[1] has effectively plagued the independent statehood of many southern world countries, their striving for a 'palingenesis', a rebirth, a new national community (after colonialism) has been usurped by the explicit identification of race and nation as biological and epistemological – an illegitimacy that affects the relationships with change and the true support of allies and intentions.

In the exhibition *Radiance, They Dream in Time* there is an array of artwork in which the placement of the works softens the gaps between craft and fine art traditions. Both artists' works are placed within reach of their promise as a universal language, stirring imaginations of a regenerative culture. Kerunen and Sekajugo's organising principles serve as a common tool through which personal and communal social status are explored.

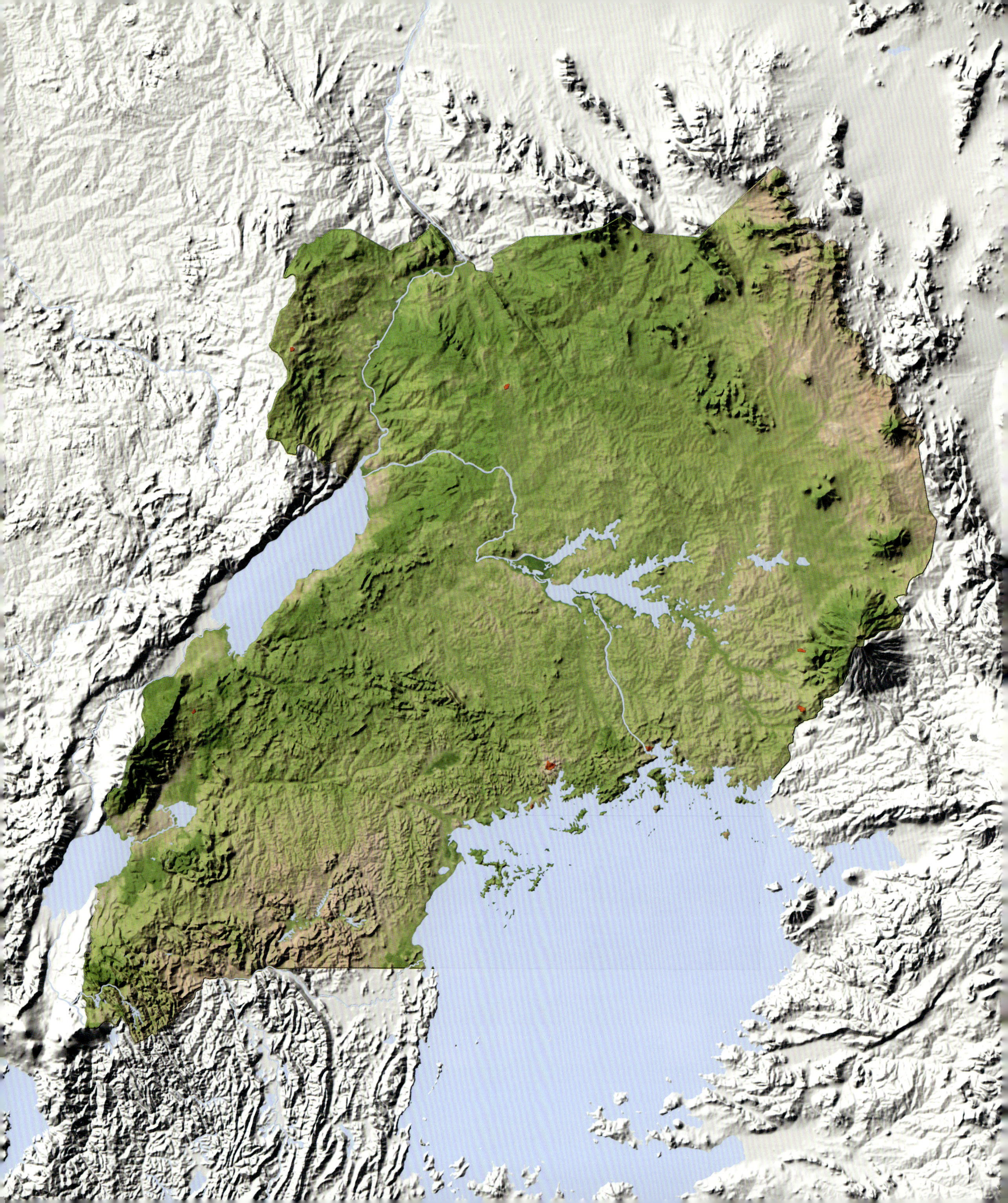

In a porous way, all the six spaces of viewing are curated to contextualise the potential to understand intellectually as well as emotively. By calling for the viewer's creative ability to combine and find their way through the symbolic symbioses offered by the artist or the presentation, the curatorial emphasises a platform for the cultural validation of Uganda's sense of inheritance. In many of the works are remnants of commercial symbols, abstracted from the management of land, its leases that are the historic colonial condition of Ugandan history. They sit side by side with a purpose-driven generation of young entrepreneurs whose traumatic experience of flourishing youth are presented for the audience to peruse in the numerous rooms and to contemplate the affects.[2]

Collin Sekajugo

The Call Centre Room by Sekajugo is a place to analyse the double materiality[3] of consumerism, a condition that has been necessitated by the formation of online services; a room for fallen champions, who deal with recurring complaints of that which is seemingly broken. Misinformation and the dysfunctional are part of the turnaround strategies to keep the users revolving through the call centres' lines of control. They stipulate, guide and make the consumers' ignorance and anxiety apparent. This sounds like a therapy centre in which a youthful creed happily embraces matters of little consequence which are always underlined by some sort of urgency. The customer and their personal finance are eased away from the foreboding hardship caused by slight discomfort or failed service.
The extraordinary workforce of the call centre is taught to identify with the callers, to create a cosy, chatty environment for the ease in which knowledge, skills, ideas and technologies are found, solutions that allow naysayers to walk back to the products inspired or less desperate and to then continue the conversation elsewhere.

The paintings based on the call centre explore expressions that become surface signifiers from the passive control that meanders in the form of information supplied by the service industry. Sekajugo's strategy of portraits which speak of the horrific backwaters central to understanding the digital plantation, defined as "a machinism rather than a structure".[4] Sekajugo manages to present the endless and, at times, fluid ways certain notions of subjectivity are cobbled together to steer the megamachine of the age of information.

The glare of lights that make teeth orange and blue lights that pulsate inside cadavers' of technology form a case study by Sekajugo that are associative narrations of spaces submerged within our mundane encounters. These types of online outposts signify the tenacity of Southern world youth in search for an equality of life. They embody access for those with contracts and standing orders whose urgent need is to rectify a technical hitch. The *Call Centre* portraits, like the stock image and identity-hacking works by Sekajugo, are unfettered in their questioning of the operational sustainability of westernised order, norms and capital advantage.

Sekajugo suggests, to act on observation, wherein aesthetic boundaries are complimented by the violence of colonial epistemes, is like the high noon sun where there is a high degree of directness. To fabricate complicated interconnections through colour variations of the palette for skin tones requires a further understanding of how complex experiments and experiences of contemporary artists from West and Central Africa become centred in global arts and auction houses. The recent Call centre portraits are subtle mind-games that Sekajugo creates, as a response to the corporate interest in African culture. The recent interest in contemporary arts from Africa has provoked feelings, not limited to the political, but one brimming with the excitement of opportunities when the centres of art's existence crosses over the ravines of difference.

Sekajugo's experience of subjects intriguingly slips between postcolonial relationalities and nightmares of the nested technologies of subjugation. Many of the imagined sitters for Sekajugo's portraits are reminiscent of German expressionism with their zombie-like Gothic gaze spuriously gazing out of bespoke wallpapered dimly lit rooms. The call centre is part of the Western order for digital nomads travelling global circus, keeping abreast of economic opportunities in their ubiquitous search for cheap labour in the southern world.
Sekajugo translates the international corporation's school of mannerisms that facilitates 24-hour Q&As or FAQs.

The portraits represent the eternal desire for the end of the nightshift (poverty) and (student loans). In the end of the world scenario palpable operators in the southern world will still serve customers as they have since the advent of 7–11 time zones. Alongside IT/ITeS outsourcing locations in the world, including the southern Indian city of Bangalore and the Hispanic bilingual call centres in cities such as Puerto Vallarta, counterparts of young graduates recruited and trained with pseudo mid-Atlantic accents guide customers to successfully install the latest upgrade for their apps or console the loss of life savings by mitigating phishing (online scamming).

The portraits by Sekajugo propose the mental anguish of the call centres' youthful hopefuls, at the edge of their patience after clearing the mess of global investments in the wilderness of bonds, equities and e-commerce across the digital doughnut. Far away from the Silicon Valley, the grumpy customer's query becomes yet another burden for this generation, clearing the digital fear for millions who are collectively forced to operate in a digital jungle of environmental destruction in our over complicated lives.

Acaye Kerunen

Collective spaces which allow the probable sharing of the same concerns bring us to the group of fabric weavers that Kampala based multivalent artist, Acaye Kerunen, works with. The encoded meaning in the traditional craft has evolved in baskets, handbags and other domestic objects routinely found in households, including floor mats, food baskets or table placemats. Kerunen takes each ubiquitous object as a project, examining references that are embedded over generations of women making craft.

Kerunen's understanding, across the wide range of vernacular diagrams, sophisticated patterns and constellations, draws on regions, tribal spaces and neighbourhoods. Kerunen has archived the differences and nuances that provide her increasingly with a space in which to develop collaborations. Shapes of decoloniality break into the space of representation where the normativity of urban life and the self in the ever-expanding modernity of westernised forms have entered as trashed tourist arts.

Disrupting the hierarchical purpose made for another class, another race of women from natural fibres and natural dyes, Kerunen deconstructs the carefully woven spatial and visually complex objects to recreate uncompassionate collages, sculptures and wall-based installations. Kerunen challenges public perception and refusing expectations by producing artwork "through weaving work by artisans who are women and their stories … how their products tell stories beyond the utilitarian objects that they eventually become … an intricate part of (Uganda's) manifestation".[5]

Kerunen's careful understanding of these narrations expands as well as challenges the taken-for-granted nature of the historical and contemporary place of work by women in Uganda. Kerunen disallows a discriminatory view, unified by bitter experiences of the binary where craft exists only in opposition to fine art. Her relationship to cultural practices is to build from a visual culture of a subterranean independent sector that detests categorisation.

Kerunen's plight in making these works revisits the feminists' phenomena of exploring women's narratives, often abandoned in the native privilege that resurfaced after independence. The actively re-imagining of the sovereign state negated the pain of mothers and sisters in patriarchal policy by supporting unequal pay and poor labour rights. The artist's interest in certain techniques and designs, particularly the ones developed in the exhibition, are created whilst its makers talk to each other, sing or chant together. In sharing and in radical listening, Kerunen realised how the lived experiences of these women, defined every stitch and knot. The very place of materials like Mikeka rolls, Biibo, woven rings and bikapuà re-shaped into non-functional pieces assumed conceptual meanings and drew on aesthetics of form, shape and texture of engaging their planet.
In the materiality of raffia or sisal, Kerunen and her views of classic feminism were redefined beyond the loss of sovereignty. If "feminist work is justice work",[6] Kerunen argues that justice

is seen in the most basic relation to the earth, its produce, its ability to sustain human growth and fertility. Property, in her case, is a launchpad to understanding value in relationship to the conflicts that independence has inherited. Many prevailing systems of violence are part of the spectrum of independence that need abolition rather than to be headed by liberal politics. In dropping classic feminism's conflicting interest in usurping capitalist leadership with liberated women, Kerunen argues the need to negate the violence of liberal capitalism. For Kerunen the white tourist gaze automatically refers to climate crisis due to its priorities, goals, history and place of privilege.

Kerunen and Sekajugo

For the many questions that both artists are agitating towards, they have provided diverse answers. Both Kerunen and Sekajugo's desire is followed by the creation of a platform through which the Ugandan sphere can be recatalysed, to reorientate and depart from games about powers pursuing coalition and mentorship with alternative systems. For both artists, other artists and craftspeople are part of the lobby aiming to mediate on Uganda as their subject matter. Recently, relationships between artists' groups and coalitions have increased as have their concerns about contributing back to the world of the arts, as well as the world that the arts has evolved out of; the reparative imaginings of life lived in liberal capitalism. Kerunen's increasing use of traditional knowledge, including working with women who forage roots, leaves and berries from the jungle in seasons and with ancestral knowledge, provides sustainable practices. Sekajugo has consistently worked with barkcloth and a concept called Kyambaro, one that is based on the design histories of Luganda or Uganda and Kinyarwanda or Rwanda.

Both artists have taken the opportunity to introduce in the inaugural pavilion Ugandan aesthesis, the elementary awareness of the stimulation of a country that links East Africa to Central Africa. Both regions have changed enormously; how much and how little has been altered can be evaluated through the work of the two artists' singular pieces or installed in rooms as series. Recent events and global discourse of the past two decades have impacted both these artists' ideas and the space and speed of consumerism is evident in their work. Moreover, the way the artists manifest the place of decoloniality allows the audience to understand common colonial and post- independence experiences affecting African lives
as local aesthesis.

The result is an increasingly hybrid materiality allowing both to research and smarten their palettes. Arguably both are producing powerful and nuanced statements, mindful of a Ugandan heritage. They dream together in time, as both painting and sculptural traditions advocate a holistic approach to the twentieth-first century global canon.

Part II

"Easily imported, but poorly translated."[7]

One of the key goals to be addressed in Venice was arriving at a transitory understanding of the artists' work and their critique of the art field for its audience. Likewise, it is important to consider the role of the artist and the curator in informing contemporary discussions of human nature and society reconstituted in the inner dynamics and role of culture. It has often been argued that, to retain a high degree of connectivity and circulation in a globalising world, it is important to consider both the circulation of forms and the forms of circulation, and to evolve a theory that relates the two. In this respect the Uganda Pavilion provides multiple entry points for the artists to address the place of ideas and forms circulating in art globally. The following considerations are based on a key question that rose at the time of an informal talk I undertook with Sanaa Gateja, wherein he raised a defiant question that remains to be considered and given the permissible attention it requires.

"Who is an artist?"[8]

Kerunen had already written one joyous entry on her social media account: "My entry onto this world stage is a fact and factor of time; time that I have spent mostly away from many eyes through the years, learning, unlearning, deconstructing, remaking… Well, I am here now. I am here to stay in my light and, to follow the light of my season and timings".[9]

I would suggest an artist spends time rethinking and interrogating, as well as examining the subtle relation to subject, object and existing complex historical entanglements. Kerunen and Sekajugo have enshrined in their work particular areas of interest which we have partially began to discuss. Arguably both artists are interested in the place of art as currently comprehended or expressed by differently positioned people in the history of art and design or art and craft histories.

Both artists have a varied base of interest including facilitating art and design/craft to expedite their differences in their own organising and studio practises. Kerunen and Sekajugo have a key interest in design culture of Uganda in which both have found and consequently show its relevance to the contemporary lived realities of its subjects.
Their response is neither monocultural nor is it mono-traditional bias. Instead, in removing the subordinated process we move outside of the given confines into an embeddednessinto visual culture which is effectual in its discourse. Their simple request remains for the democratisation of conversations between Ugandan visual culture and exhibition-making as a form of cultural activism so to influence the place for resourcing ideas within sustainable tribal and regional sensorial fields.
In the Western realm the arts are generally led by singularly minded artists whilst designers are guided by the character of guidelines and technologies of briefs, plans and production. In

both cases these artists are dismantling the subordinated status of African traditions assigned by dominant groups including museums, curators, art critics and art education. Kerunen and Sekajugo come from a lineage of multiple experiments carried out in the Southern World artistic community who have established workshops with craftsmen, designers and folk artists to create an artistic pedagogy. These attempts are not perceived as revivalism nor progressive but rather the continuation of traditions as living knowledge, sometimes aptly entitled as living traditions. For the inaugural Uganda Pavilion, the work by Kerunen and Sekajugo provides an exhibition as an experience in which to mediate on living traditions through the complex interaction of motifs and human values presented as the mutable realities of ancient divisions. Professor Mahmood Mamdani from Makerere University has suggested colonial modernity can be similarly effective:"After the British took over in the early 20th century, they politicised ethnic boundaries, reconstituting cultural difference as tribal difference. The inheritors of this colonial mentality govern as the British did, not as their ancestors did."[10]

At the time of the Architectural Biennale, 2014, in a talk with the architect Rem Koolhaas and curator Hans Ulrich Obrist, held outside the Swiss Pavilion in the Giardini, Okwui Enwezor suggested the exhibition could be viewed as "an object".[11] The fact that this particular emphasis of exhibition as an object emerged out of the Venice Biennale, with its multiple conversations and references drawn from its rotating programme, speaks to the importance of ideas of Venice as a meditative probe which draws on diversity. To dismantle conflicting states of cultural difference as the logic of indirect colonial rule, artists need to advance decoloniality, "characterized by a relation to the real (to earth, world and ourselves)".[12]

Moreover, at a time of multiple impacts and the gradual demise of political stability, both artists are manifesting themselves by advancing post- independence experiences affecting African lives and aesthesis. Building and contributing from Uganda, by assembling networks they undo the divisions that forced separations between epistemologies, genres and intellectual engagement. This condition has previously hindered caring and honouring by confining experiences to Western modernity to produce global realities. In the period of the Venice Biennale for approximately seven months, the exhibitions maintain the sphere of influence for the objects and archives as a point of multiple enquiries that emerge in the year. The sustained enquiry about representation of the extreme weather, inequality crises, extractive histories and fuel poverty is part of a roster of a global audience reignited or triggered by its own experiences. The institutional record of any public space, including the Venice Biennale, is now more than ever before trusted to align its resources to explore the profound shifts in thinking by evoking (and provoking) further forms of address and creative as well as distinct lines of inquiry. Yet the "staggering amounts involved for countries taking up a stand at the Venice Biennale has been the bane of most African countries, restricting Africa's active participation at the Venice Biennale. Apart from a few sporadic appearances, African countries have been largely missing at the Venice Biennale".[13]

Since its first International Art Exhibition treatise in 1895, each iteration of the Venice Biennale persistently ruptures and dismantles former enquiries, as well as bringing through the city an arborescent model of fascinating artistic enquiries. The Biennale exists as a multiple point of entry into the art history orbit; each iteration provides a contemporaneous focus through fascinating curatorial and artistic contemplation and invention. For the audience who flock to the Venice Biennales (Films, Art, Architecture and Dance) who walk miles, often circumventing the official venue, to finally enter the exhibit, the performance, the screening, or the seminar tabulating the artists and viewing of the artwork or event, can never be underestimated. Dan Karlholm, Professor and Head of Art History at Södertörn University in Stockholm outlines *All the World's Futures*, the 56th Venice Biennale (2015) central theme and exhibition curated by Okwui Enwezor as "an exhibition that is summarized by three keywords: disorder, liveness and capital".[14]

Of course, these three words are extracted from the curator's text that summarises the exhibition's intent with the summative *All* in the title: "*All the World's Futures* is informed by a layer of three intersecting *Filters*, namely *Garden of Disorder, Liveness: On Epic Duration* and *Reading Capital*. The three *Filters*, in their iterative choreography across the exhibition, represent a constellation of para-meters, which will be touched upon in order to imagine and realize a diversity of practices".[15] There are filters and preconceptions present in every exhibition-making, conditions that exhaust the very breath out of curatorial intention. The para-meters that Enwezor refers to remains central to Kerunen and Sekajugo's diverse and palimpsest's work in *Radiance, They Dream in Time* of a Ugandan world returning to loss of heritage and trust as most African subjects were imposed by an "international system (which) provided different norms and rationalizations, as well as alternative opportunities for African actors in the colonies, continuity was nonetheless more commonly experienced and dominated societal currents more so than the shifts".[16]

The Post-war Colonial Administration (Africa) set up in the inter-war years between 1914–18 seems long ago, yet many scholars even in the 1960s and 1970s have pointed out the mandate set up of "indirect rule" and *mise en valeur*[17] for imperial continuities for international administration. One has to only examine the role of France to its former colonies as a moral osmosis maintaining a hegemonic foothold in Francophone Africa. Seen through these frames, the Venice Biennale acts as a system to both defend a mode of production (of objects and exhibitions) and "build on those emancipatory and/or creative futures that lie dormant within the many diversely conflictual presences of the world" (Karlholm 2015). Interestingly, Enwezor separates parameters into a hyphenated word, para-meter.
In Italian the word para relates to the warding off, from the Latin 'parare' to make ready. It figures in parachute, parasol, parapet, etc., as well as parasite. Para can be used for the "defence, protection against; that which protects from" and parameter defines a system or sets the conditions of its operation.

The exhibition as an object is both an osmosis and for African artists and artists from former colonies the desire to consider the intrinsic contradictions of intimate dialogues. To consider one such ongoing dialogue, we must consider the 58th Venice Art Biennale, where the inaugural Nigeria Pavilion presented the work by Victor Ehikhamenor, who has since had a tremendous presence in events organised in a number of countries. These included several contested debates, one of which was held at Jesus College at the University of Cambridge, over the site of the college benefactor Tobias Rustat's connections to slavery. Ehikhamenor's recent installation *Still Standing* at St Paul's Cathedral in London (Feb. 2022) is a tapestry image of the oba, or king, of Benin made from Rosary beads. *Still Standing*, acts as a rebuttal to the legacy of "Harry Holdsworth Rawson, whose bronze and marble memorial has been installed in the cathedral's crypt since 1913. Rawson was instrumental in not only the punitive expedition in Benin City, but a number of other highly controversial 19th-century military campaigns including the Second Opium War in China".[18] In an interview with Kabir Jhala published on 17 February 2022 in *The Art Newspaper* the artist stated: "Not to believe in full restitution is for me not believe in full justice", he says. "Any country or kingdom or state asking for what has been looted from their ancestral land should be obliged without long story. We must now shift from 'retain and explain' to what I call 'return and explain … add[ing] contemporary artists to the conversation so it is clear to the world that African artists who started making works post-colonialism didn't emerge from a vacuum."[19]

These types of assertions have been part of artists' research in Africa and many parts of the Southern world. It is common practice to use often controversial and misrepresented truths which include the restitution of cultural artefacts as located in the base of Sekajugo's use of stock imagery to stalk the foundational legacy of whiteness. Photography has a particular place with a particular ability that reverses the gaze implicating both the viewer and the maker. The particularity of technologies of viewing and yet not seeing is part of the box of tricks for the canon and Western imperial aesthetics. Artists from the diaspora have often presented evidence of the best examples of how political Black art can be created through the chequered history of Western imperialism as the vanishing point of its canon. The strange relationship to the Benin bronzes has its roots in Western aesthetics for it presents "a peculiar sensation, this double-consciousness, this sense of always looking at one's self through the eyes of others, of measuring one's soul by the tape of a world that looks on in amused contempt and pity".[20]

The Benin bronzes are spectacular representations, from the thirteenth century onwards by artists, in this case by the Edo people from Benin. Their formal realisation as portraits and the method in which they have been created are unsurpassable. Heritage held as hostage is part of the colonial arrangement that often relocates the global historical record of kingdom and civilisations to their museum and royal collections.

What interests me as an artist-curator is the place of the artist in the political world. The octogenarian South African poet and artist, Pitika Ntuli, associates the act of creativity, in relationship to cultural experience, as an impulse that is provoked by destruction. African culture and landscape are still transmitted through colonial exploit and pillages which trigger the artist as "the creative act is a titanic battle between flesh and spirit. Each artwork is a diversion of the flesh, the body. Each time the artist dies, a new work is born, or rather the opposite: each time a work of art is born the artist dies a little. A little death invokes a greater desire to live and thus creates another artwork. When the artist dies finally, she continues to live through her offspring – her children and her artworks".[21]

As Sekajugo and Kerunen have allowed us to contemplate over-hauling the system by relocating historical doubts and the locus of 'facts'. Through artistic independence wrapped and led by personal and impersonal relationship "attuned to the cracks and disjunctures we sense but may not yet be able to articulate in relation to the things we think we know well".[22]

In terms of the 2,000 bronze and wooden objects recently repatriated more than a century later, Cosme Houegbe Lo Behanzin, great grandson of King Behazin, commented: "We didn't have books, but we had these objects, these are the objects that told our story before they were taken from us".[23] A further focus organised for the Beninese was to invite them "to discover the second part of the exhibition, where 34 contemporary Beninese artists present around a hundred works". Collectively the recent exhibitions by contemporary artists from the African continent escalate the recovery of these stolen works, moving towards change with positive benefits from contemporary problem-solving of Africa's significant heritage through contemporary artists' efforts.

The intentions of the inaugural Uganda Pavilion at the 59th Art Exhibition La Biennale di Venezia 2022 were made possible by the work of the first curator from Africa Okwui Enwezor as well as the reconfiguration of his concerns, addressed by the artistic director of the 59th La Biennale di Venezia, Cecilia Alemani, whose considered interest in this transformative period is suggestive of a further para-meter in the remapping of "subjectivities, hierarchies, and anatomies".[24]

Alemani has placed the witnesses, centring the testimonies of formerly subjectivities whose site in this planetary convergence has become a necessity. These subjectivities had remained absent in the cosmopolitan elite hierarchies that overlooked the Southern world perspectives. The indigenous communities in the northern world were deemed of little relevance and struggled to intervene in the Western assault on planetary resources.
In the reconvening of a planet hurtling towards the extinction of multiple species and inhabitations, a brokered space in which to overcome the coronavirus pandemic and the rise of racial justice has become an existential battle over history. This a moment to partly salvage the remains left by white achievement and white glory signified as colonialisation that yielded mass extraction and the preoccupation with power. The first Prime Minister of the independent Democratic Republic of the Congo (then Republic of the Congo) was Patrice Émery Lumumba, who played a significant role in the transformation of ideological structure of pan-Africanism and African nationalism, leading the Congolese Nationalist Movement (CNM) from 1958 until his assassination in 1962 after independence from Belgium.

Lumumba's last letter to his wife Pauline Lumumba stated many of the facts that remain pertinent to all Africans in the struggle for the continents' independence and independent thinking. "Neither brutal assaults, nor cruel mistreatment, nor torture have ever led me to beg for mercy, for I prefer to die with my head held high, unshakable faith and the greatest confidence in the destiny of my country rather than live in slavery and contempt for sacred principles. History will one day have its say; it will not be the history taught in the United Nations, Washington, Paris, or Brussels, however, but the history taught in the countries that have rid themselves of colonialism and its puppets. Africa will write its own history and both north and south of the Sahara it will be a history full of glory and dignity."[25]

The artistic director of the 59th Venice Art Biennale has outlined the current planetary struggle of understanding and contemplating "subjectivities, hierarchies, and anatomies".[26]

Kerunen provides a unique and complex response. Her African experiences in transcribing natural environments into artistic contexts helps the audience to explore new junctures at which craft traditions remain in balance with the natural environment, rather than increasing suffering from an environmentally caused pandemic. Sekajugo enlarges the ground by expressing the views from his own experiences of Western forms of consumerism and turns to new ecologies of thinking and sensing to present poverty and inequality as linked to extractive capitalism.

Both artists are stretching the boundaries of subjectivities and hierarchies by developing within the new ecologies of the aesthesis of solidarity. Thus, they contribute to our understanding of the emergence of decoloniality in Uganda as a nationalist aspiration. There is a little bit of Kerunen and Sekajugo in every one of us, a commitment to action in each of us as we search for ways to legitimise the value of a more sustainable future together.

Footnotes

1 https://www.marxists.org/subject/africa/fanon/pitfalls-national.html (accessed 24 March 2022).

2 Sabiiti, H., *Young and Flourishing: A Rising Fearless Cop of a Purpose Driven Generation* (Kampala: Xlibris, 2020), 33.

3 The concept of double materiality acknowledges that a company should report simultaneously on sustainability matters that are: 1) financially material in influencing business value, and 2) material to the market, the environment and the people. https://www.greenstoneplus.com/blog/what-is-double-materiality-and-why-should-you-consider-it (accessed 26 February 2022).

4 Lazzarato, M., *Signs and Machines: Capitalism and the Production of Subjectivity*, translated by J. D. Jordan (Los Angeles: Semiotext(e), 2014), 33.

5 Unpublished conversation with the artist, 3 February 2022.

6 Olufemi, L., *Feminism, Interrupted: Disrupting Power* (London: Pluto Press: 2020), 5.

7 "The exhibition challenges the manner in which art is traditionally curated. It questions how art is contextualized and raises the bar not just for the way in which modern African art needs to be understood and discussed, not only for how all postcolonial art needs to be displayed, but for how all art is contextualized and then understood. All art exists in history, not only within a given moment and not only in the history of art. The inspiration for art and popular culture at any given time is infinitely complex." Becker, C., "Interview with Okwui Enwezor", *Art Journal* 57, no. 2 (Summer 1998): 101–7.

8 Unpublished conversation with Sanaa Gateja, 10 February 2022.

9 Acaye Kerunen on her Facebook page, 13 February 2022.

10 https://www.thebritishacademy.ac.uk/blog/book-prize-2021-neither-settler-nor-native-mahmood-mamdani/

11 Okwui Enwezor in conversation with Rem Koolhaas and Hans Ulrich Obrist at the Swiss Pavilion, 14th International Architecture Biennale in Venice, 2014, https://www.youtube.com/watch?v=z8uyl0eenDk

12 Vázquez, R., "The Question of Precedence", lecture at "Thinking Together", Haus der Berliner Festspiele, Berlin, 18 March 2017, https://time-issues.org/vazquez-the-question-of-precedence/

13 Rikki Wemega-Kwamu on his Facebook page, 27 January 2022.

14 Karlholm, D., "Filtering Futures: La Biennale di Venezia. 56th International Art Exhibition, 2015. All the World's Futures. Artistic director and curator: Okwui Enwezor", *Konsthistorisk tidskrift/Journal of Art History* 84, no. 4 (2015): 248–51.

15 Enwezor, O., "Introduction", in *All the World's Futures: Short Guide*, edited by O. Enwezor (Venice: Marsilio, 2015), 18.

16 https://encyclopedia.1914-1918-online.net/article/postwar_colonial_administration_africa

17 See Lugard, F. D., *The Dual Mandate in British Tropical Africa*, 1922, online, http://archive.org/details/cu31924028741175, and Sarraut, A., *La mise en valeur des colonies françaises*, 1923, online, http://archive.org/details/lamiseenvaleurde00sarr

18 https://www.theartnewspaper.com/2022/02/17/nigerian-installation-in-londons-st-pauls-cathedral-provokes-debate-around-restitution-and-colonial-monuments

19 Ibid.

20 Du Bois, W. E. B., *The Souls of Black Folk* (New York: Vintage Books/Library of America, 1990), 5. First published 1903.

21 https://themelrosegallery.com/artists/30-pitika-ntuli/biography/

22 Hammar, A., "The Concept and Paradoxes of Displacement", in *Framing African Development: Challenging Concepts*, edited by K. Havnevik, T. Oestigaard, E. Tobisson and T. Virtanen (Leiden, Netherlands and Boston, MA: Brill, 2015), 111.

23 Ibid.

24 Statement by Cecilia Alemani, https://www.labiennale.org/en/art/2022/statement-cecilia-alemani (accessed 20 September 2021).

25 https://www.blackpast.org/global-african-history/primary-documents-global-african-history/patrice-lumumbas-letter-pauline-lumumba-1960/

26 Statement by Cecilia Alemani.

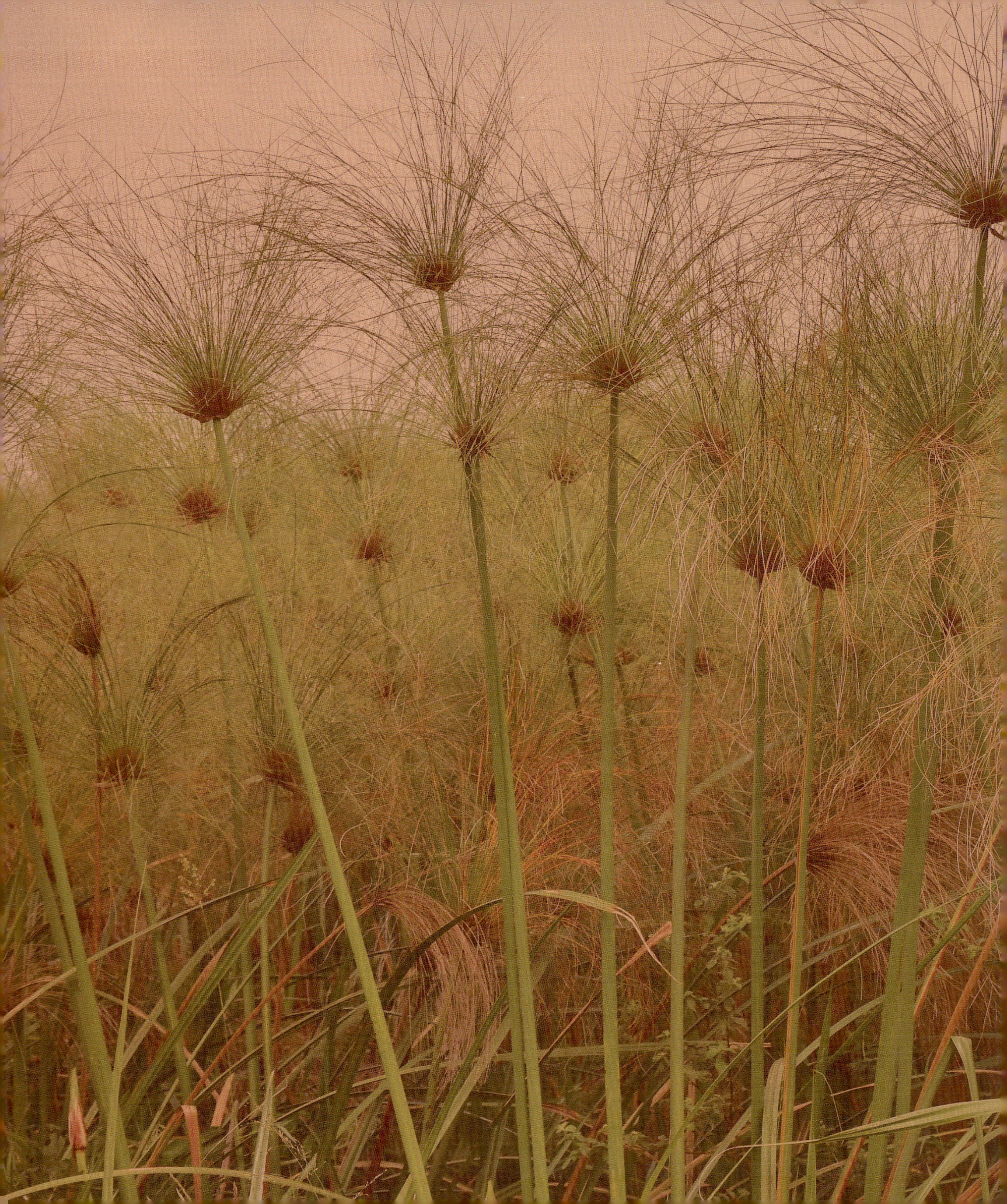

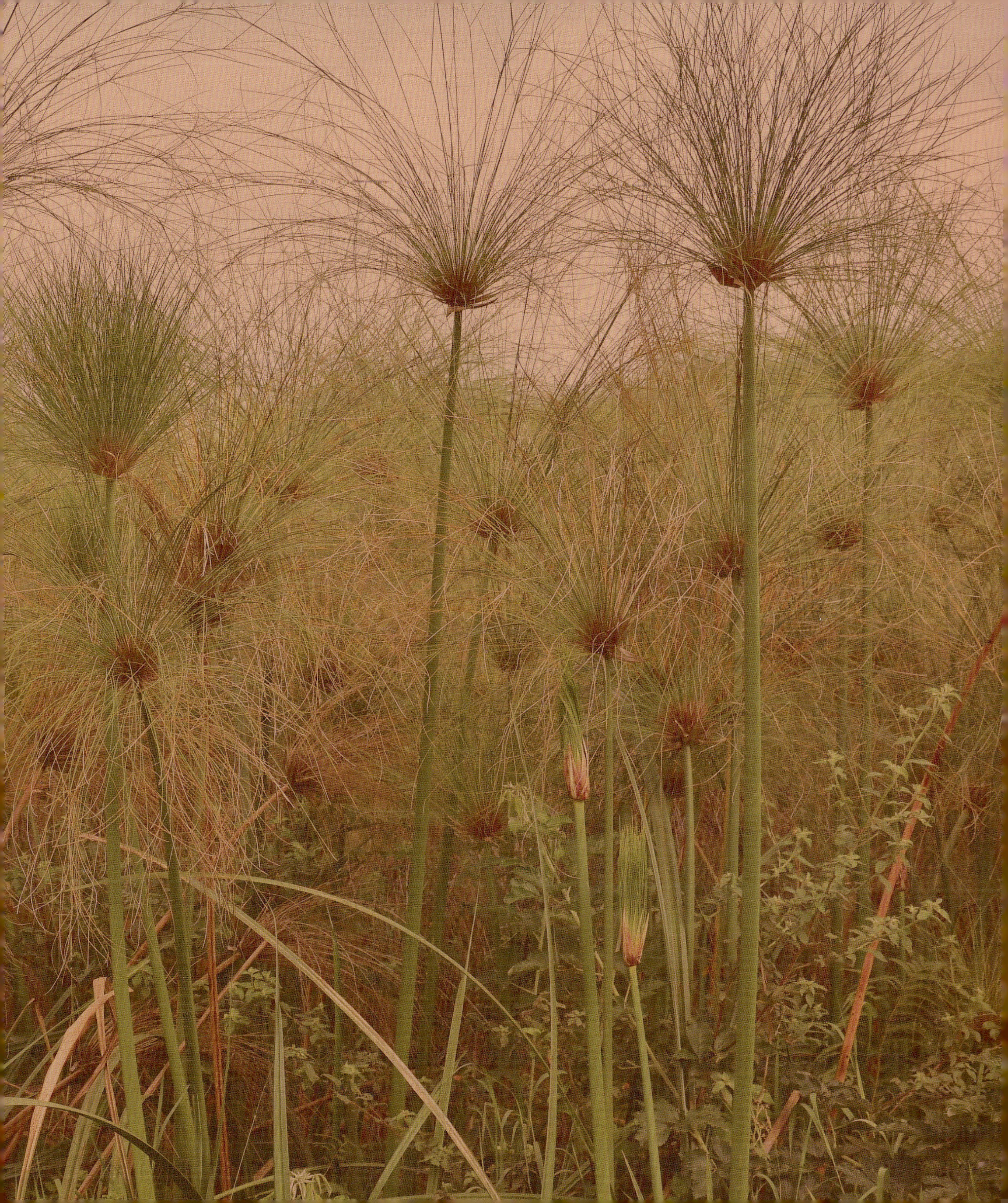

Acaye Kerunen in the Eye of Time

On Sunday, 31 October 2021, I received a message from Uganda. It read: "Greetings. This is Acaye Kerunen from Uganda. I am an artist/curator exploring natural woven fibre in installations".[1]

This was a start of a series of fabulous conversations over Zoom, gmail, WhatsApp; any way possible so we could virtually meet and organise her participation in the evolving exhibition, *Radiance, They Dream in Time*. Of course, the pronoun *they* was apt for both Kerunen and Sekajugo as the conversations evolved with many others reclaiming their power in the cultural frontlines of Kampala, Brussels, London, New York, etc.

On Sunday, 31 October 2021, it felt like entering a Kerunen sphere of control, a cyclone that she was observing which she stated "I am building". Consistently disrupting, Kerunen seemed to be building on the spiral forms of contemporary lives with a base in the middle and emerging outwards, resisting gravity and all the natural forces she once described as "a proper storm".

Kerunen, aka Acaye. E. Pamela, is a polymath artist, well versed in the public domain of Uganda, having performed, written, composed and, more recently, worked closely with weaving-craft artisans to conceptually interpret women's labour. For her first comprehensive solo exhibition entitled *Iwang Sawa* (Alur-Swahili for "In the eye of time") at the Afriart Gallery, Kampala, Kerunen presented repurposed functional objects such as placemats and baskets made of natural materials. The result was a startling series of wall-based works and installations. It garnered local attention that inspired many others from abroad to speculate on its strong symbolism. Themes related to commodification and craft culture embedded in a series of assemblages made from natural fibres were a focus triggering feminine symbols of labour. In her work one recognised pathways of regional networks where the conditions at play were based on transformative justice for the genealogy of modern women. Ebiso (raffia), sisal, byayi (bananafibre), reeds, stripped sorghum stems and ensansa (palm leaves) all assumed conceptual meanings and drew on an aesthesis of form, shape and texture. Aesthesis, an unelaborated elementary awareness of stimulation, was found in her declarations of independence from colonial heritage. It ignored boundaries and freed the surface of these artisan objects from their truly authentic and characteristically East African lineage to create the hybrid fabrication she called *Iwang Sawa: In the Eye of Time*.

Kerunen thus, takes on the role of artist/curator to relocate woven natural fibres, which she commissions from groups of community women weavers. Through her process of repurposing these functional objects such as placemats, winnowing trays and baskets she re-creates *zones of one thing*. The author Lola Olufemi argues: "Art is best utilised as a weapon, a writing back, as evidence that we were here".

For Kerunen, art and craft co-exist to provide a strategic way to map the here as Uganda, a writing as Ugandans, and the evidence to be resolved of her borders and her relationship to the Great Lake region. She liberates craft objects by providing a rich transitional surface in which

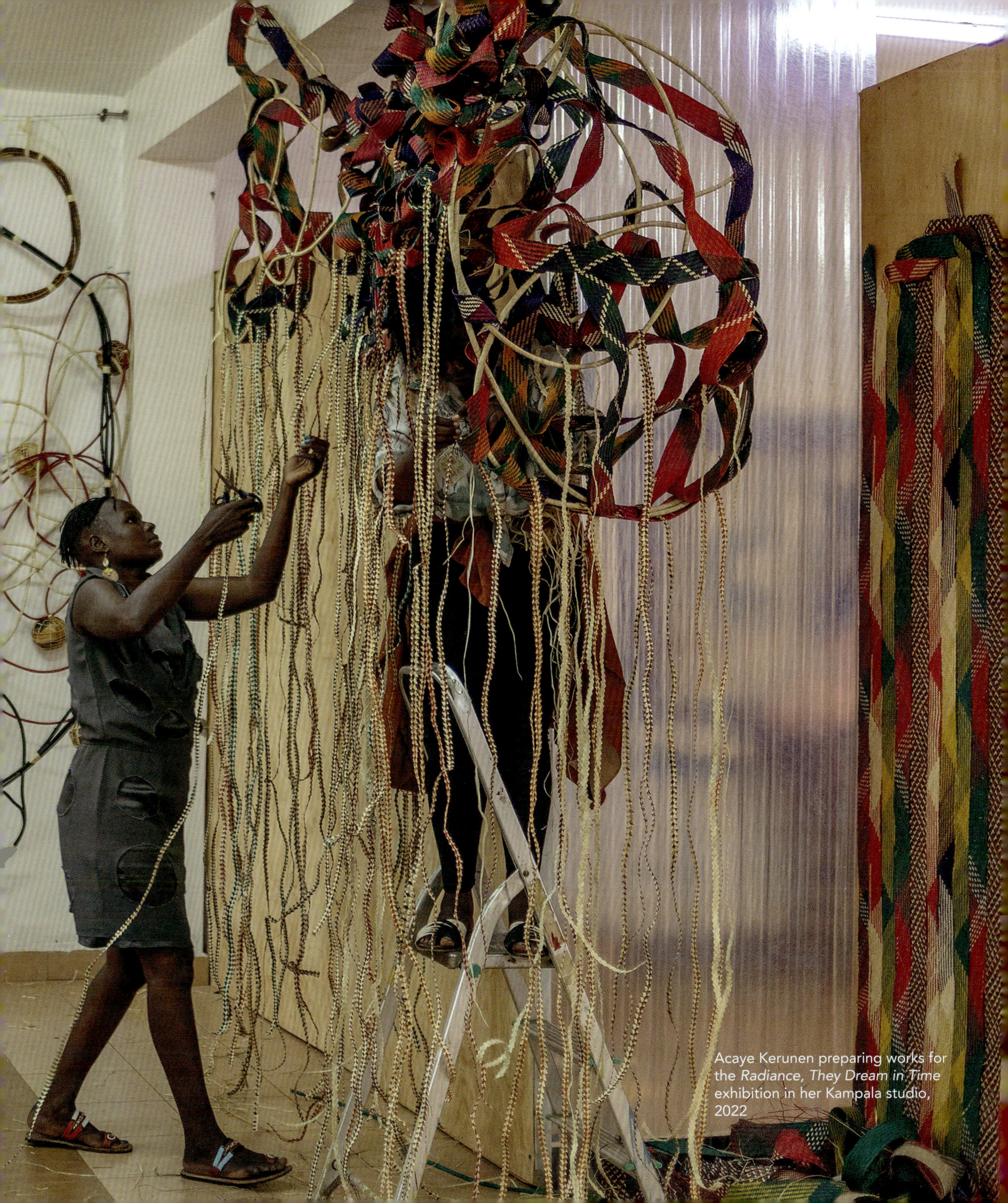

Acaye Kerunen preparing works for the *Radiance, They Dream in Time* exhibition in her Kampala studio, 2022

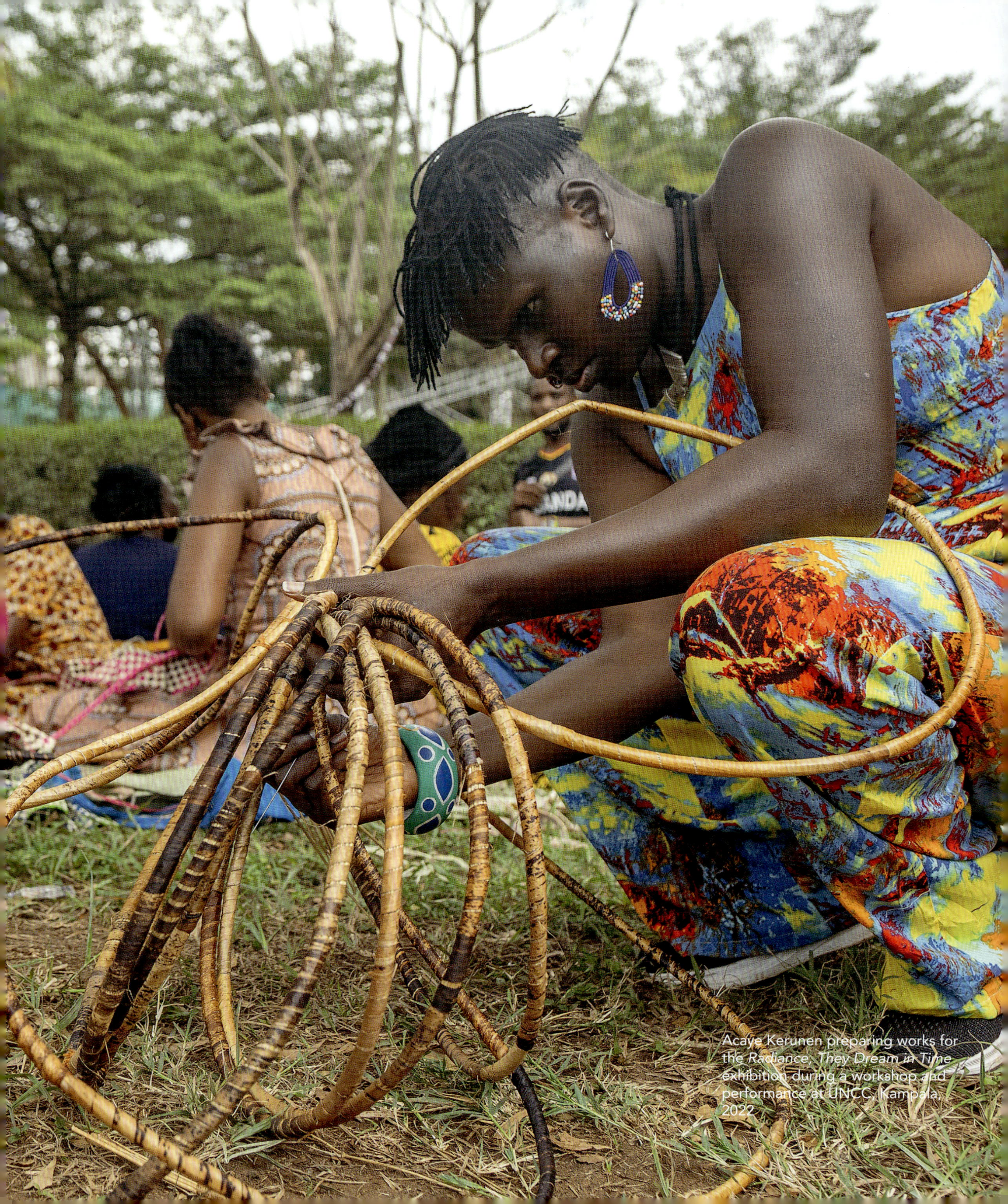

Acaye Kerunen preparing works for the *Radiance, They Dream in Time* exhibition during a workshop and performance at UNCC, Kampala, 2022

she manages to discuss differences with political meaning including Uganda's history; its stories about borders and women, its smart responses to climate change and its part in East African tribal cultures and languages. This allows the audience to re-interpret not only the long-established artisan expertise of women weavers from Uganda, but also the place of labour within the craft tradition. The installation "Ouganda" is partly informed by the politics of European colonial desire where commissioned household goods accommodated their Western styles and lifestyles. The dining room and dining table placement used in the artwork, are a perfect example; the furniture and the tableware are a composite that she explores in the matrix of European traditions and the extensive skills of the women, who created hospitality through their labour and impressive proficiency as makers. In the liberal feminist rationale, all Black women remain in the soft focus. Kerunen invites us to make connections to a black feminist critique that has existed and is documented by many who remained unafraid and explored political agency through multiple responses including crafting and mapping outside of the limits of whiteness.

Kerunen has embodied multiple mechanisms beyond art's control or states' patriarchal surveillance concentrating on the constructive ambiguity of Western discourses and emotions. Kerunen's aim, based on the fate of the earth, is to search for colours spectrums and forms from the forest, the great lakes and the flaneur in her has been greatly affected by the leadership and intuition of her people compromised and still chronicling the century of African independence through interventions.

Recently, she has brought together women making natural dyes, leaves and bark collected from foothills and beyond the planned limitations of wild farming, combining the painful storms with plastic coated fibre optic cables that run below the Indian Ocean bringing technology to Africa. She sculpts along the meridians on the inside of East Africa to locate the carriers of faith, thought processes, in transition and to find revolution in the duality. "That is what I am trying to represent with connectivity."

The meridians

Beyond the current arrangement of the mainstreams, Kerunen's spirituality finds its fate tied to deities, feminine twin goddesses, twinning in increasing duality dreaming in time. These deities guide those seeking shelter through affordable housing for the homeless, preparing fresh food and safety for those living on the streets. These existential realities and philosophies remain relational to both connectivity by Wi-Fi and to the dye made by a woman from Kisoro for the colour of raffia for the new age.

Kerunen stages her work as signal routers for the southern world psyche, the portraits of ancestors and those who mentor hung at an angle away from the wall, looking downwards, towards the ground and onto strolling selves on every Independence Day. That is a proper storm.

Shaheen Merali, February 2022

[1] Unpublished text from the artist to the curator.

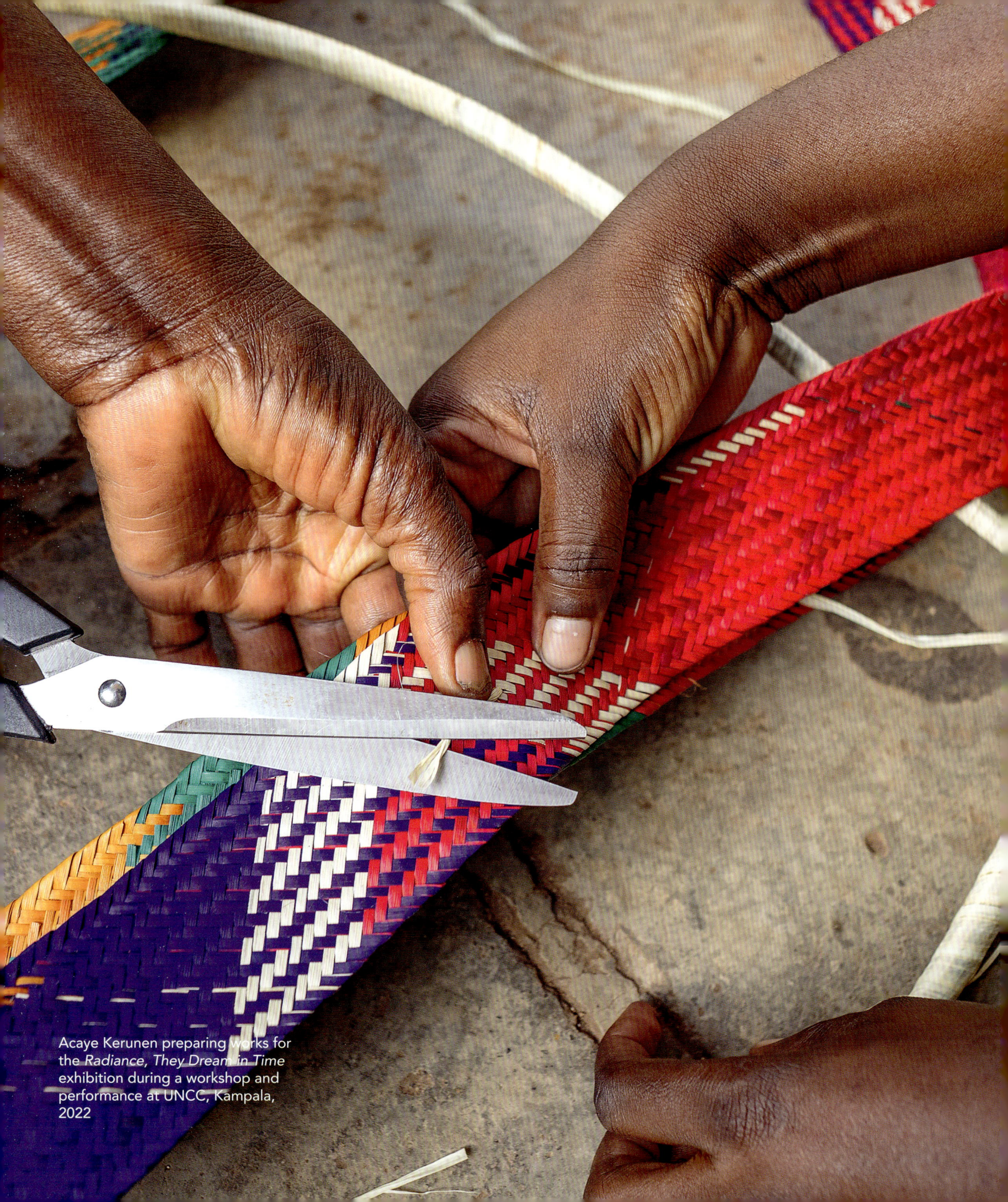

Acaye Kerunen preparing works for the *Radiance, They Dream in Time* exhibition during a workshop and performance at UNCC, Kampala, 2022

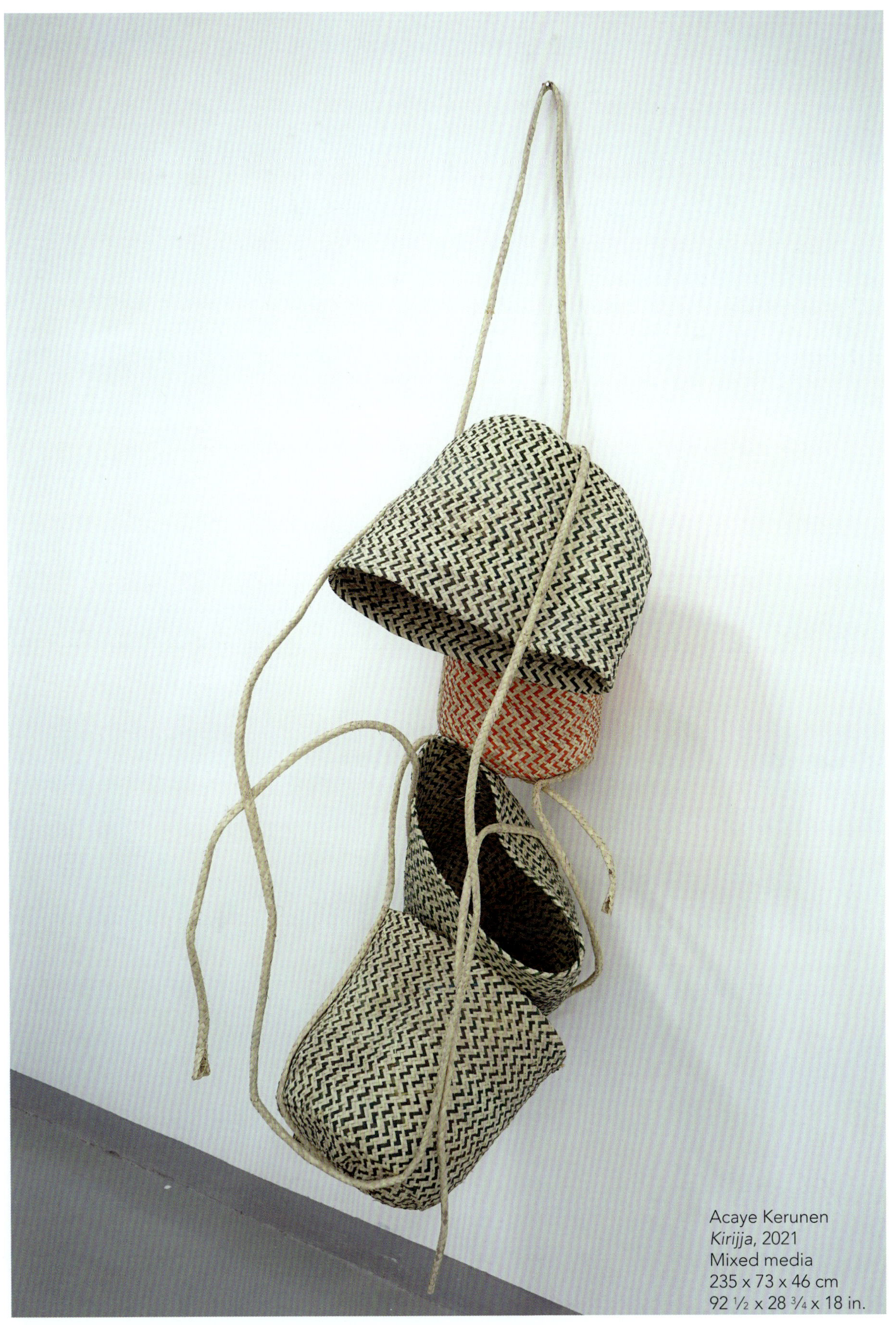

Acaye Kerunen
Kirijja, 2021
Mixed media
235 x 73 x 46 cm
92 ½ x 28 ¾ x 18 in.

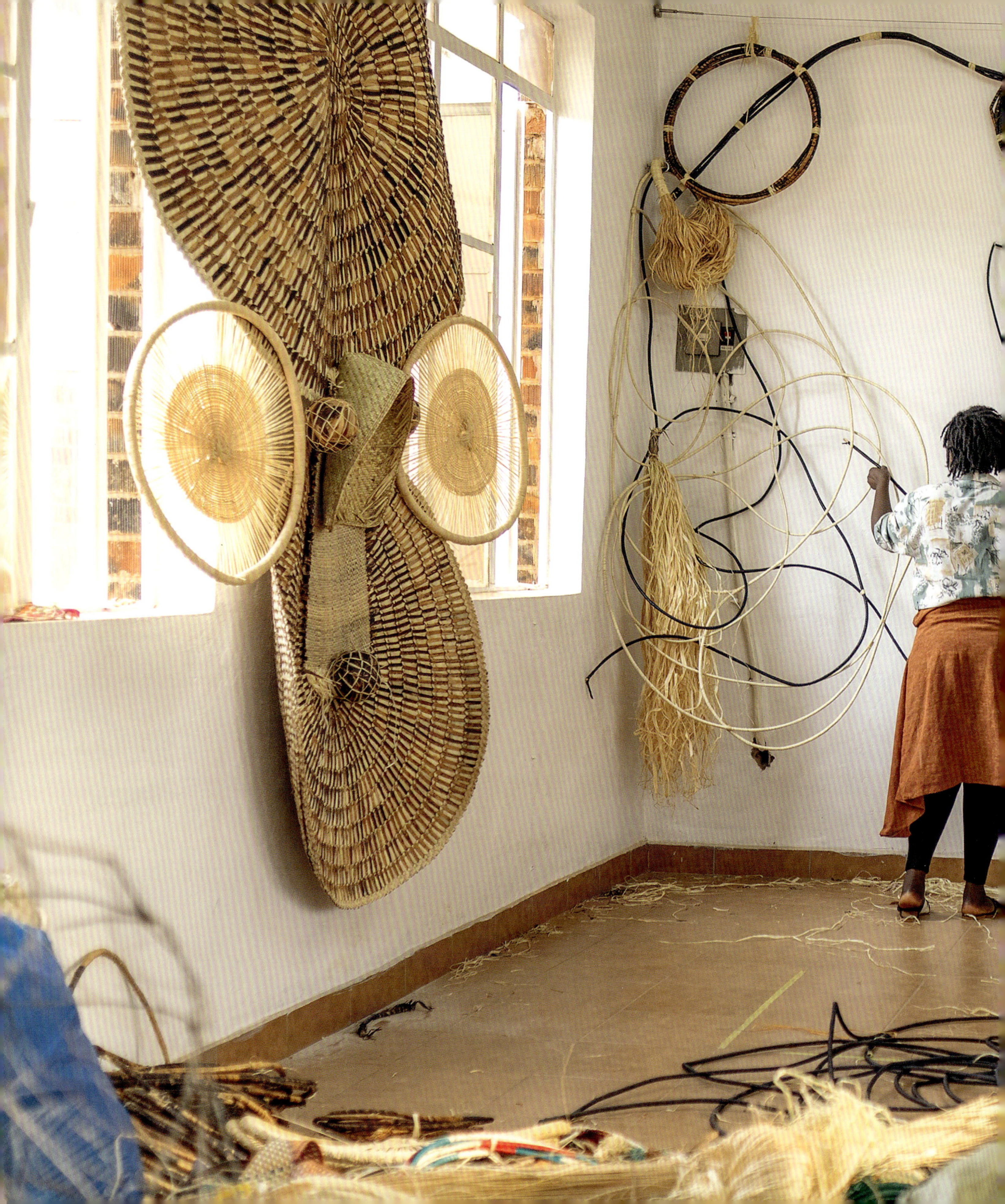

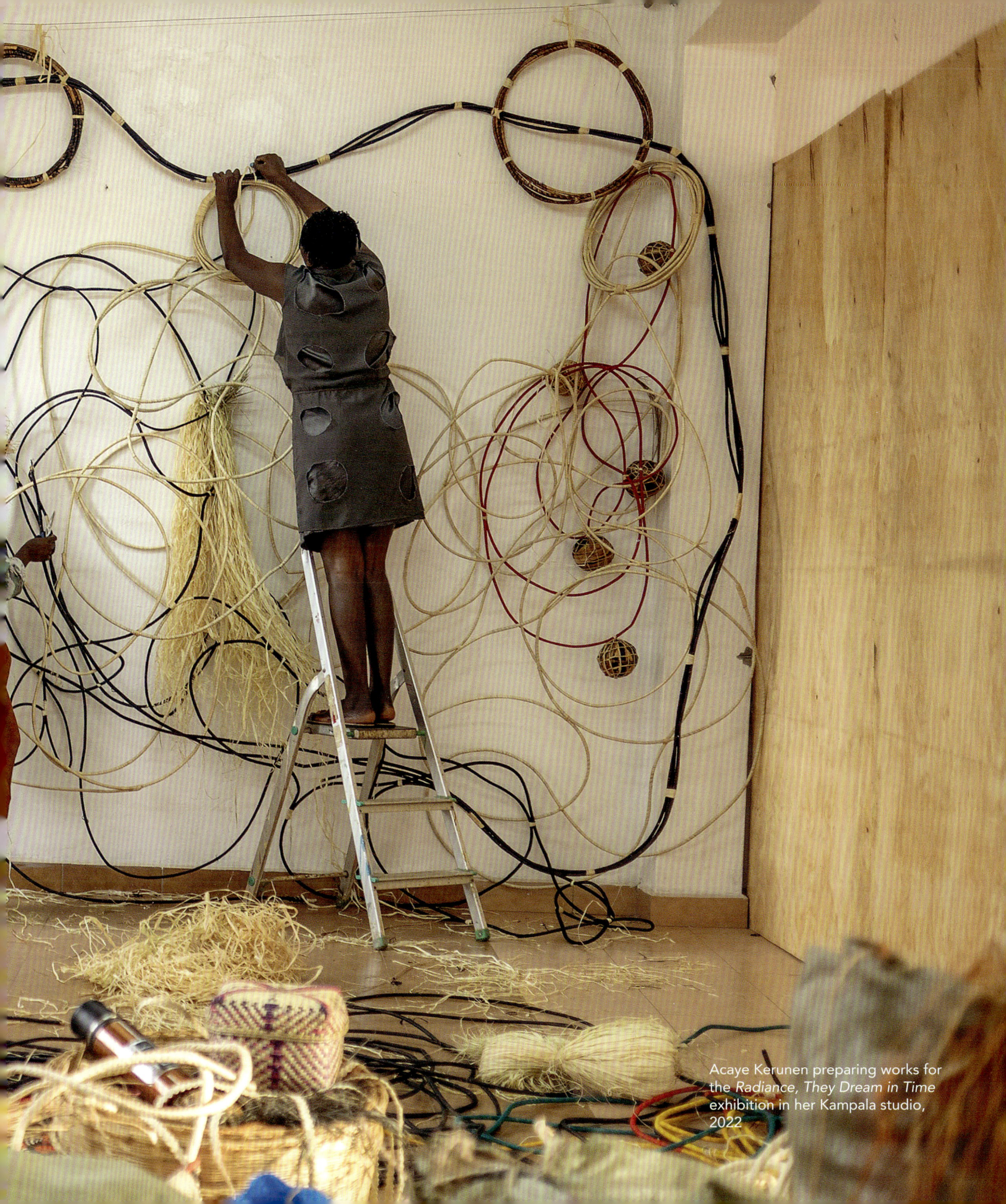

Acaye Kerunen preparing works for the *Radiance, They Dream in Time* exhibition in her Kampala studio, 2022

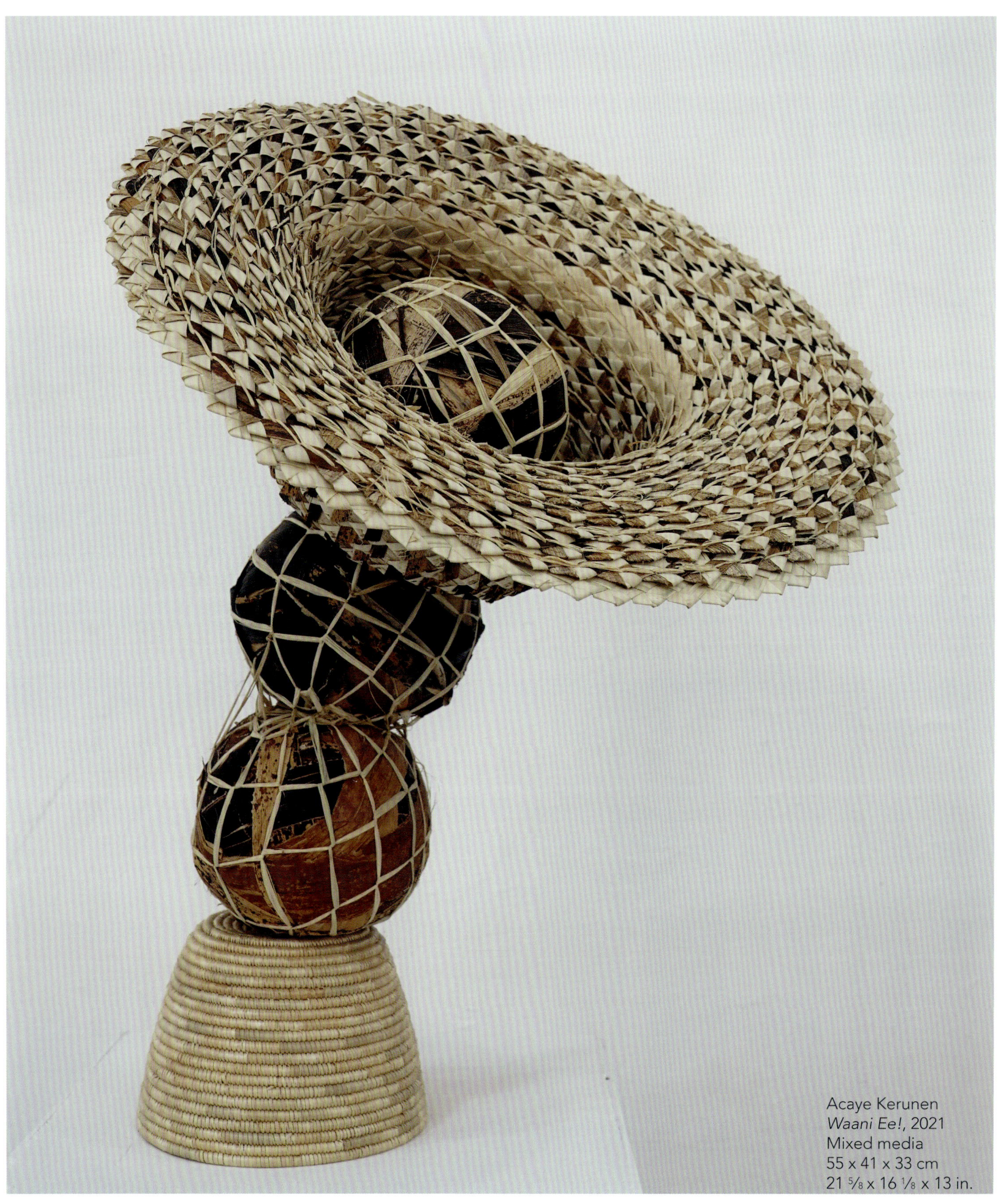

Acaye Kerunen
Waani Ee!, 2021
Mixed media
55 x 41 x 33 cm
21 5/8 x 16 1/8 x 13 in.

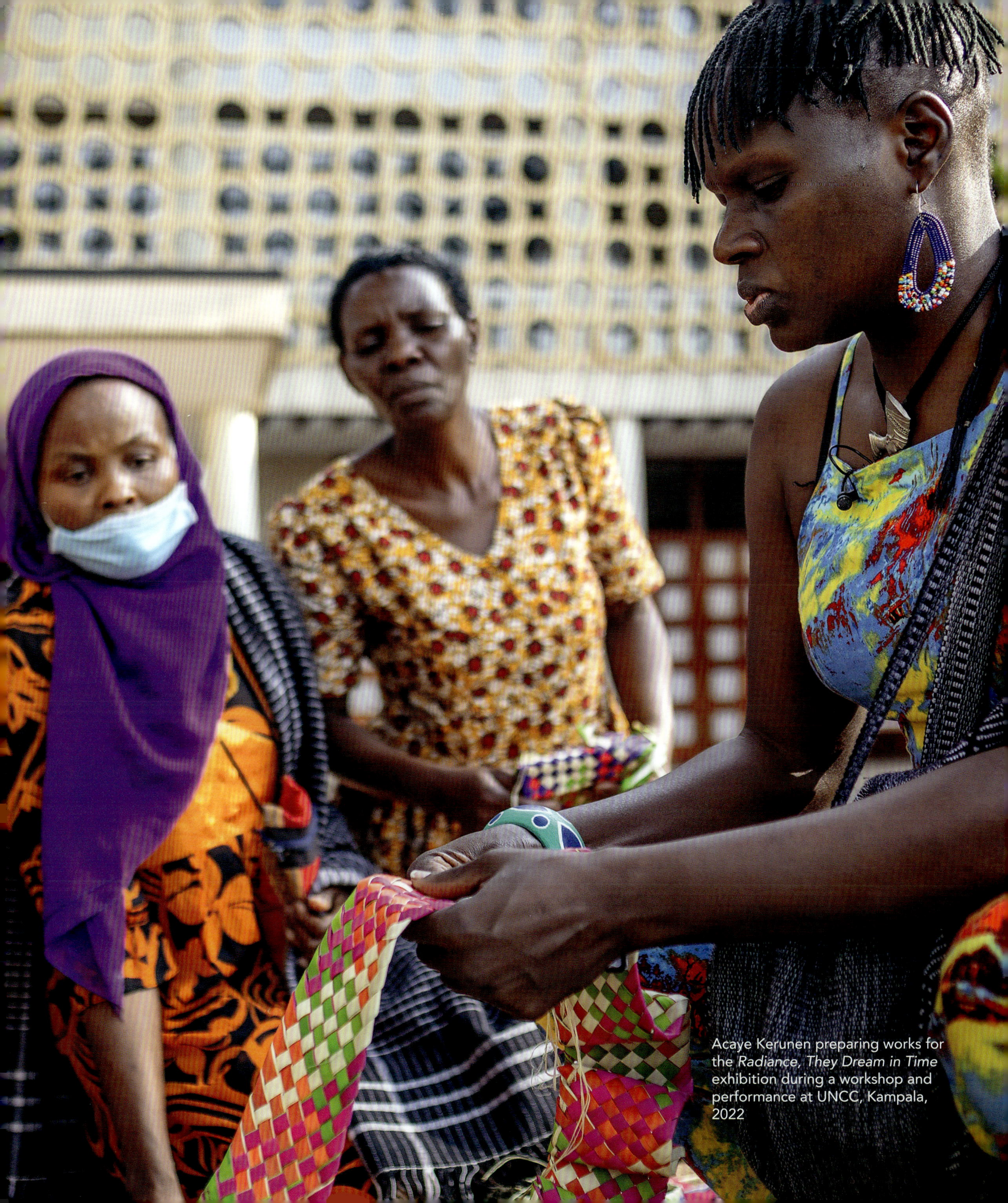

Acaye Kerunen preparing works for the *Radiance, They Dream in Time* exhibition during a workshop and performance at UNCC, Kampala, 2022

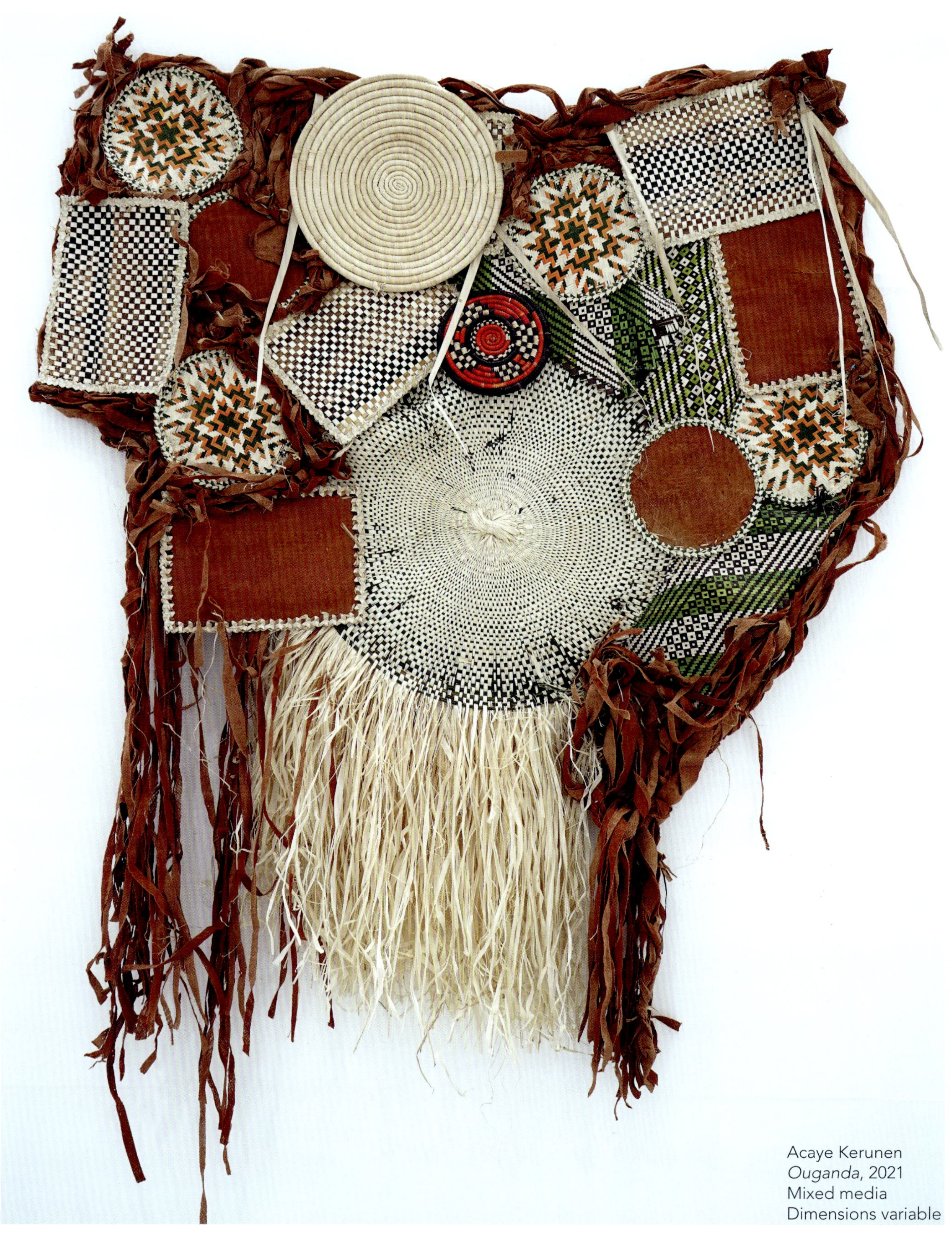

Acaye Kerunen
Ouganda, 2021
Mixed media
Dimensions variable

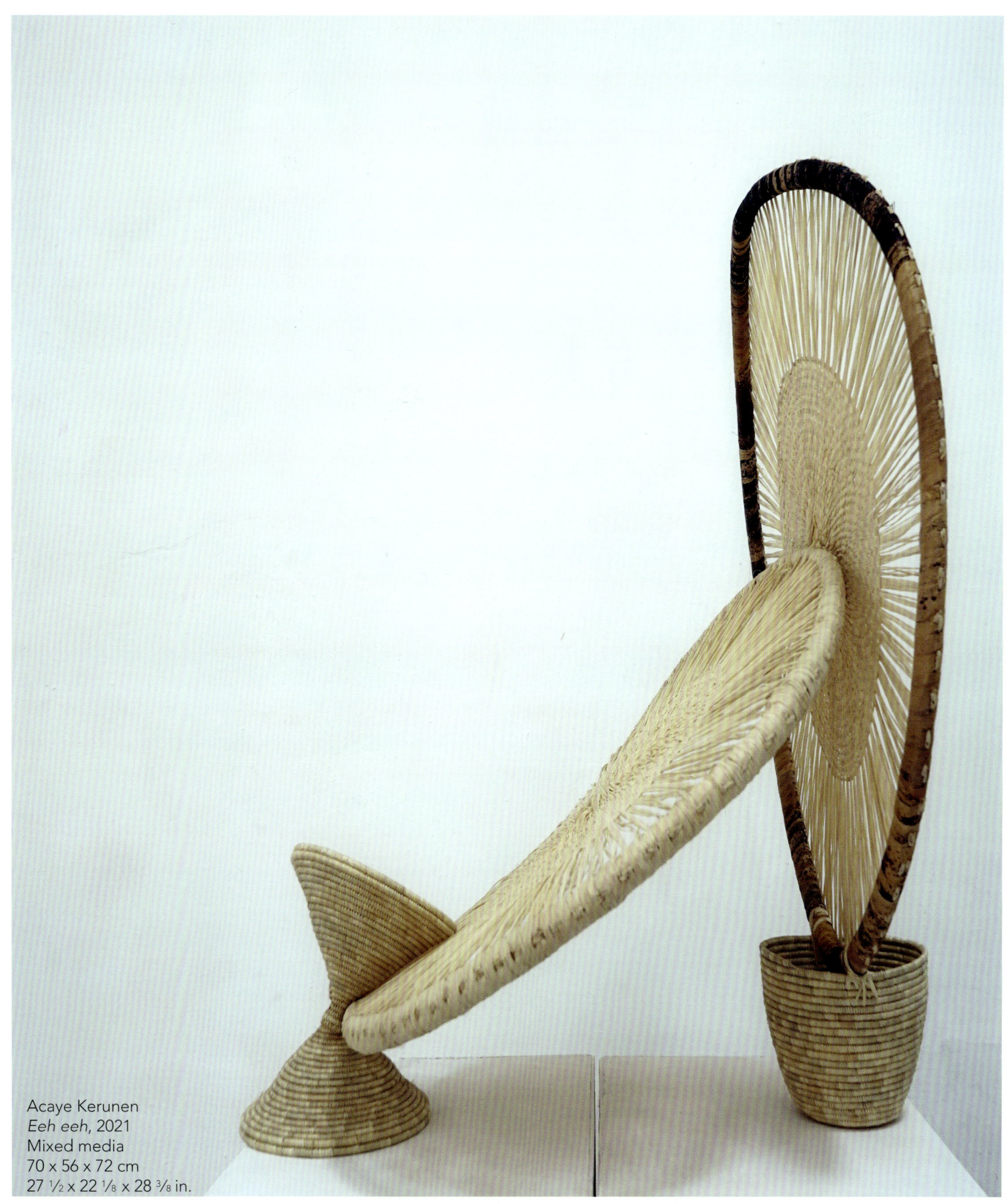

Acaye Kerunen
Eeh eeh, 2021
Mixed media
70 x 56 x 72 cm
27 ½ x 22 ⅛ x 28 ⅜ in.

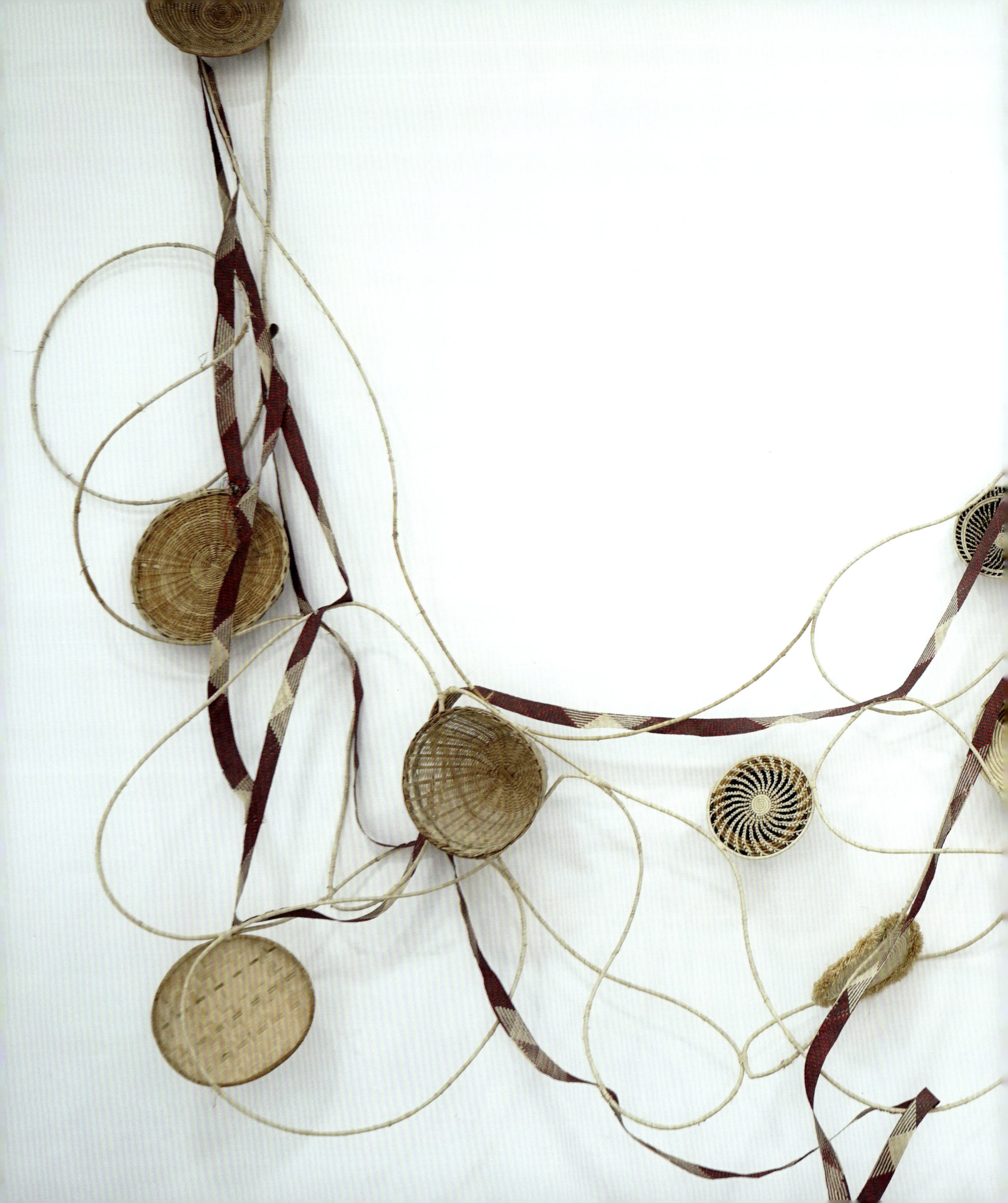

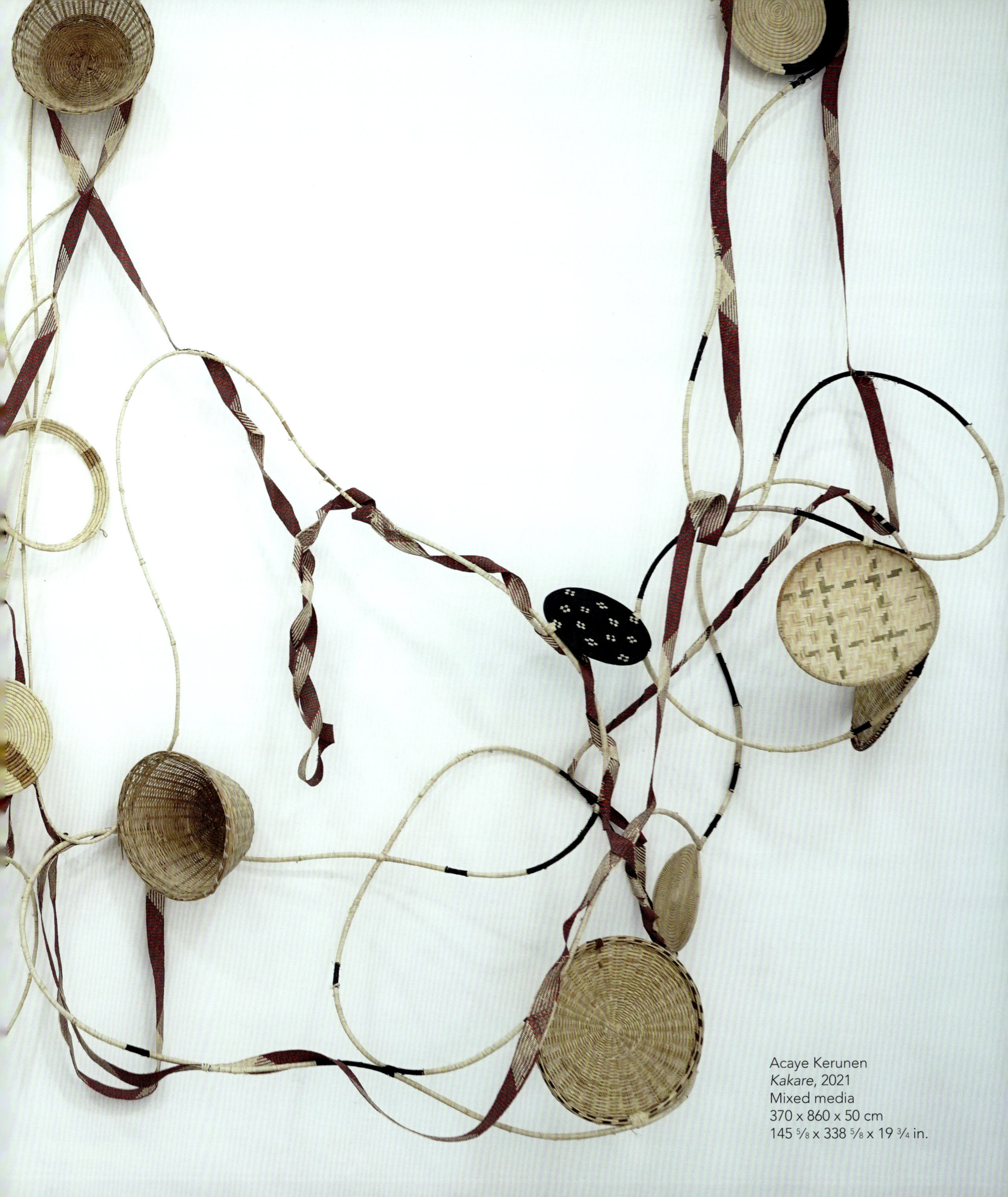

Acaye Kerunen
Kakare, 2021
Mixed media
370 x 860 x 50 cm
145 ⅝ x 338 ⅝ x 19 ¾ in.

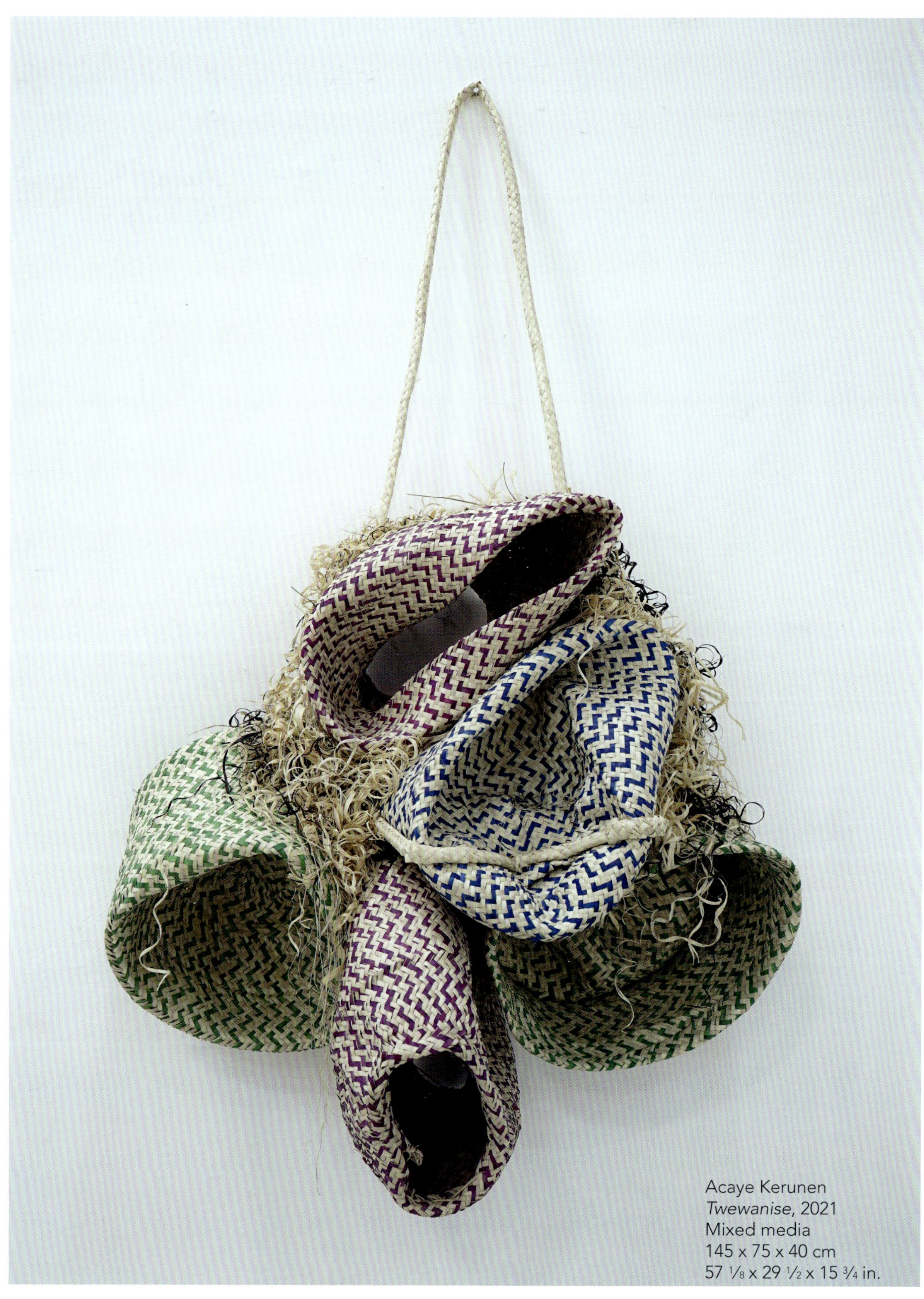

Acaye Kerunen
Twewanise, 2021
Mixed media
145 x 75 x 40 cm
57 1/8 x 29 1/2 x 15 3/4 in.

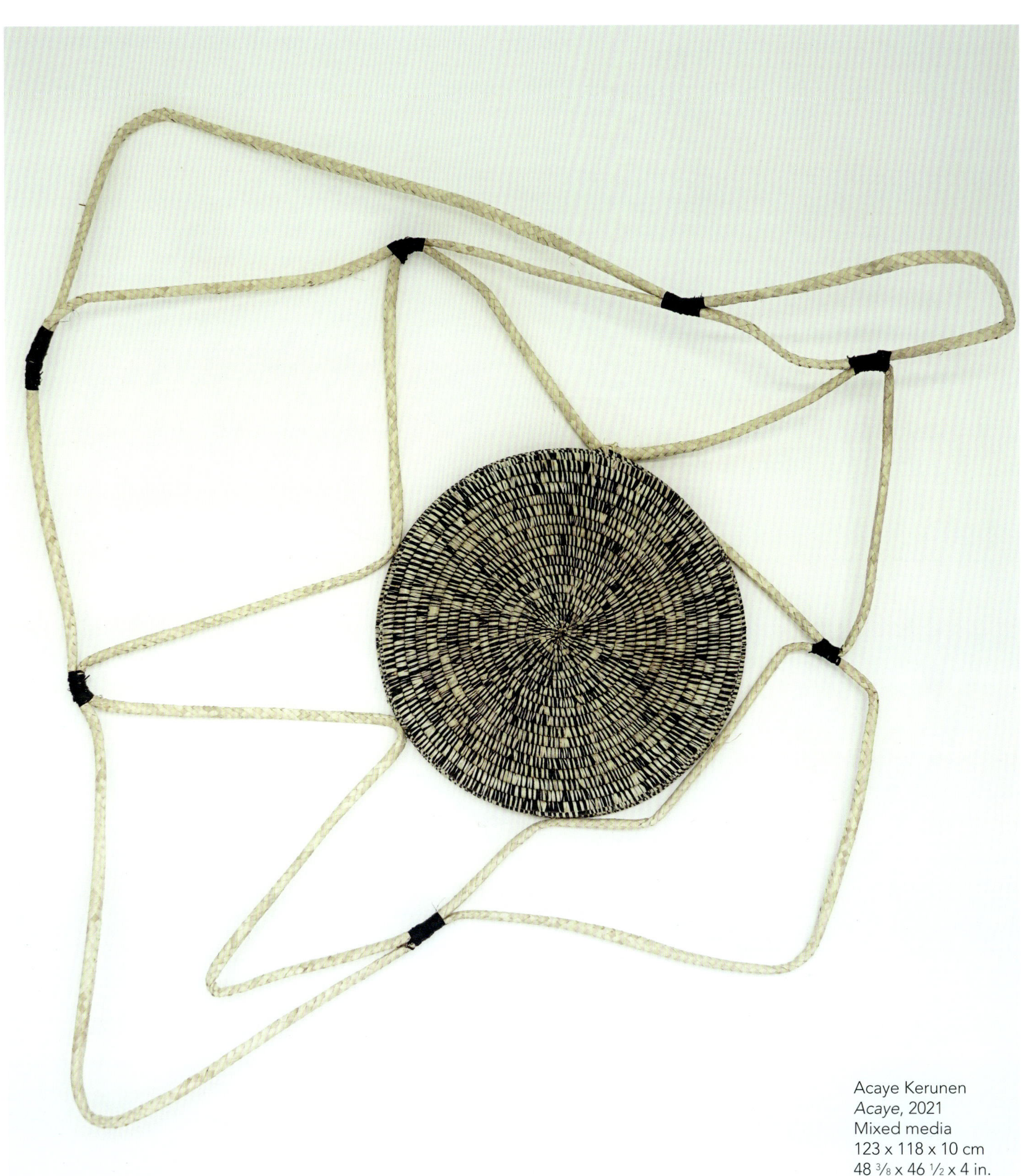

Acaye Kerunen
Acaye, 2021
Mixed media
123 x 118 x 10 cm
48 ³⁄₈ x 46 ¹⁄₂ x 4 in.

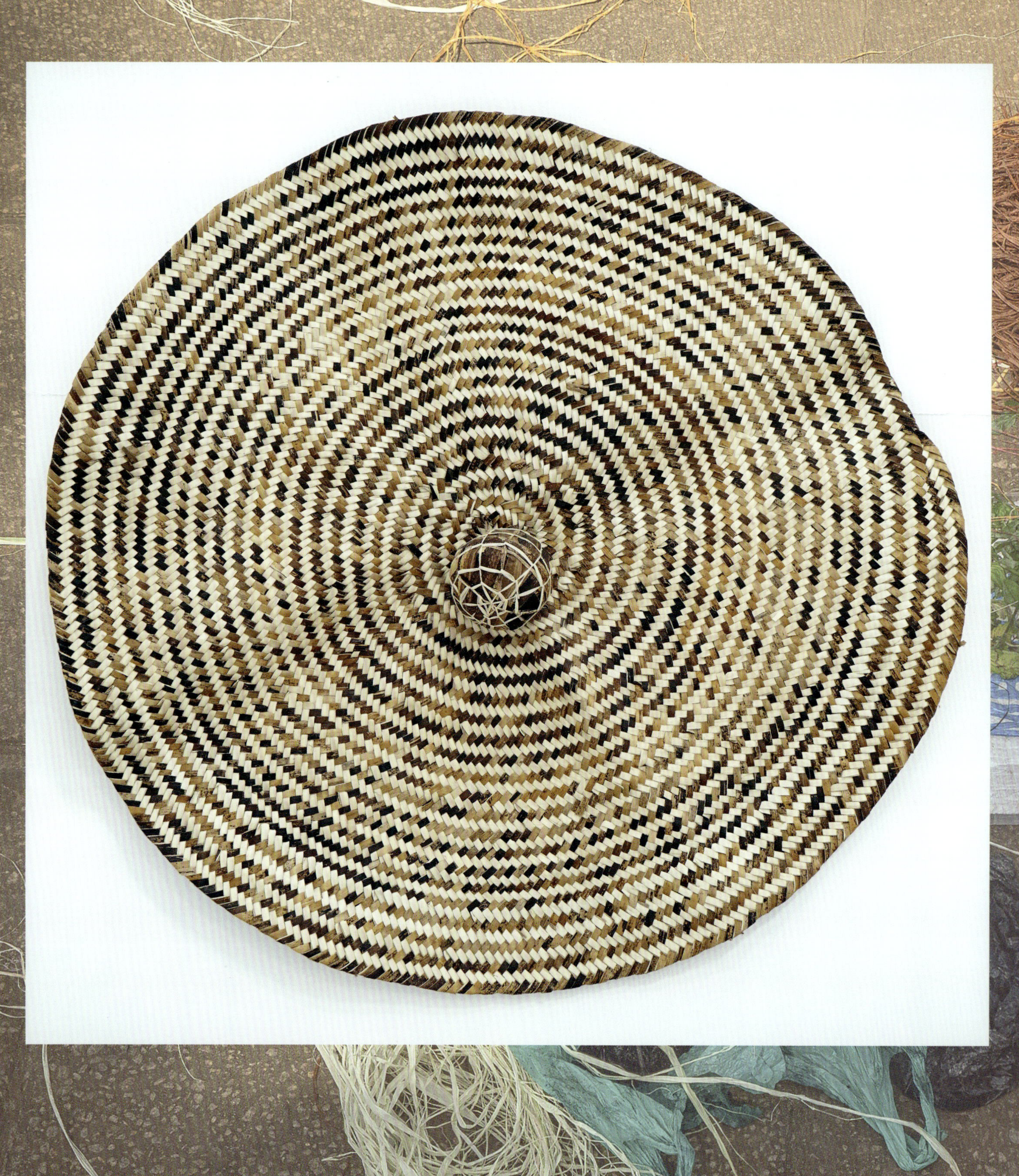

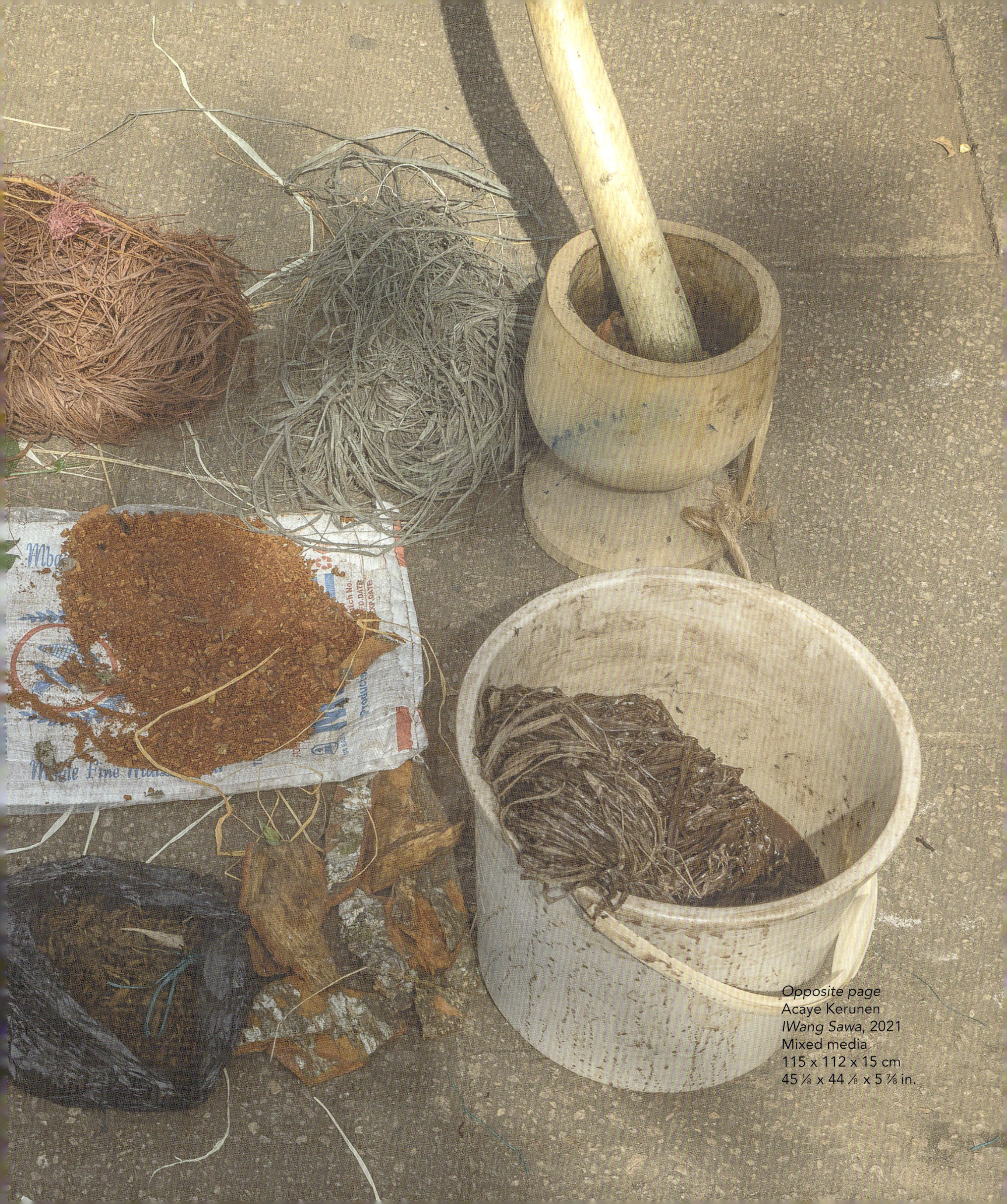

Opposite page
Acaye Kerunen
IWang Sawa, 2021
Mixed media
115 x 112 x 15 cm
45 ⅛ x 44 ⅛ x 5 ⅞ in.

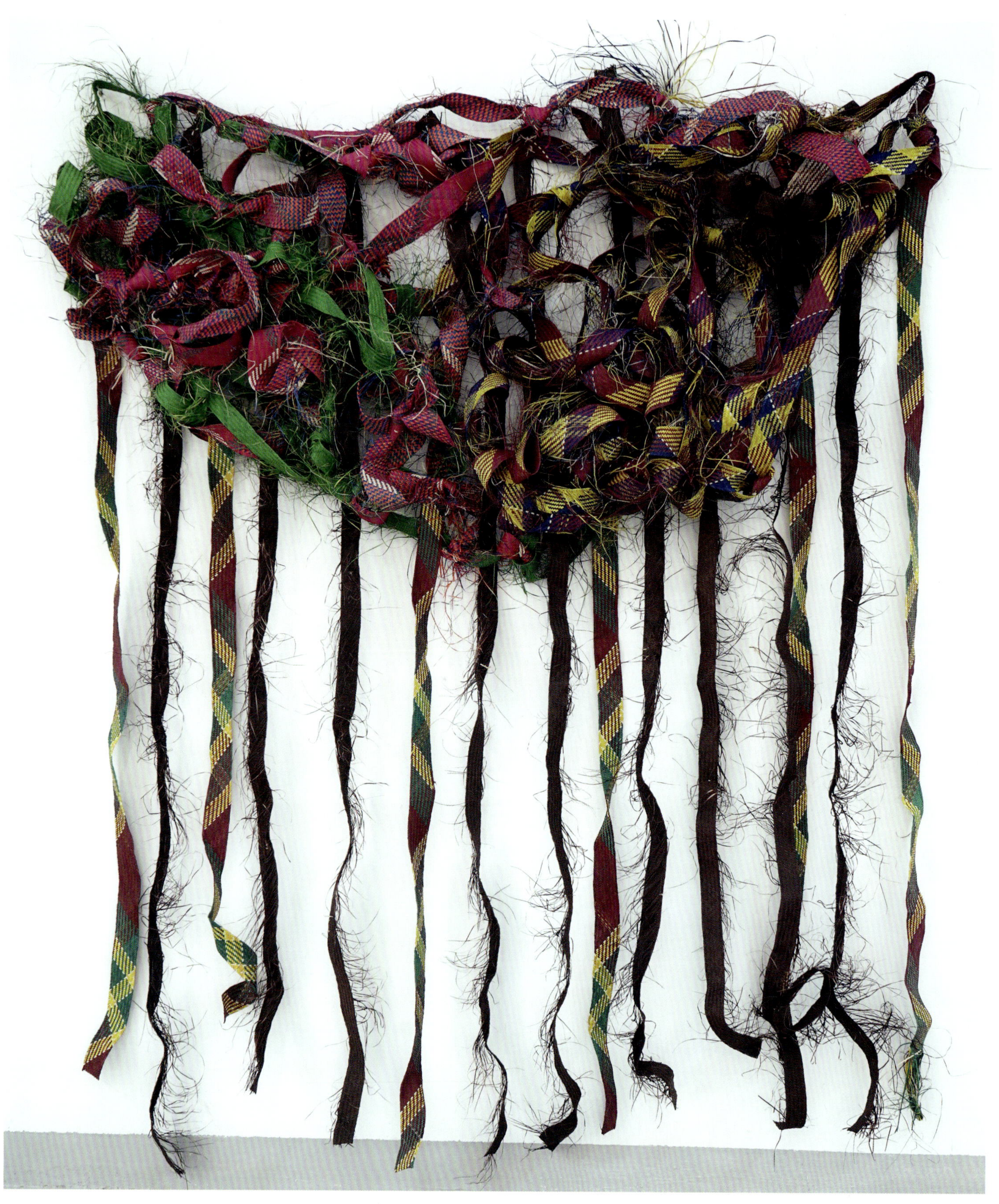

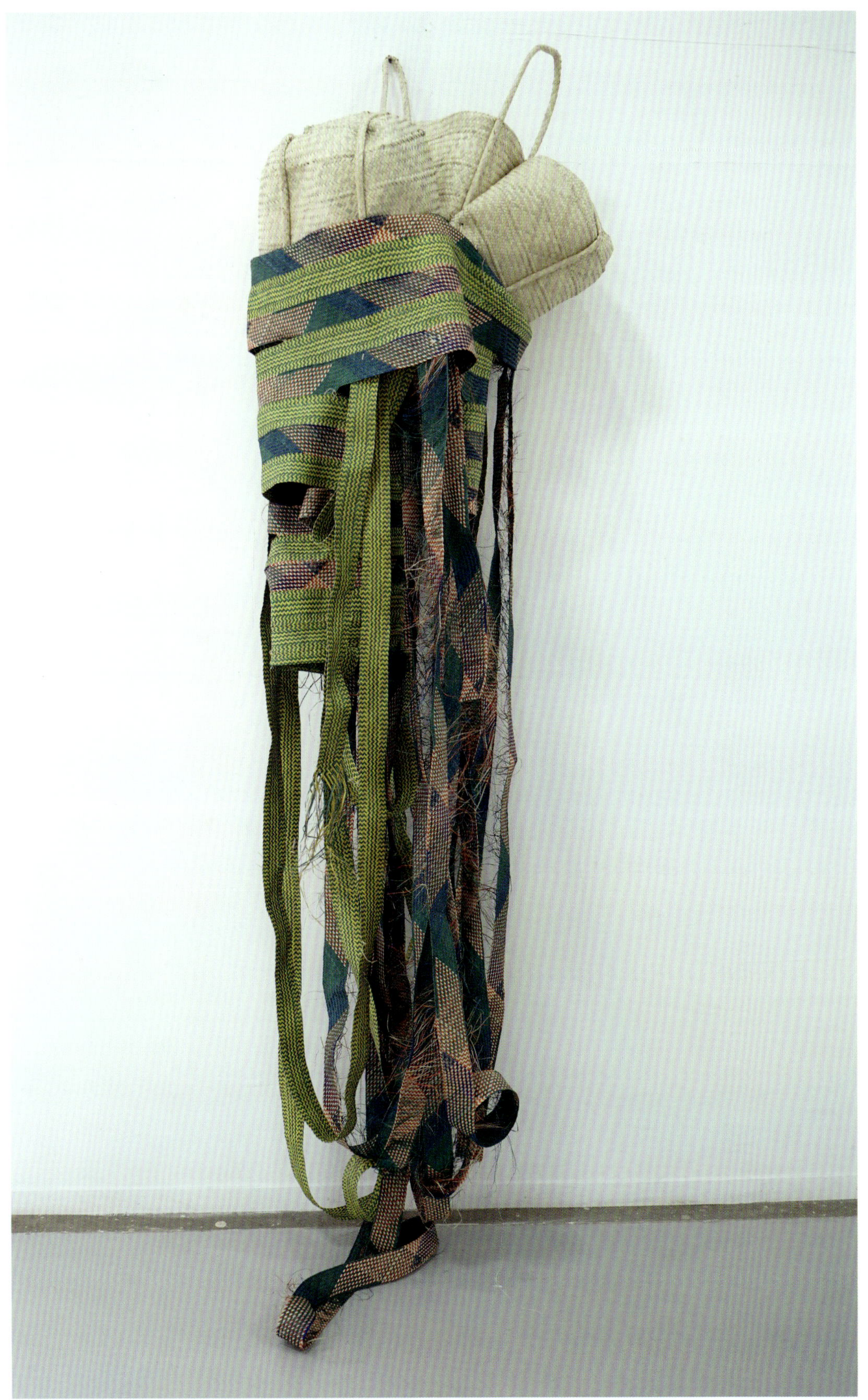

Opposite page
Acaye Kerunen
Ayera, 2021
Mixed Media
210 x 155 x 28 cm
82 ⅝ x 61 ⅛ x 11 ⅛ in.

Acaye Kerunen
Bamutenda!, 2021
Mixed media
275 x 118 x 40 cm
108 ¼ x 46 ½ x 15 ¾ in.

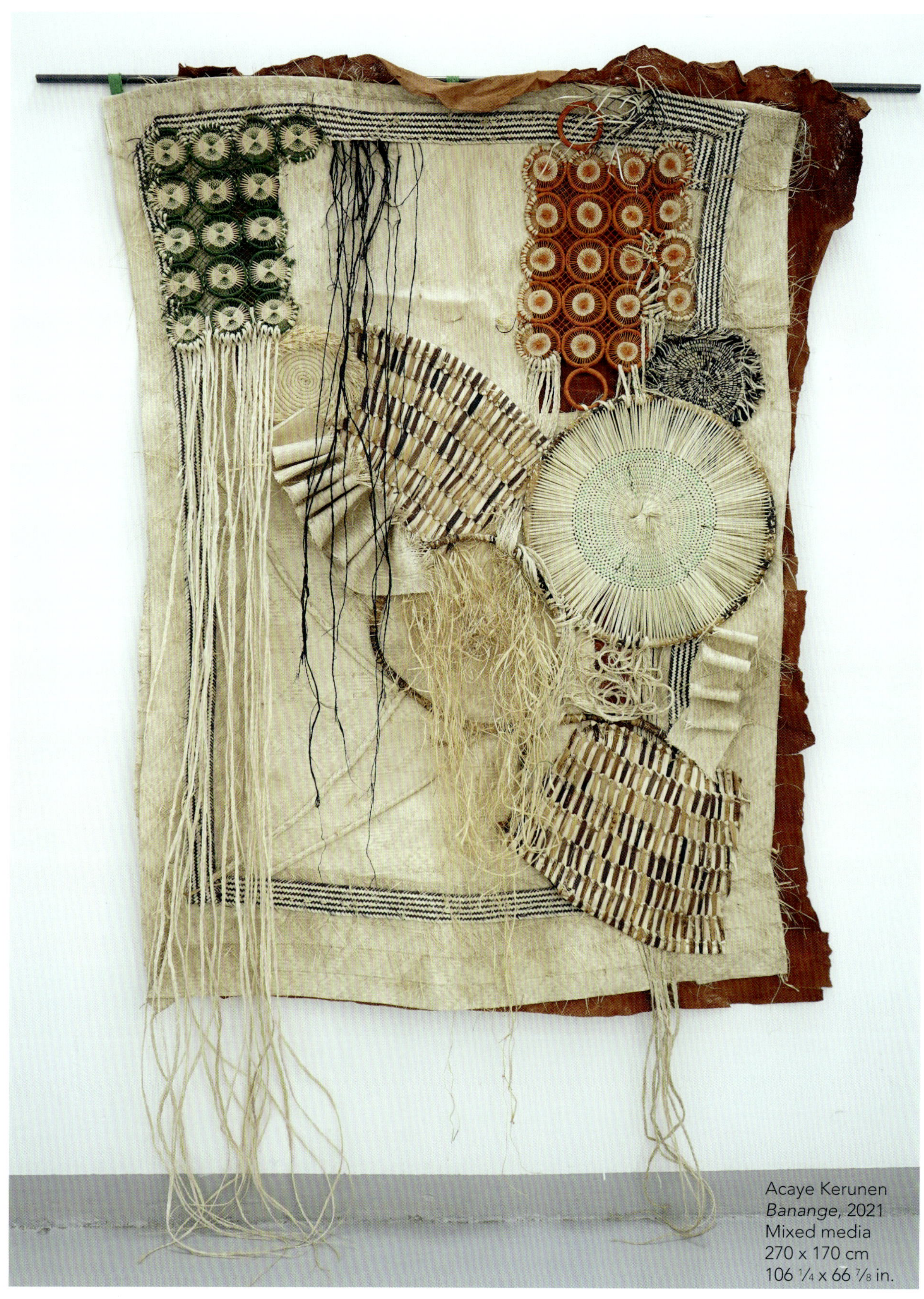

Acaye Kerunen
Banange, 2021
Mixed media
270 x 170 cm
106 ¼ x 66 ⅞ in.

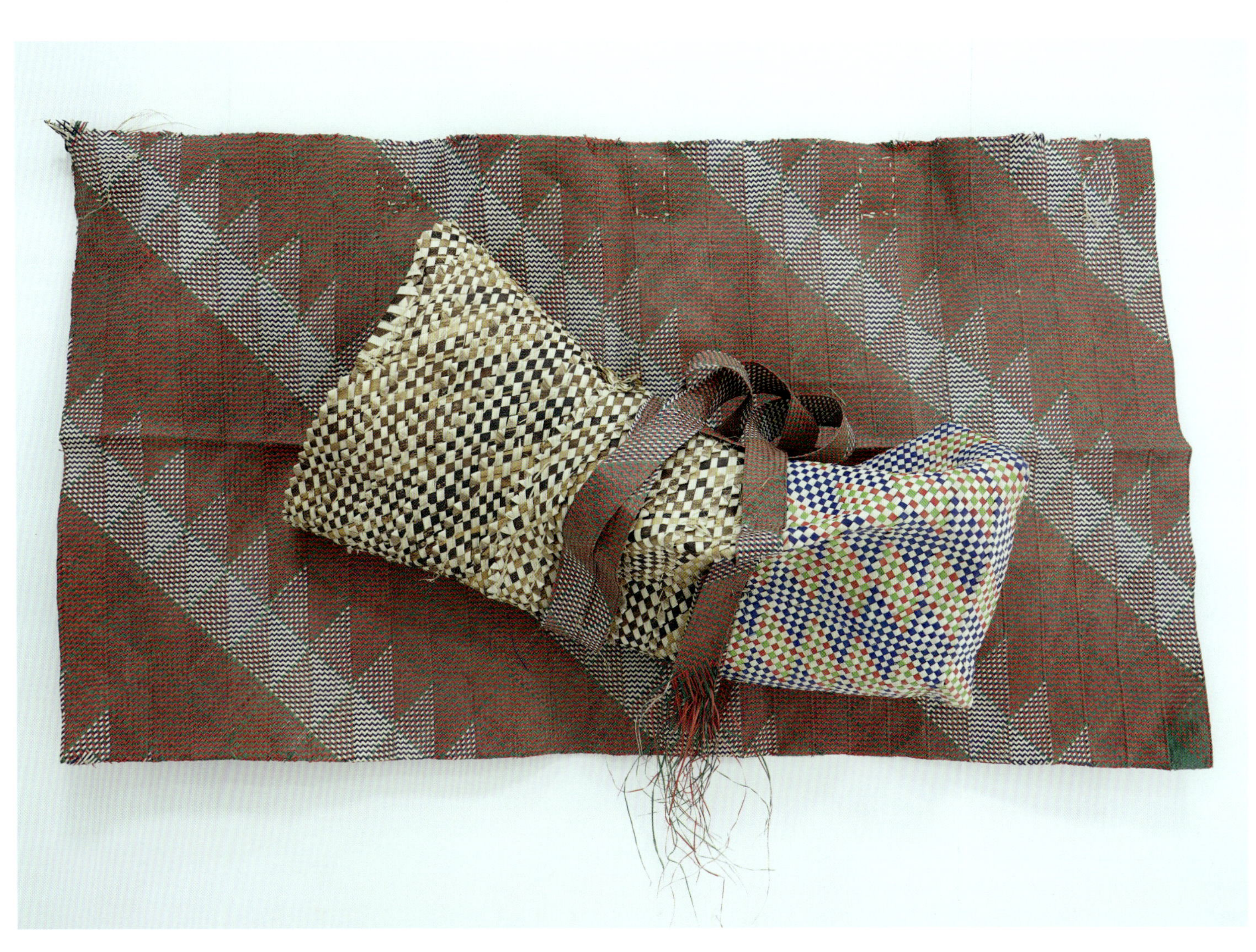

Acaye Kerunen
Nterede, 2021
Mixed media
130 x 180 x 40 cm
51 ⅛ x 70 ⅞ x 15 ¾ in.

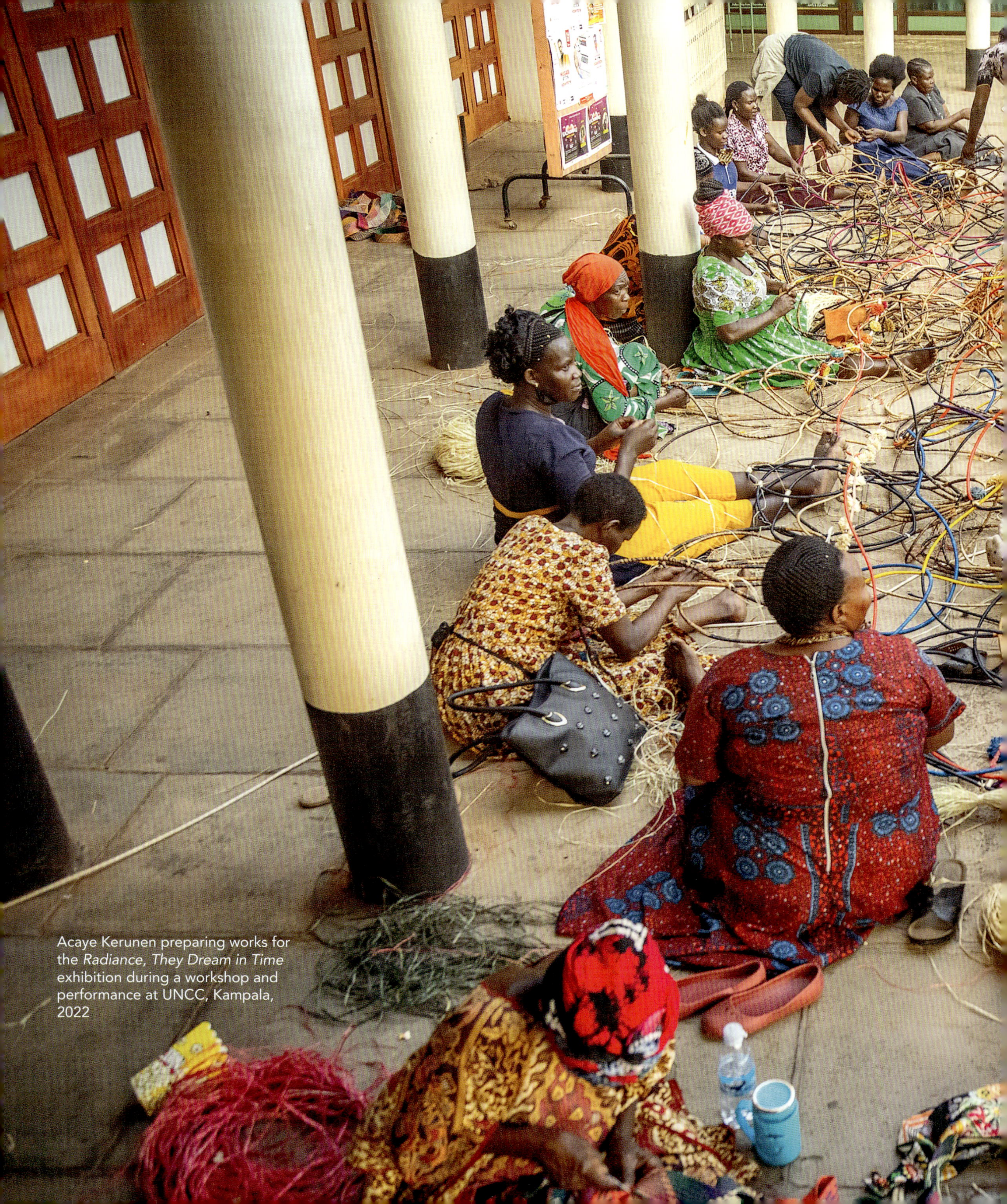

Acaye Kerunen preparing works for the *Radiance, They Dream in Time* exhibition during a workshop and performance at UNCC, Kampala, 2022

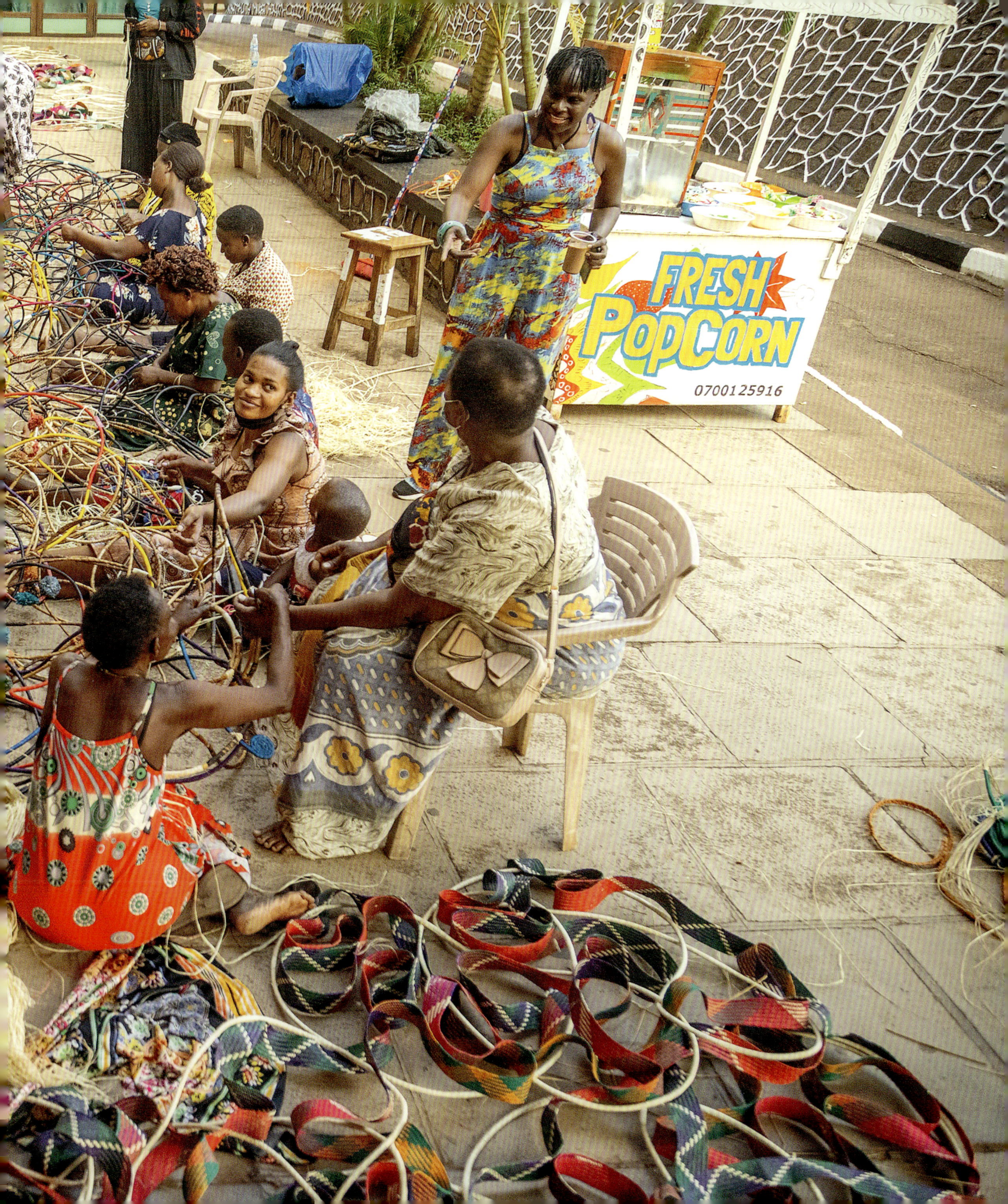

FRESH
POPCORN
0700125916

Sekajugo on Stalking Images

What we experience in these modern portraits is pure theatre against a backdrop of radial wallpapers, designed in a matrix of stripes, with a setting for figures that have awkwardly re-dreamed doubt and certainty in the metropole. One such figure leans towards the viewer, wide smile, thumbs raised, a discombobulated Blackened image of Richard Branson instead of some twentieth-century Black revolutionary preacher that has served as a wailing wall. Sekajugo's paintings remain in the intermediary distance of having dreamt of Black radiance, one that has surged (with the brilliance of the Black tradition) in the twentieth century and which has returned recently in racial justice demands with great zeal as publications and speech, emboldening visions of afrofuturisms and parlance about afropessimisms.

Sekajugo's concerns are of truth over fact and conspiracies; misrepresentation is without doubt a collective reality in this puzzling time of human history. The more considered artists are beginning to offer us art that can help us shape our experience of late capitalism's antagonisms; its geometry of trade, in which the majority existed as generic tribes, sects and ethnicities, is no longer viable.

Since 2012 Sekajugo's paintings have radically evolved, as a de-canonising tool, situating his palette to examine a particular cultural strand that remains populated by any-bodies, created by unforced errors in photographic studios and labs all over the white sphere of affluence. His paintings are a response to this archive of stock images that had proliferated like a festering infestation over every mode of human communication. From newspapers, magazines, flyers, posters, still photography of white dudes and young trendy gals, the progeny of heroin chic and laddism, have been rejected from his court.

Instead, a Black cast are performing a Ugandan version of Spike Lee's minstrelisation in his championing of role reversals. In Sekajugo's canvasses these mostly young, savvily dressed people have sauntered in and stood in the same spot, with a semi-relaxed gaze, performing a changing of the guard. In some cases, they re-exist in nostalgic surroundings, reminding one of British and German photographs of pre-independence East Africa. Often the gaze of these remarkable paintings works in lieu of trending objects from an Etsy-type market, mesmerised by the system that continuously recycles to institute its dominance as value in the secondary and tertiary market presence.

In one way or another we are witnessing a planetary convergence, creating a transformative period where there is an unprecedented remapping of "subjectivities, hierarchies, and anatomies".[1]

How is this sharpening our ability to understand the work by often unfamiliar artists, without always reducing their work through wavering conclusions based on 'short termism'? In appreciating the intriguing desire by Sekajugo "to create alternative cosmologies"[2], we are preparing

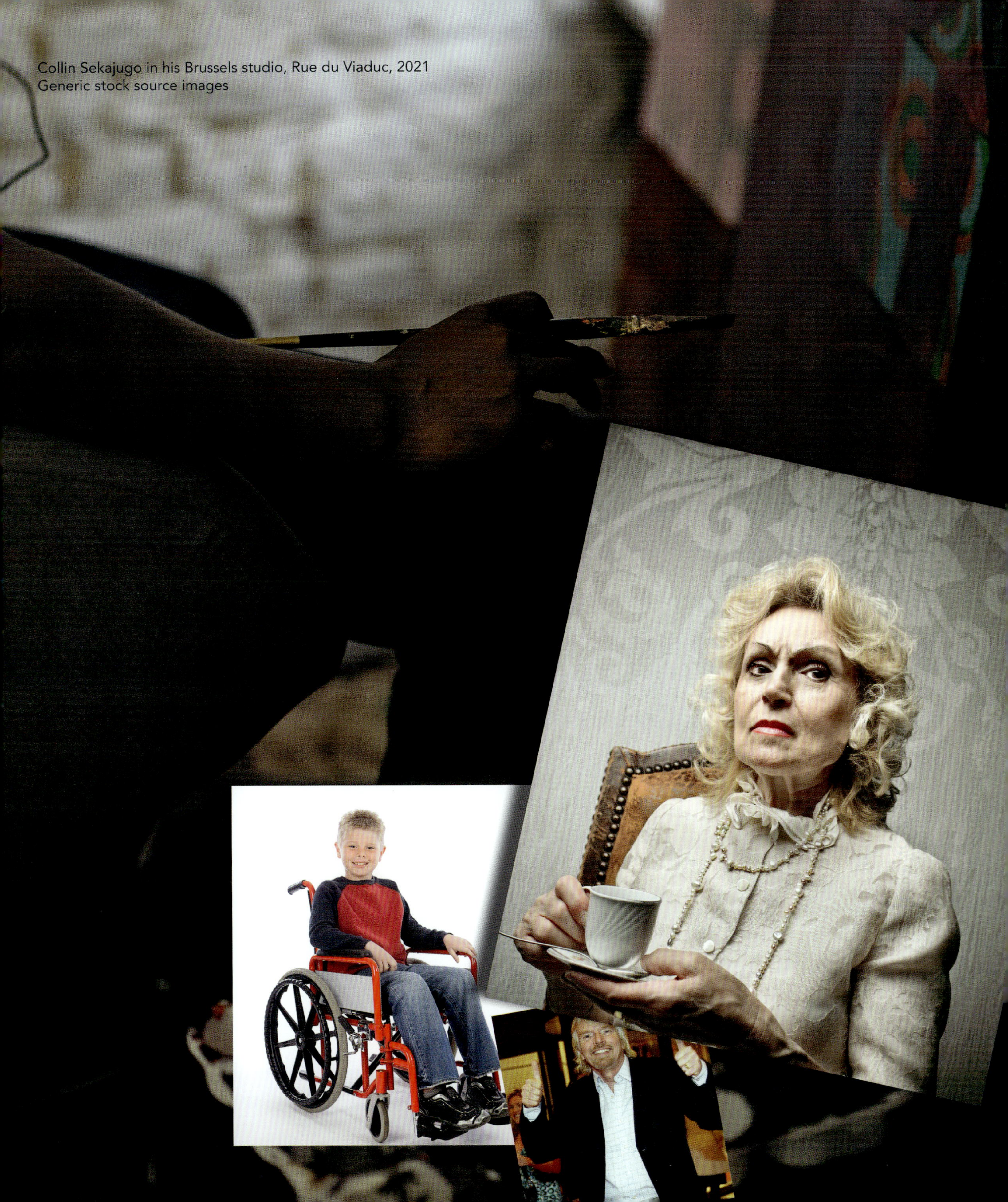

Collin Sekajugo in his Brussels studio, Rue du Viaduc, 2021
Generic stock source images

for different "knowledge and new politics of identity"[3] in civic engagement and in the changing meanings of race. The imagery with strong vernacular language, creates motifs of longing, striking restrained commentaries of Anglosphere aspirations.

The material psyche lies in the lives of the global majority who have been paradoxically excluded from participating in employment structures, invisible from our screens, excluded from academia or as so fervently noted by Sekajugo, excluded from stock photography. As young Black professionals are beginning to take their rightful place from white stereotypes, they are not being replaced by the doe-eyed, perfect teeth and 'washed behind the ears' look, but in fact, as Barbara Kruger indicates, "in the end, history happens".[4]

The installations will consider this logos-phallocentric history of privilege, to arrive at a transitory understanding of Baldwin's concept of "talented ruins… as discipline, love, luck, but most of all, endurance" that assists heightened state of the "accuracy and completeness of our knowledge of the world".[5]

Shaheen Merali, March 2022

[1] Statement by Cecilia Alemani, https://www.labiennale.org/en/art/2022/statement-cecilia-alemani (accessed 20 September 2021).
[2] Ibid.
[3] Ibid.
[4] Barbara Kruger, Stedelijk Museum Amsterdam, 2021.
[5] https://www.universityworldnews.com/post-mobilphp?story=20210907132356331&fbclid=IwAR2XY38U-fFqprpTS0KJ0chLgoEnHfEz5kw2w5hCAtdIAkwSw3EY-w36AKLag

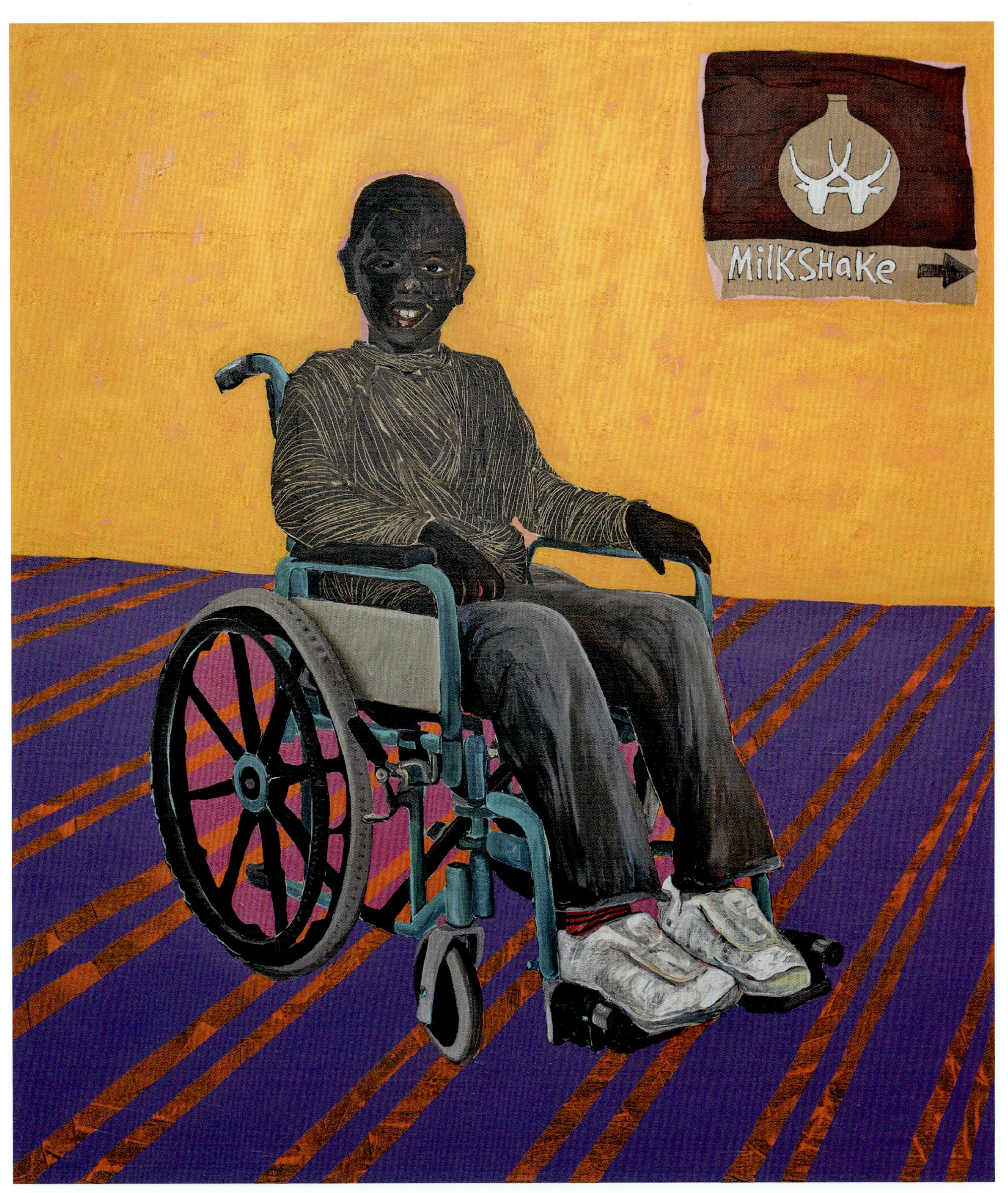

Collin Sekajugo, *Stock Image 001 – Boy in Wheelchair*, 2017/2021, acrylic and mixed media on canvas, 140 x 120 cm (55 1/8 x 47 1/4 in.)

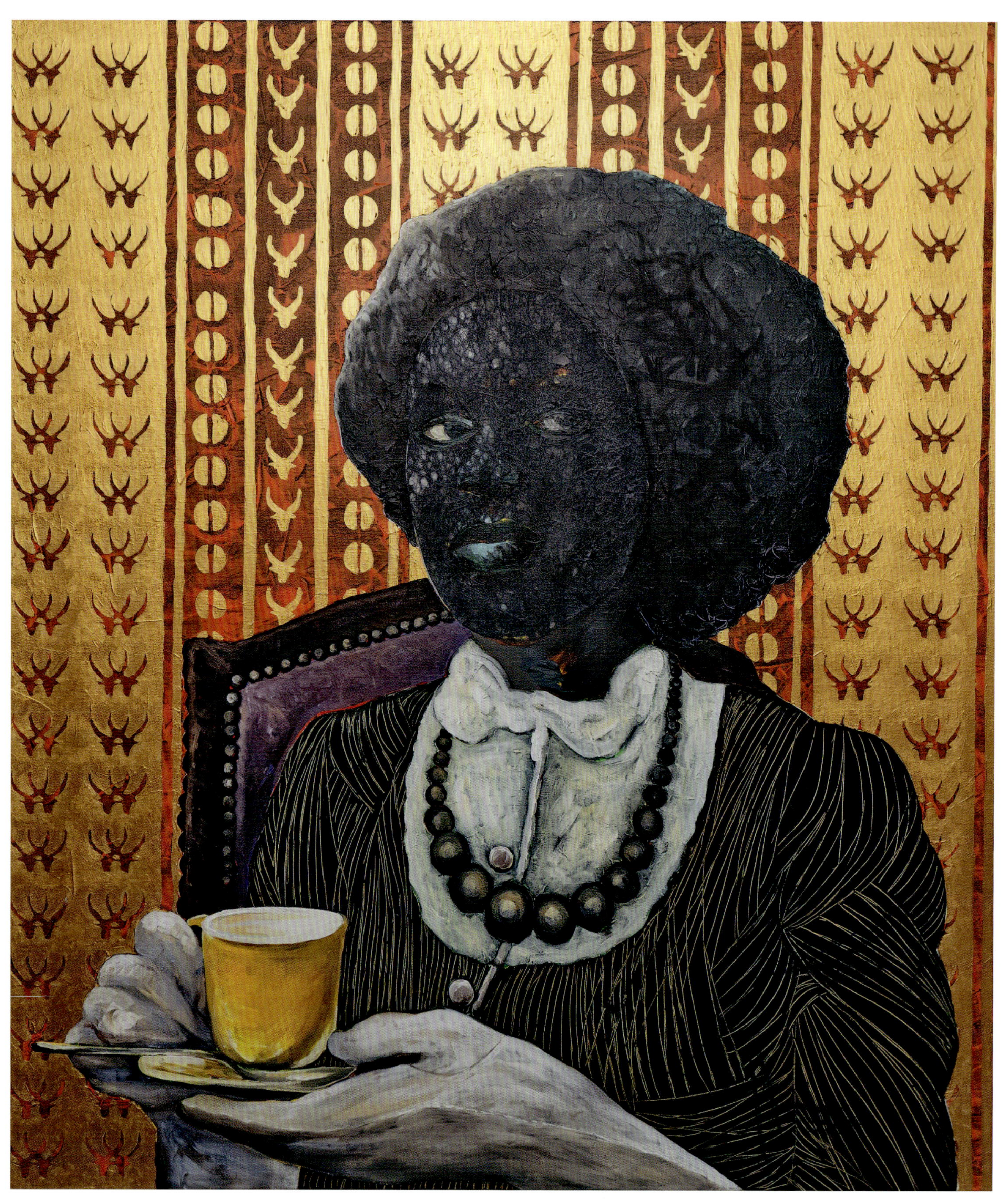

Collin Sekajugo, *Stock Image 002 – Rich Woman Drinking Tea*, 2015/2021, acrylic and mixed media on canvas, 140 x 120 cm (55 $\frac{1}{8}$ x 47 $\frac{1}{4}$ in.)

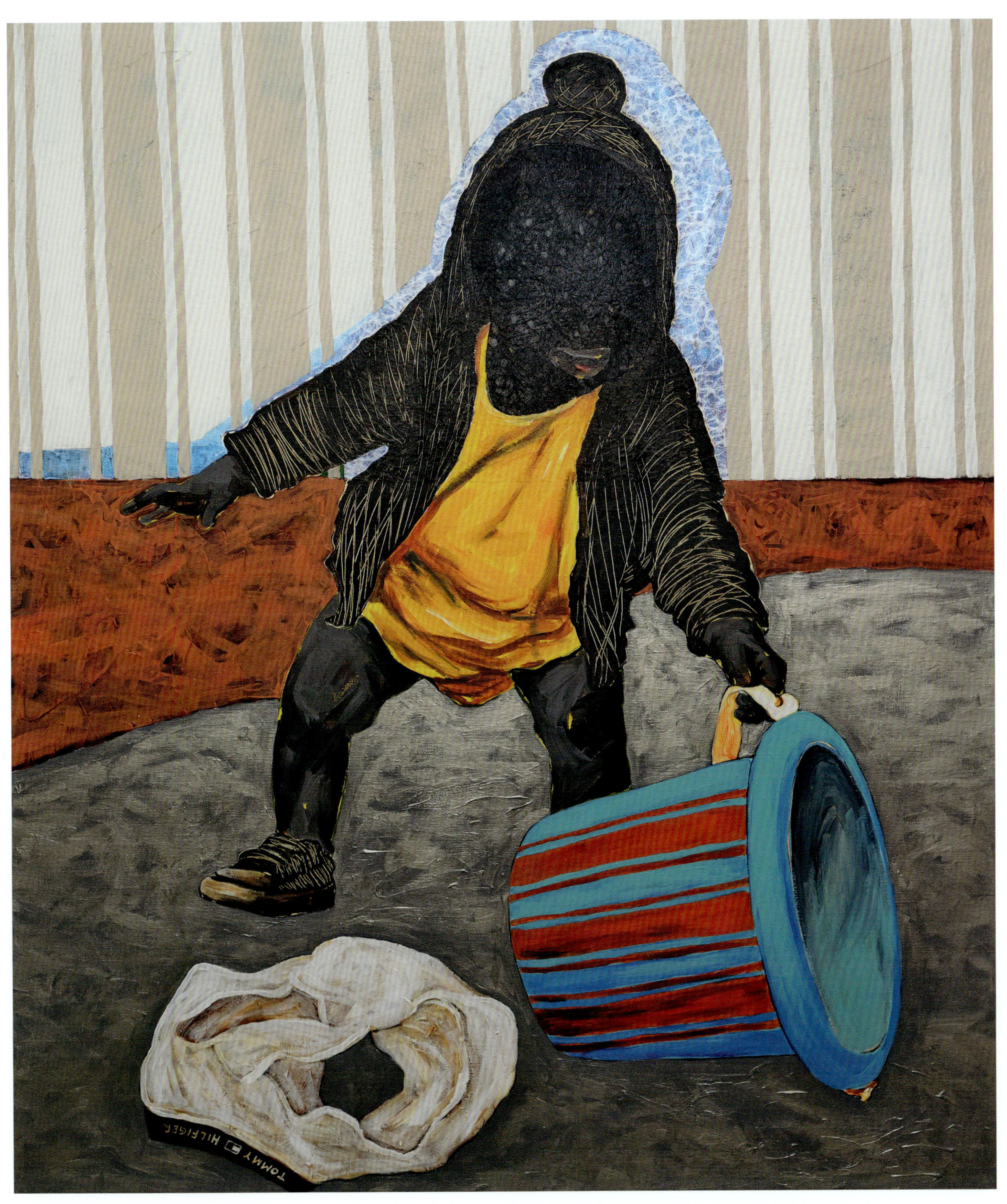

Collin Sekajugo, *Stock Image 003 – Baby with Bucket*, 2018/2021, acrylic and mixed media on canvas, 140 x 120 cm (55 ⅛ x 47 ¼ in.)

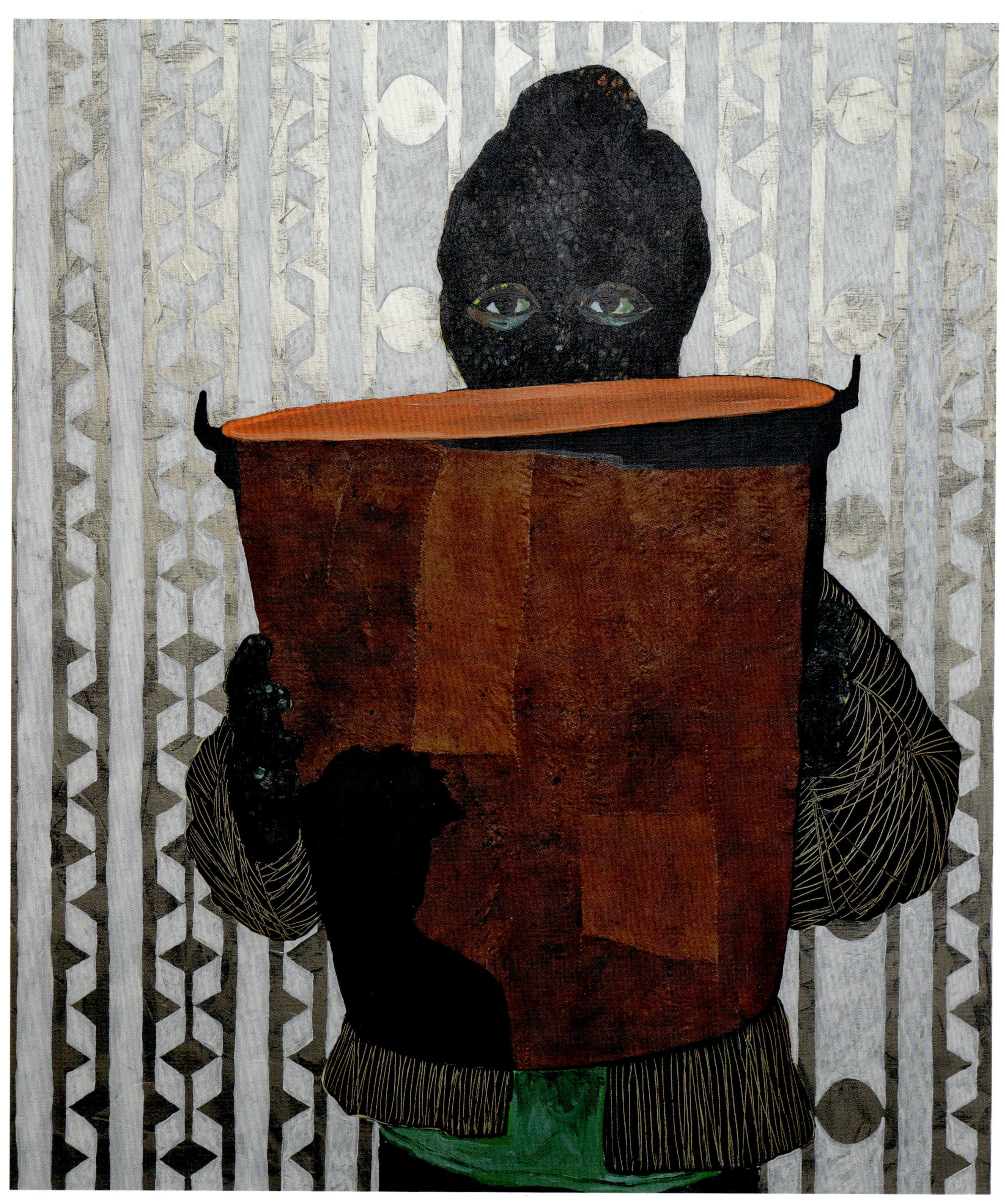

Collin Sekajugo, *Stock Image 004 – Child with Recycling Bin*, 2018/2021, acrylic, barkcloth and mixed media on canvas, 140 x 120 cm (55 ⅛ x 47 ¼ in.)

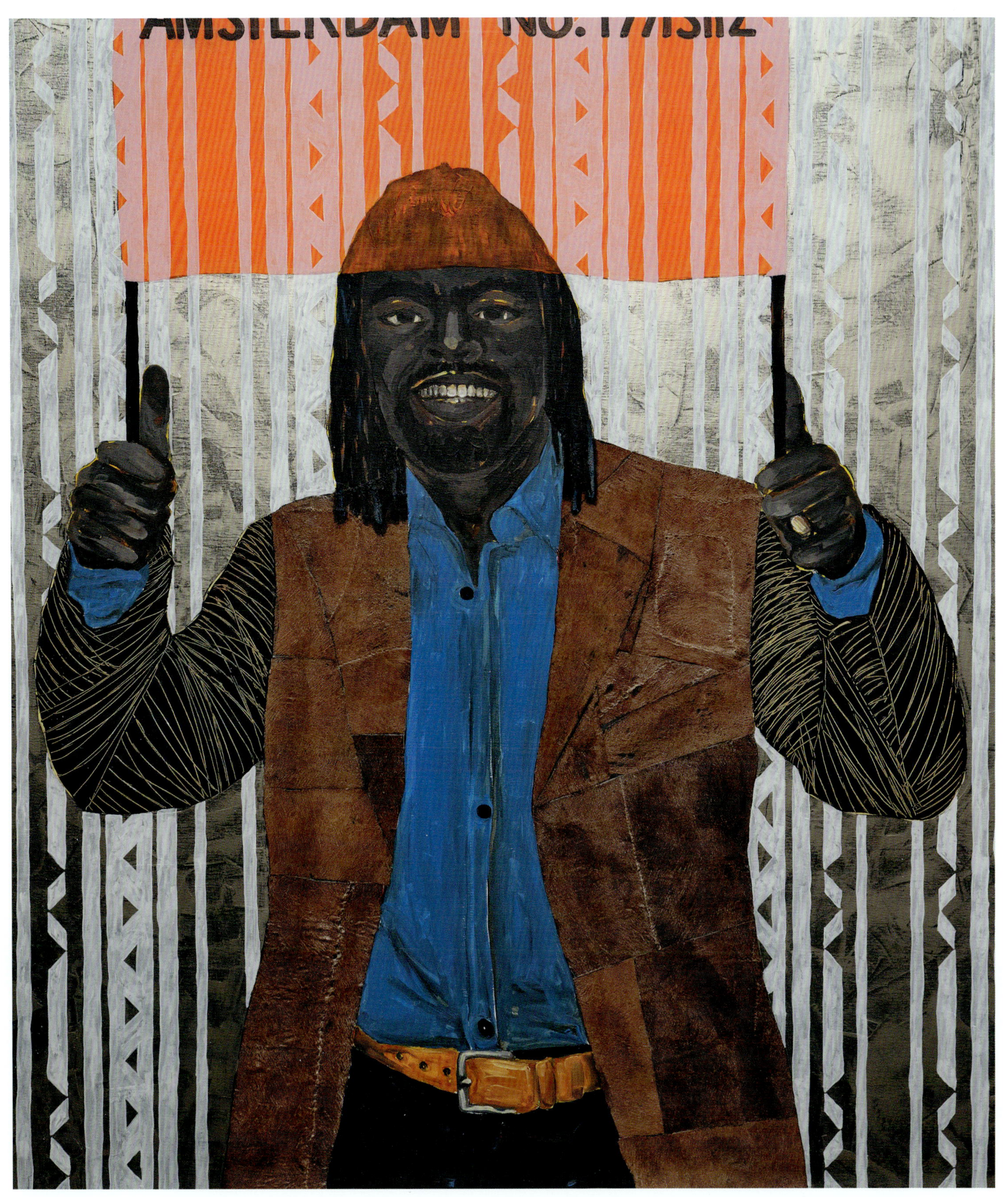

Collin Sekajugo, *Stock Image 005 – Richard Branson*, 2021, acrylic, barkcloth and mixed media on canvas, 140 x 120 cm (55 ⅛ x 47 ¼ in.)

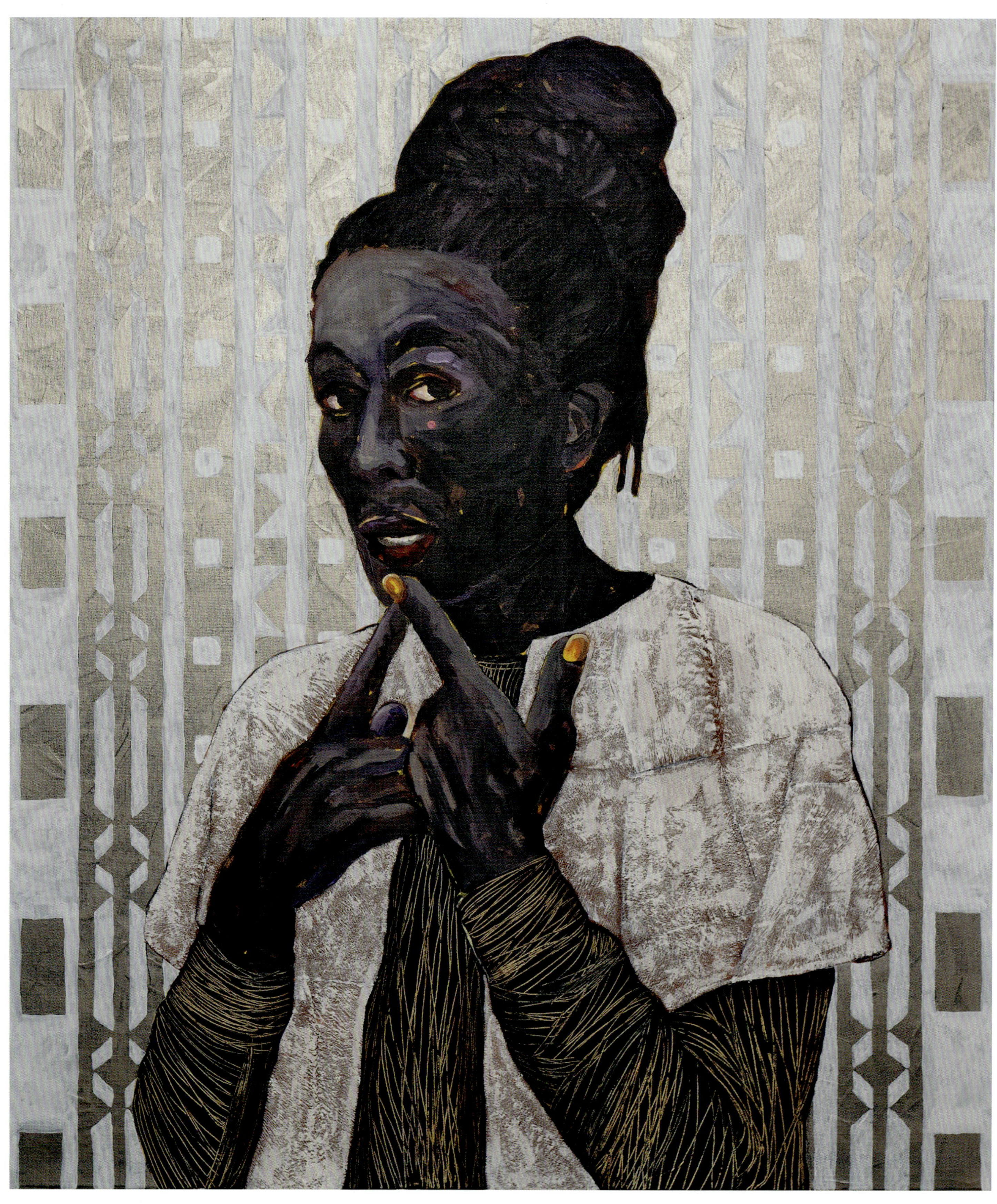

Collin Sekajugo, *Stock Image 006 – Woman in Surprise*, 2018/2021, acrylic, barkcloth and mixed media on canvas, 120 x 100 cm (47 ¼ x 39 ⅜ in.)

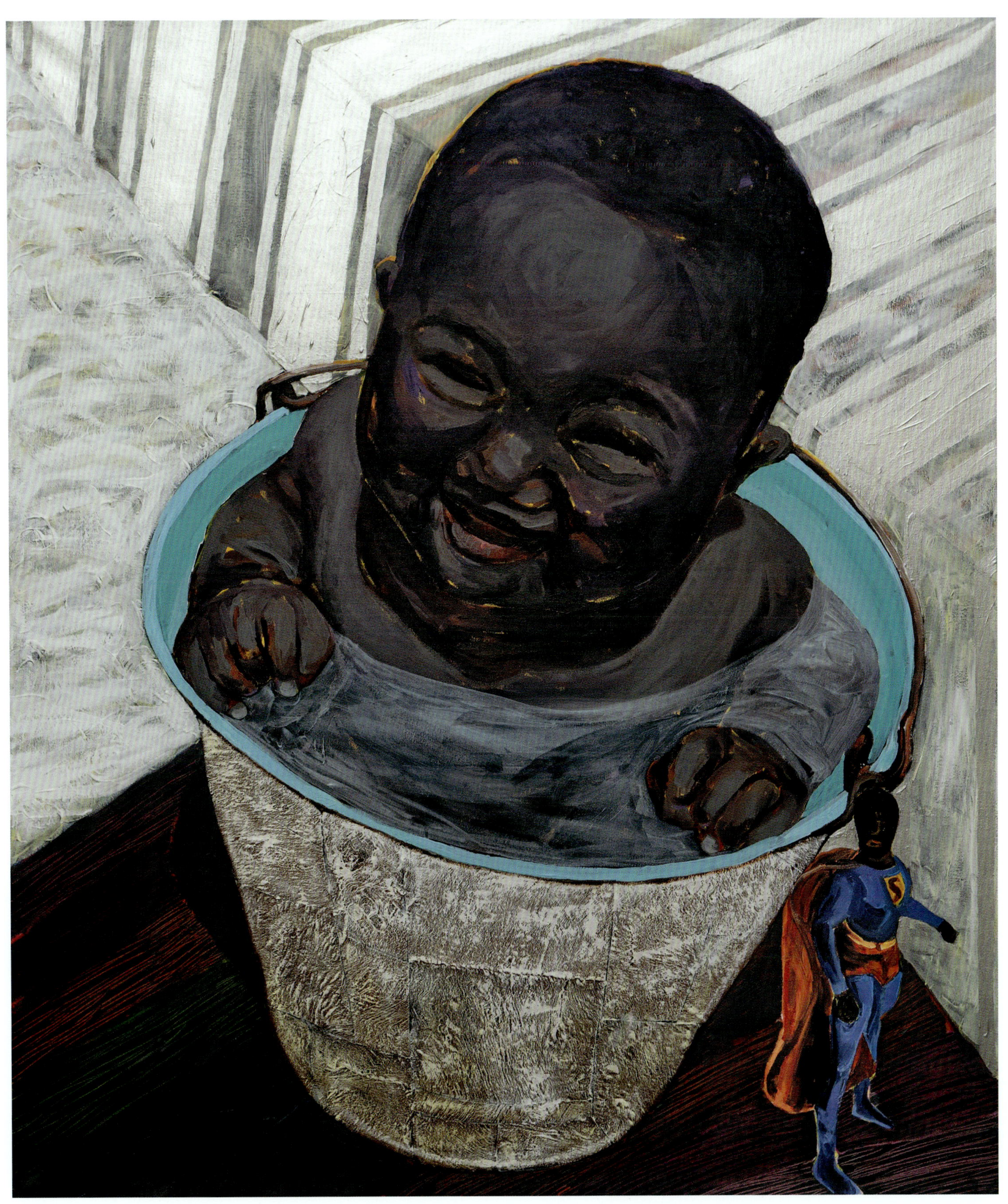

Collin Sekajugo, *Stock Image 007 – Baby in Bucket*, 2018/2021, acrylic, barkcloth and mixed media on canvas, 120 x 100 cm (47 ¼ x 39 ⅜ in.)

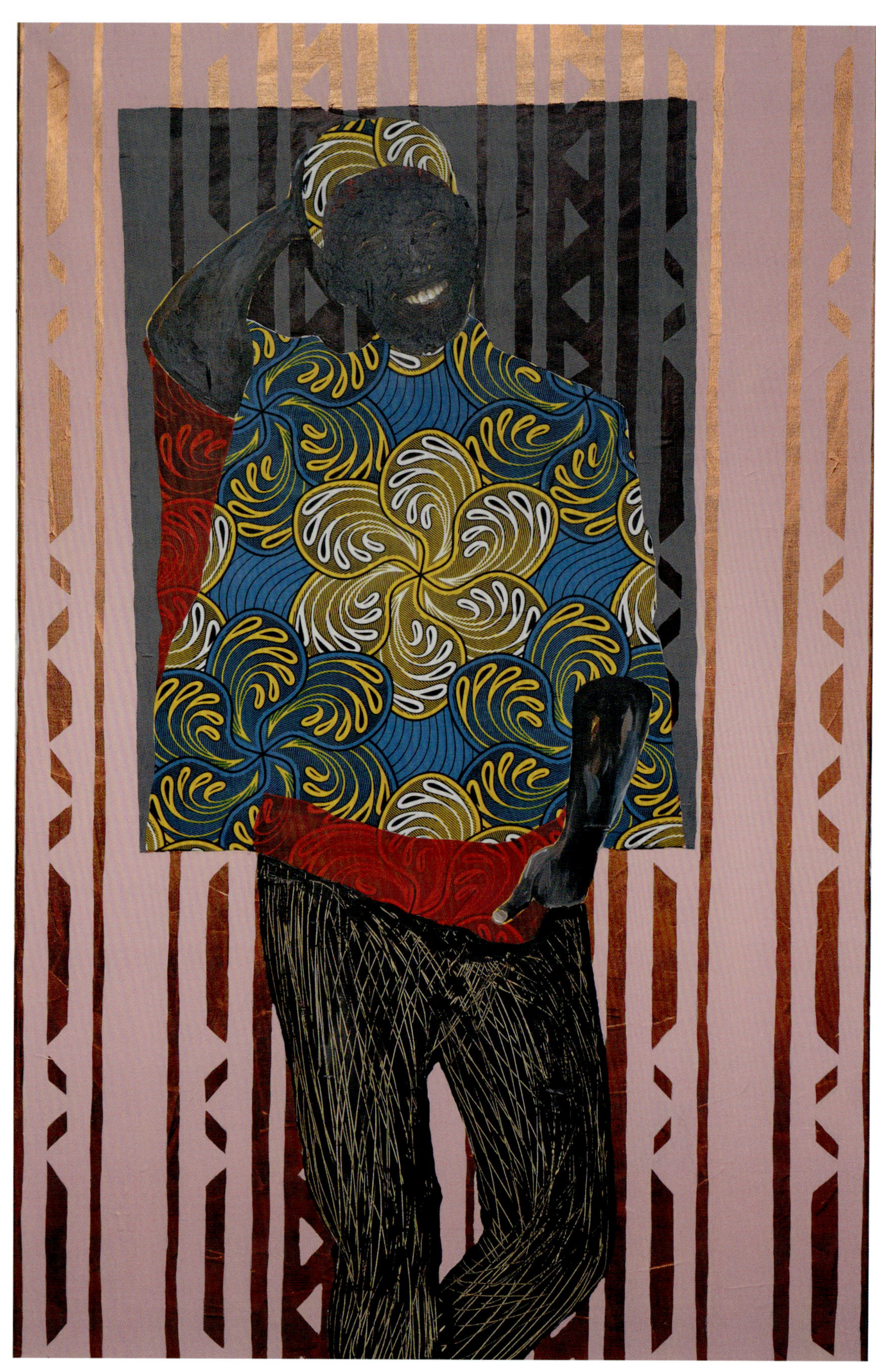

Collin Sekajugo, *Stock Image 008 – Relaxed and Smiling*, 2021, acrylic, wax cloth and mixed media on canvas, 160 x 100 cm (63 x 39 ⅜ in.)

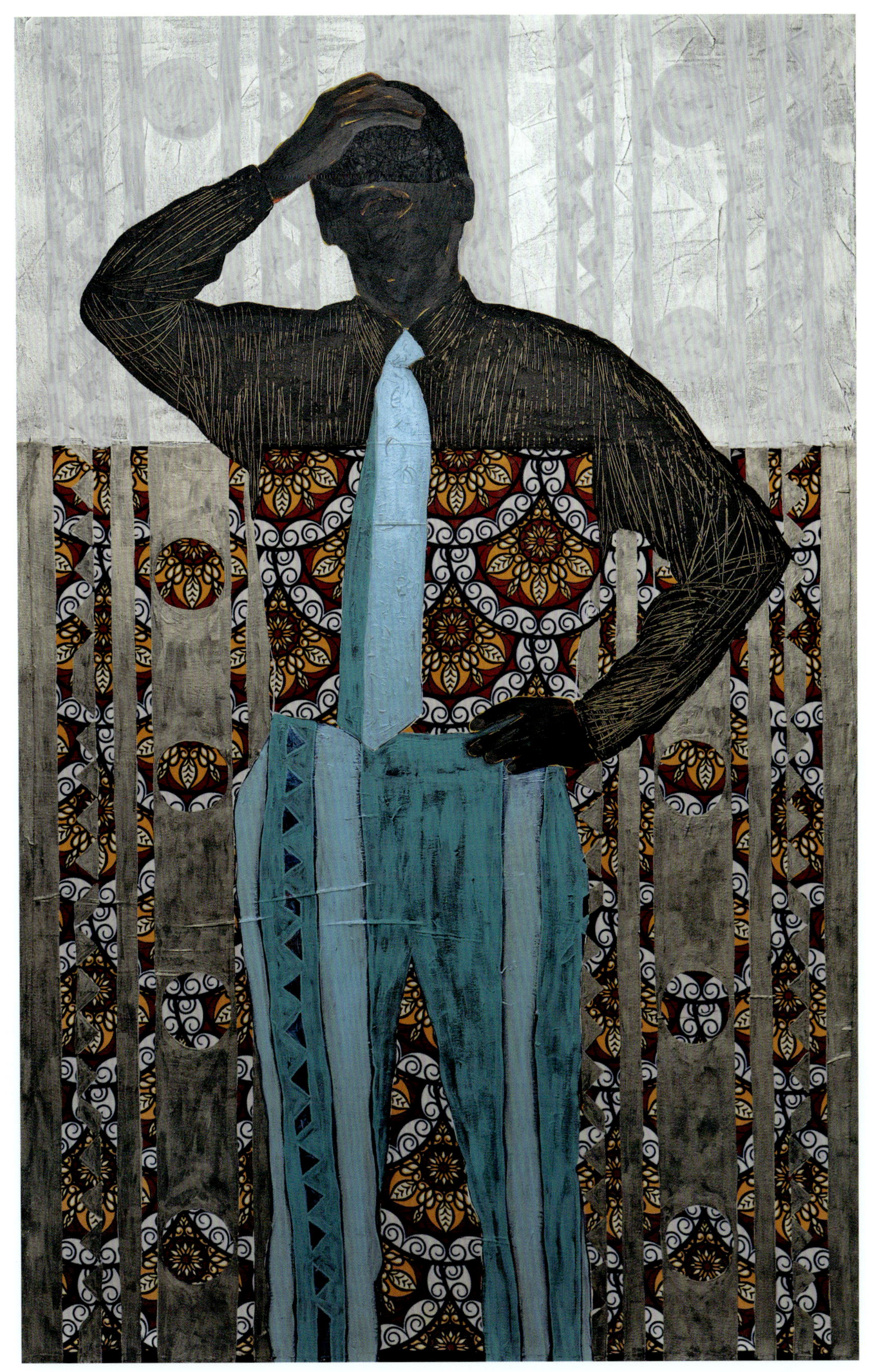

Collin Sekajugo, *Stock Image 009 – Oh No!*, 2021, acrylic, wax cloth and mixed media on canvas, 160 x 100 cm (63 x 39 ⅜ in.)

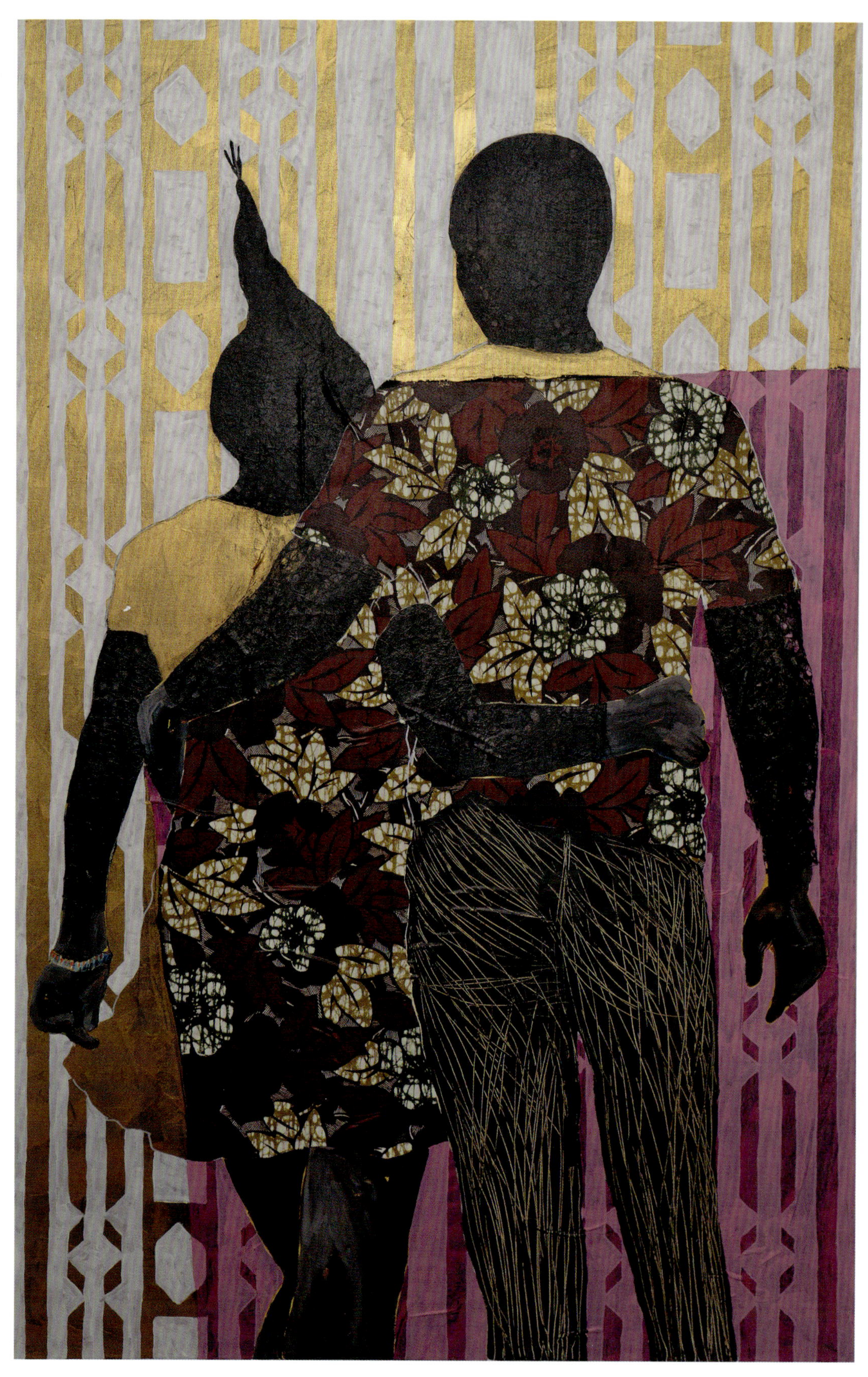

Collin Sekajugo, *Stock Image 010 – Falling in Love*, 2021, acrylic, wax cloth and mixed media on canvas, 160 x 100 cm (63 x 39 ⅜ in.)

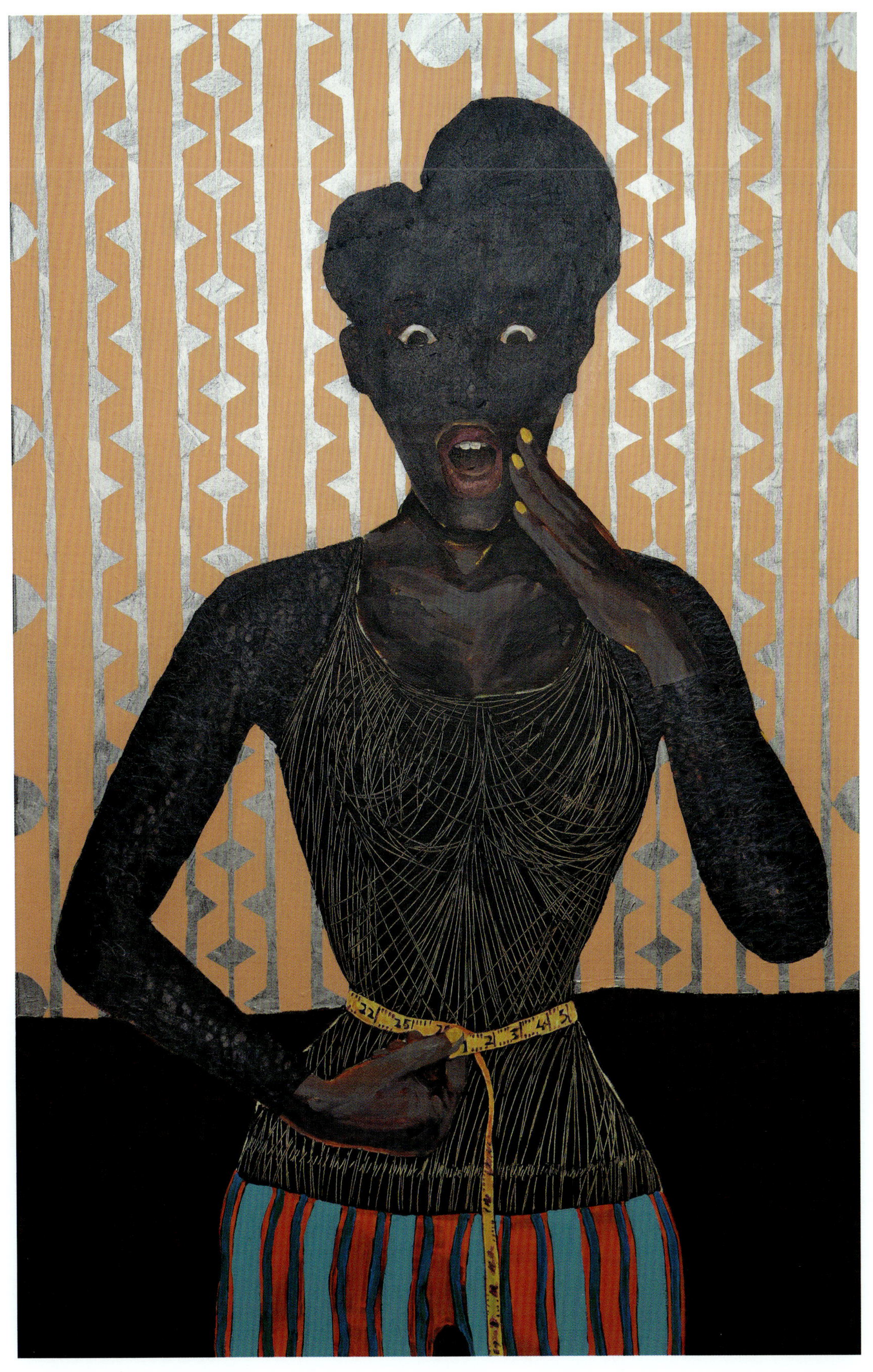

Collin Sekajugo, *Stock Image 011- Ariane's Weightloss*, 2021, acrylic, barkcloth and mixed media on canvas, 160 x 100 cm (63 x 39 3/8 in.)

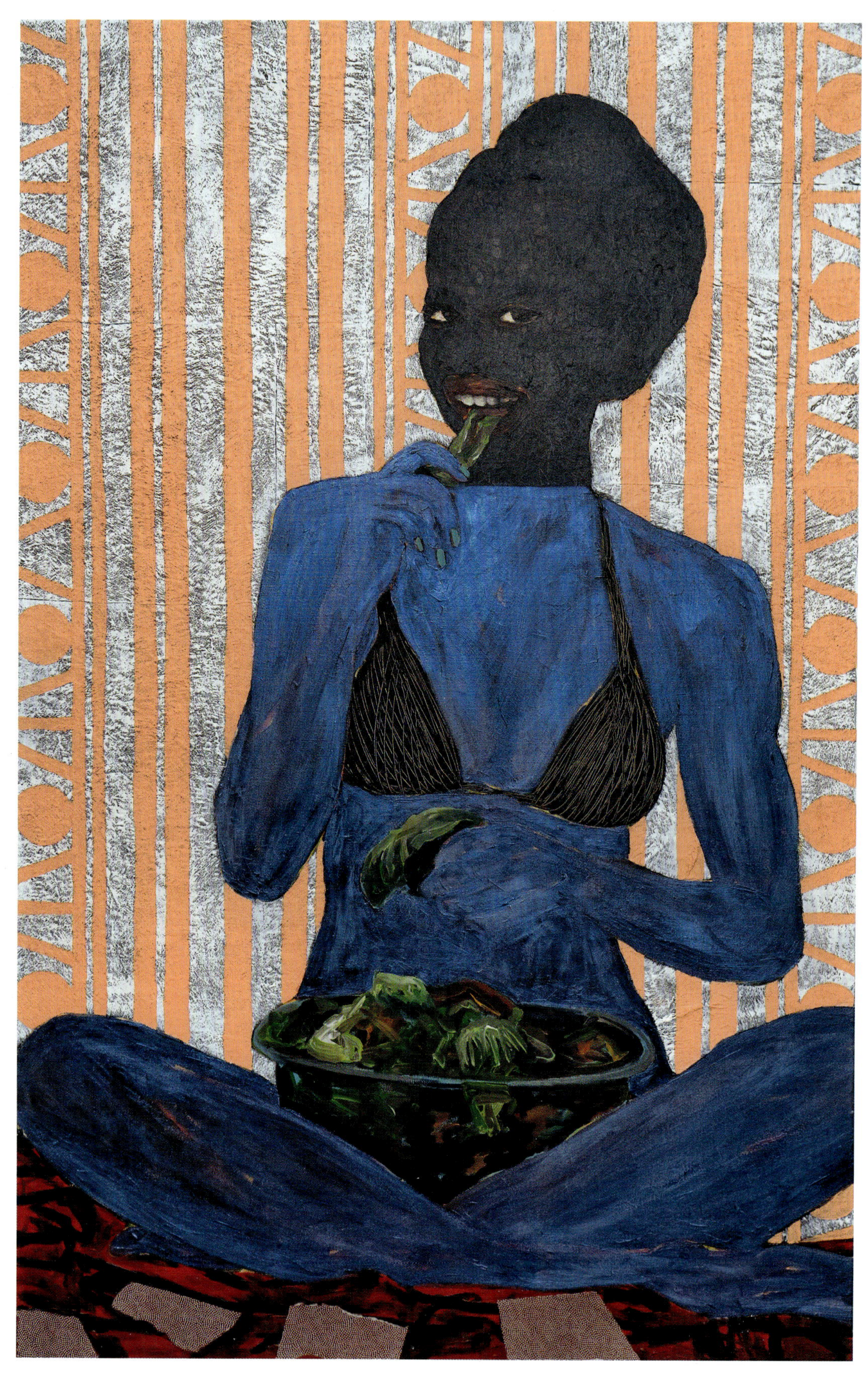

Collin Sekajugo, *Stock Image 012 – Smiling Girl Eating Salad*, 2021, acrylic, barkcloth and mixed media on canvas, 160 x 100 cm (63 x 39 ⅜ in.)

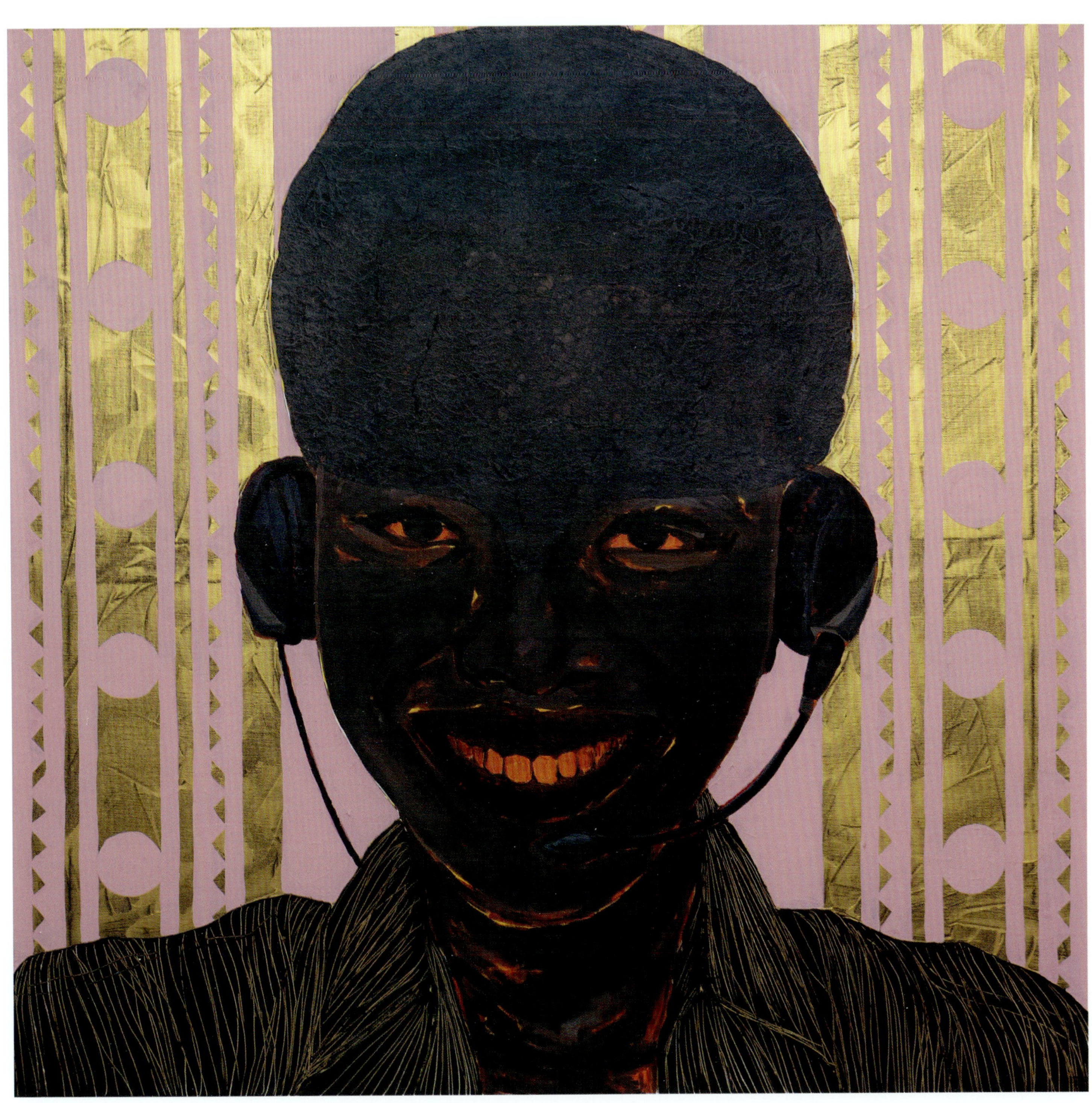

Collin Sekajugo, *Stock Image 013 – Engaged*, 2018/2021, acrylic and mixed media on canvas, 120 x 120 cm (47 ¼ x 47 ¼ in.)

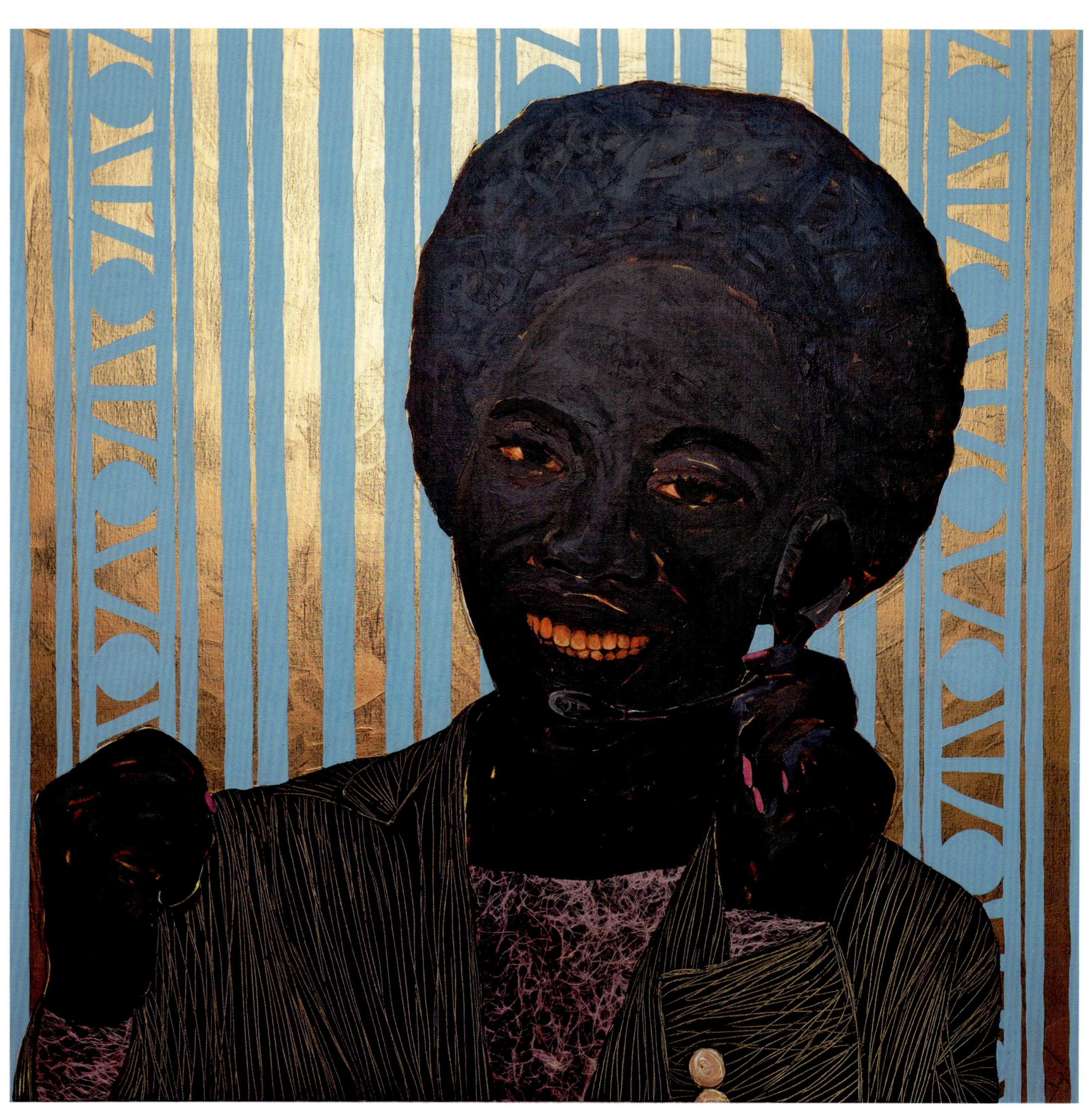

Collin Sekajugo, *Stock Image 014 – How may I direct Your Call*, 2018/2021, acrylic and mixed media on canvas, 120 x 120 cm (47 ¼ x 47 ¼ in.)

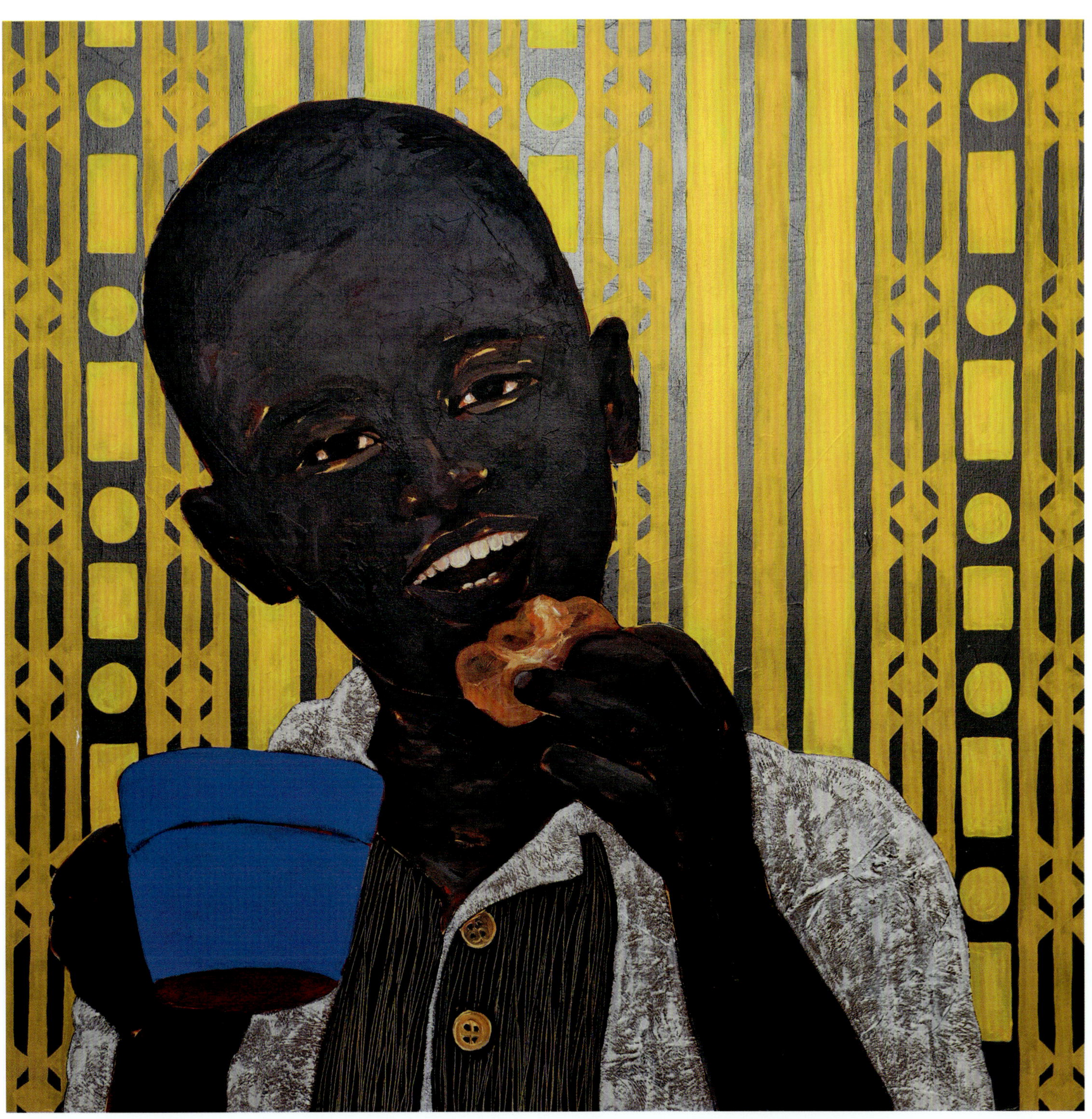

Collin Sekajugo, *Stock Image 015 – Milk and Cookies*, 2018/2021, acrylic, barkcloth and mixed media on canvas, 120 x 120 cm (47 ¼ x 47 ¼ in.)

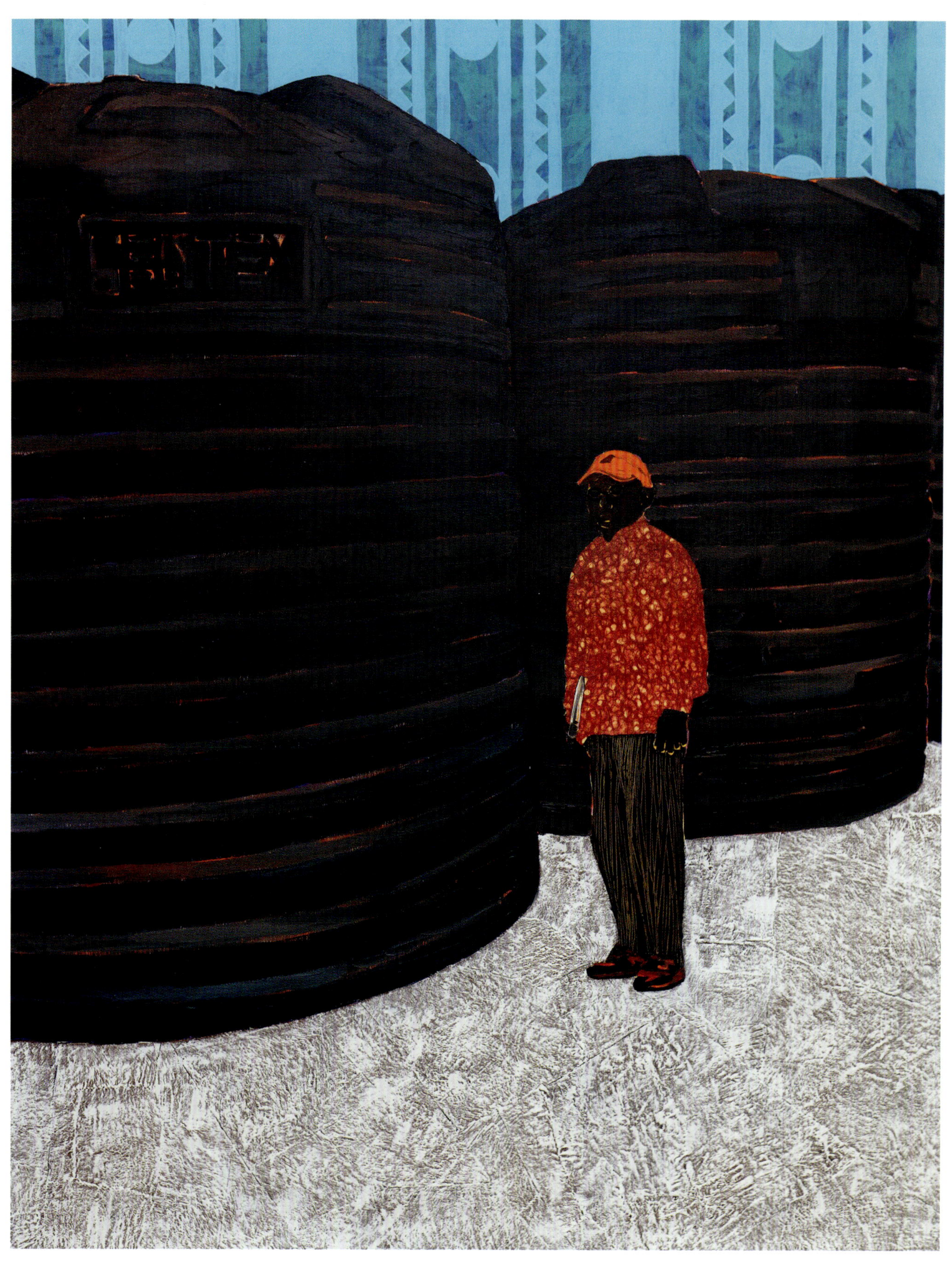

Collin Sekajugo, *Stock Image 016 – Water Tanks Kampala*, 2022, acrylic, barkcloth and mixed media on canvas, 194 x 145 cm (76 $\frac{3}{8}$ x 57 $\frac{1}{8}$ in.)

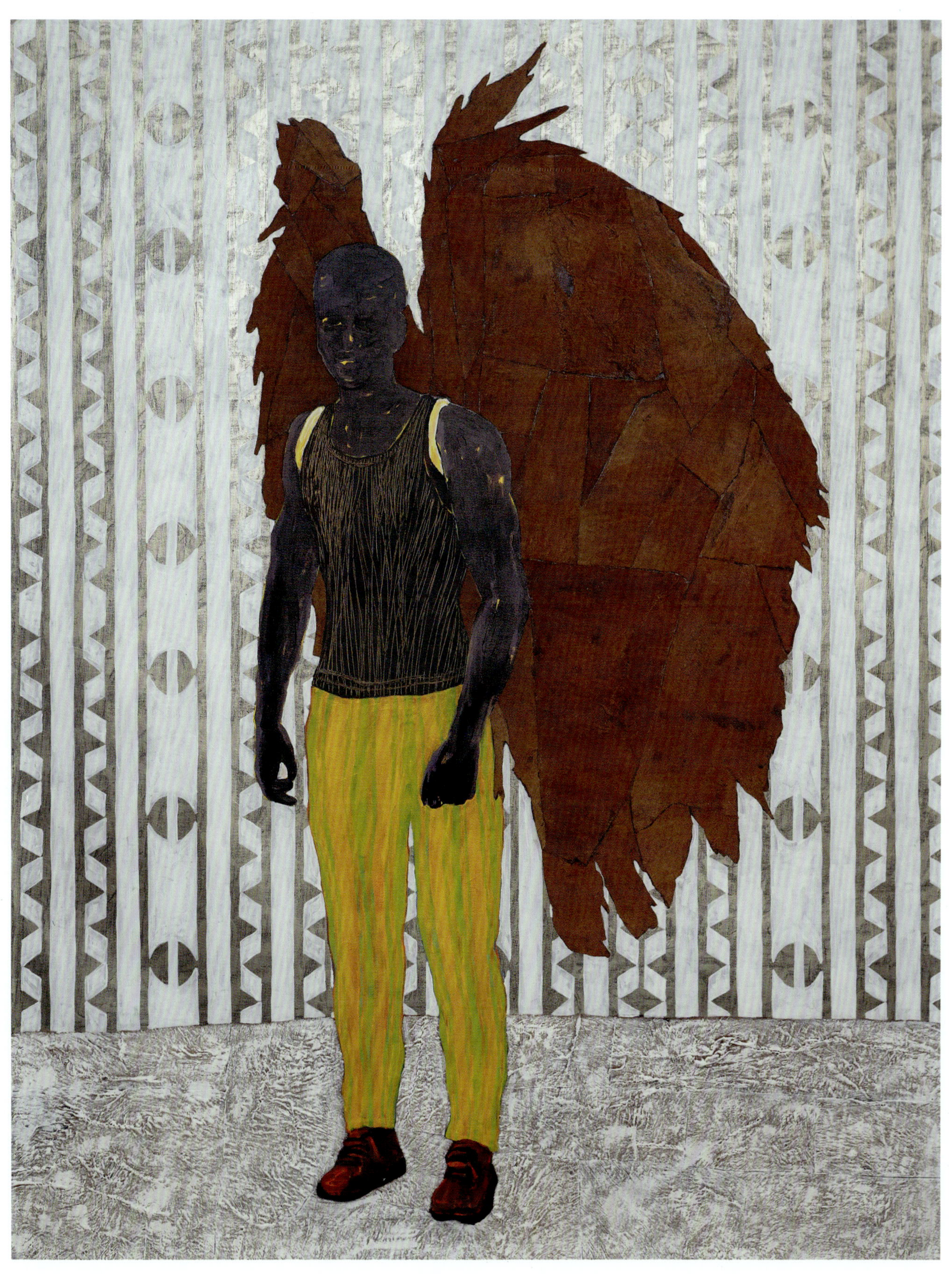

Collin Sekajugo, *Stock Image 019 – Party Monster*, 2022, acrylic, barkcloth and mixed media on canvas, 194 x 145 cm (76 ³⁄₈ x 57 ¹⁄₈ in.)

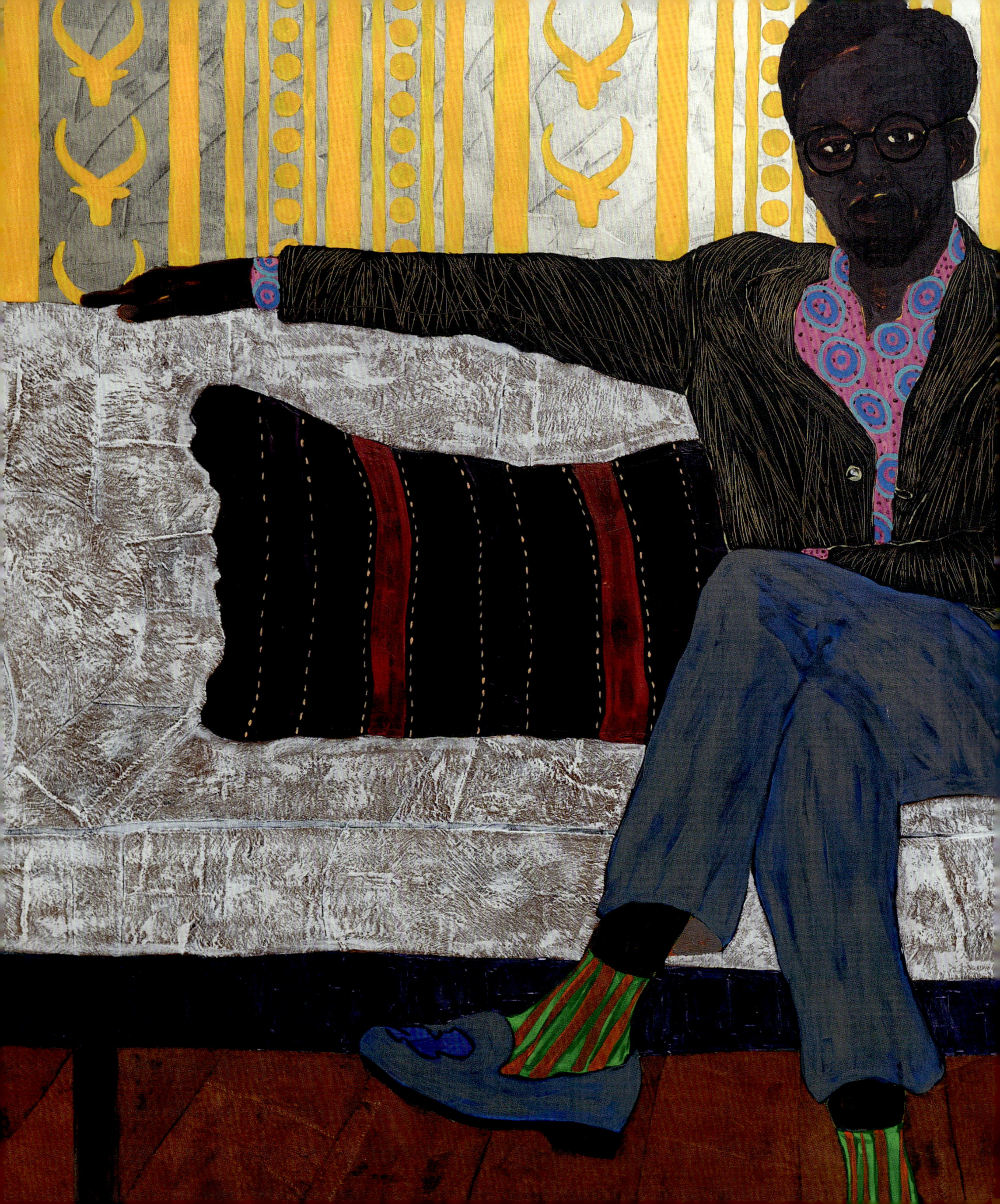

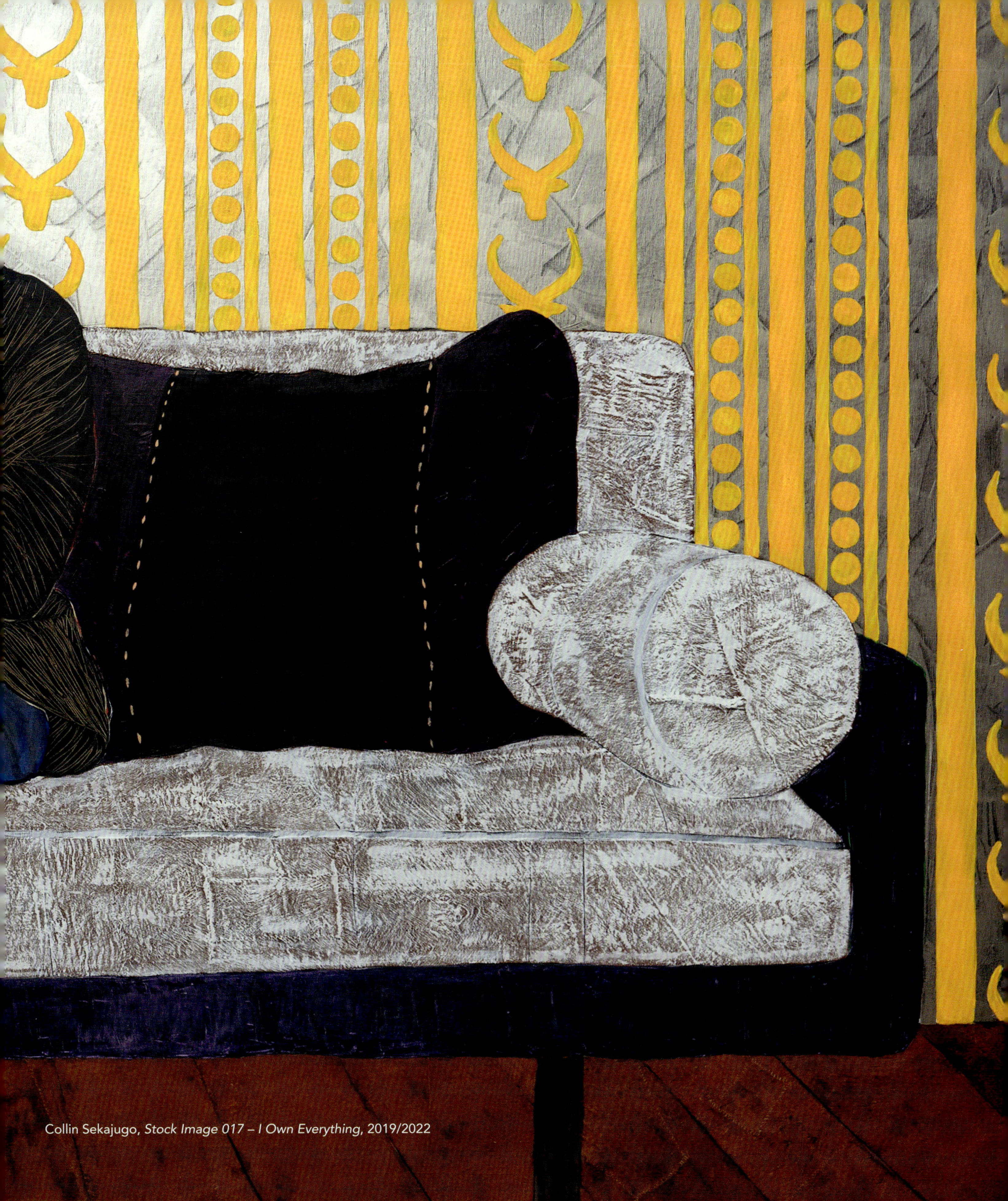

Collin Sekajugo, *Stock Image 017 – I Own Everything*, 2019/2022

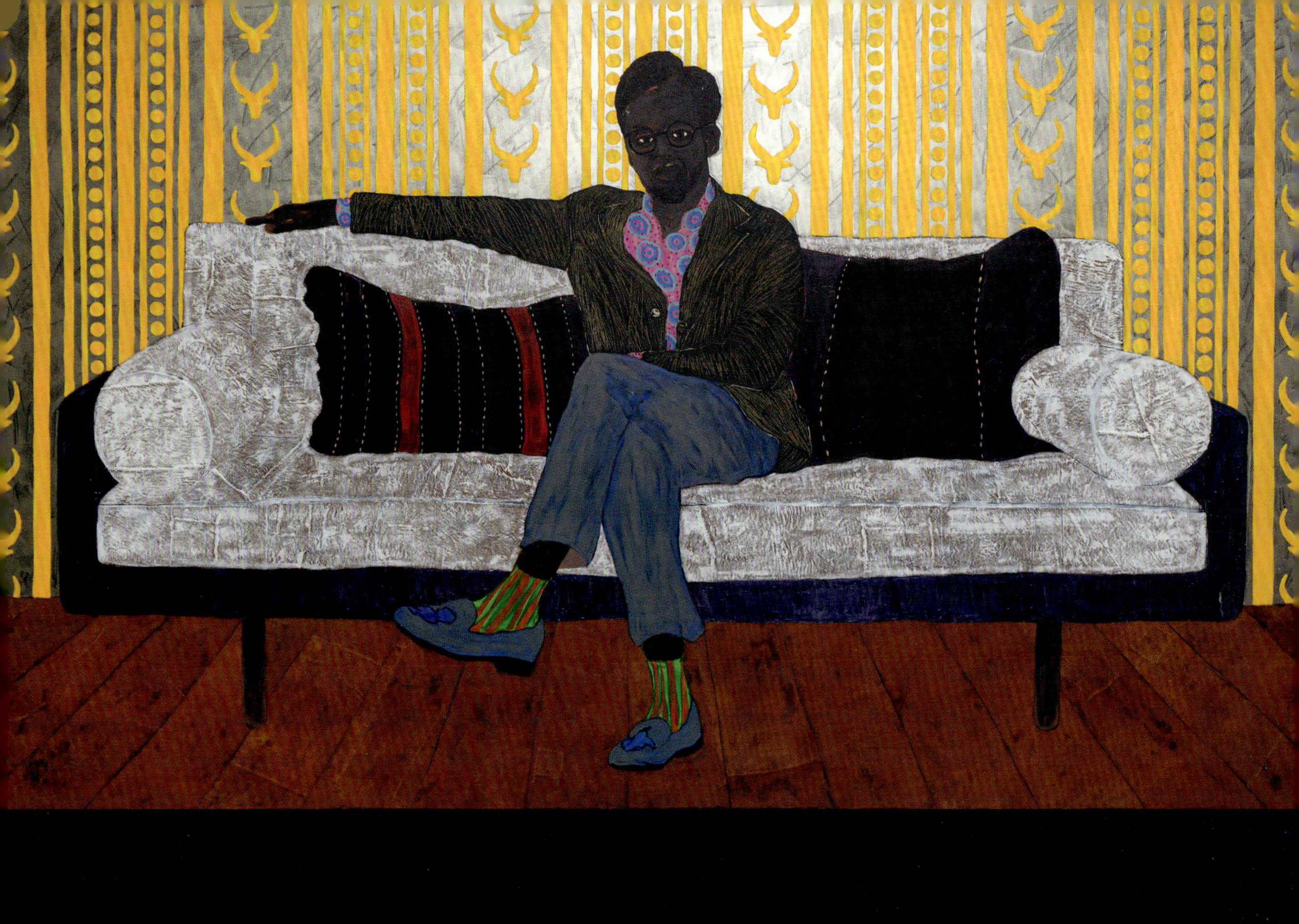

Collin Sekajugo, *Stock Image 017 – I Own Everything*, 2019/2022, acrylic, barkcloth and mixed media on canvas, 190 x 300 cm (74 ¾ x 118 ⅛ in.)

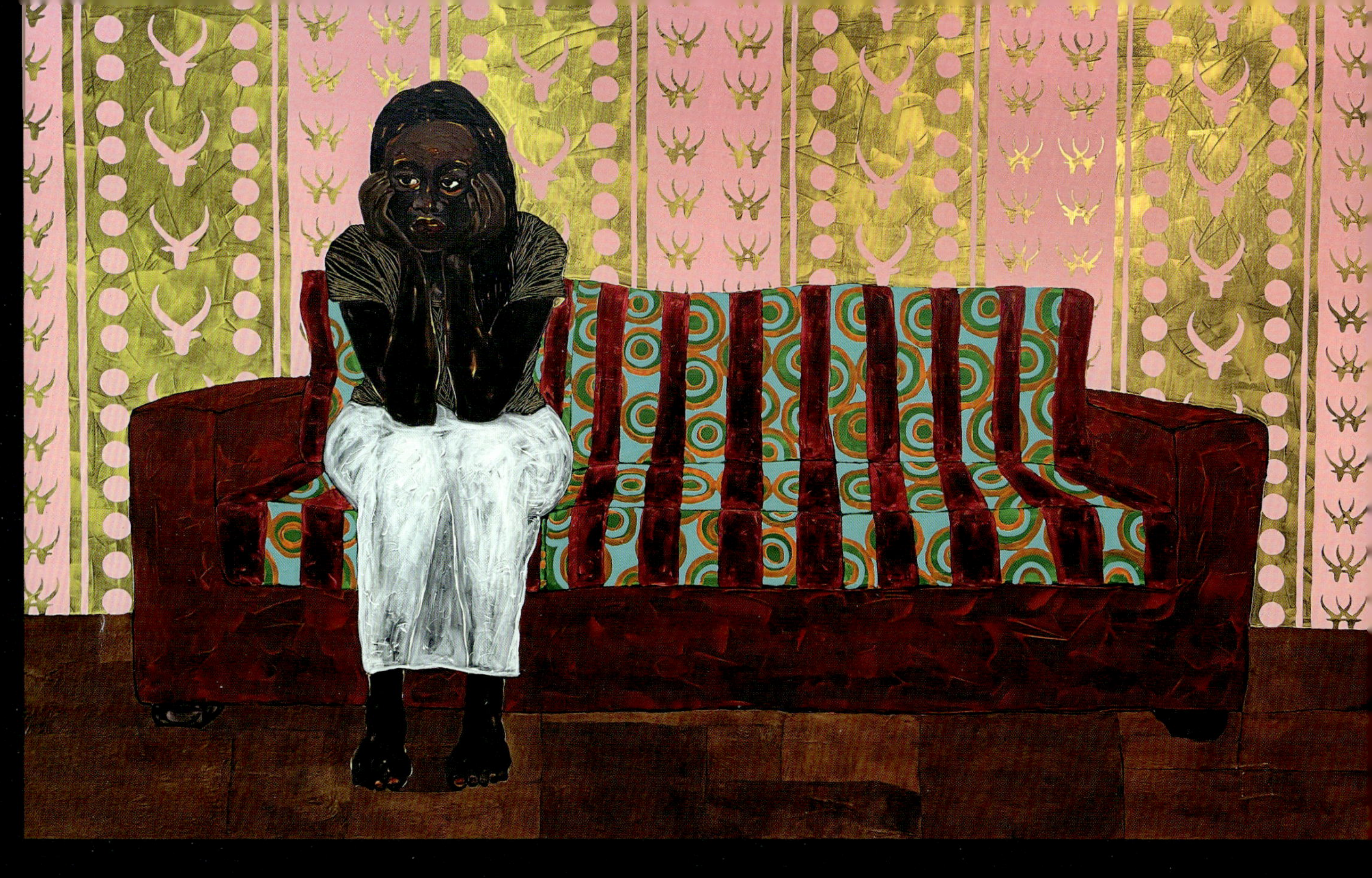

Collin Sekajugo, *Stock Image 018 – Sad, Seated to Left*, 2019/2022, acrylic, barkcloth and mixed media on canvas, 190 x 300 cm (74 ¾ x 118 ⅛ in.)

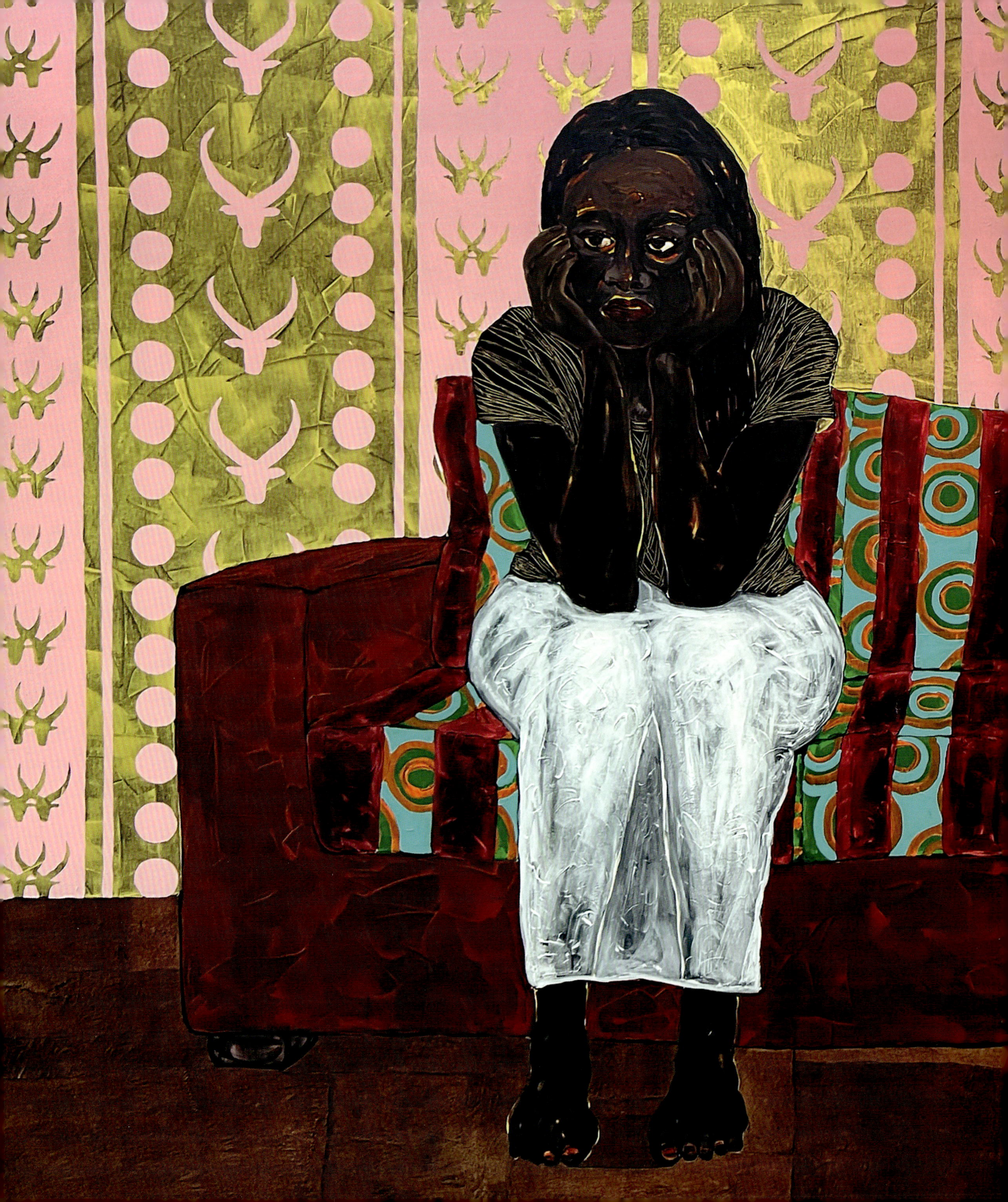

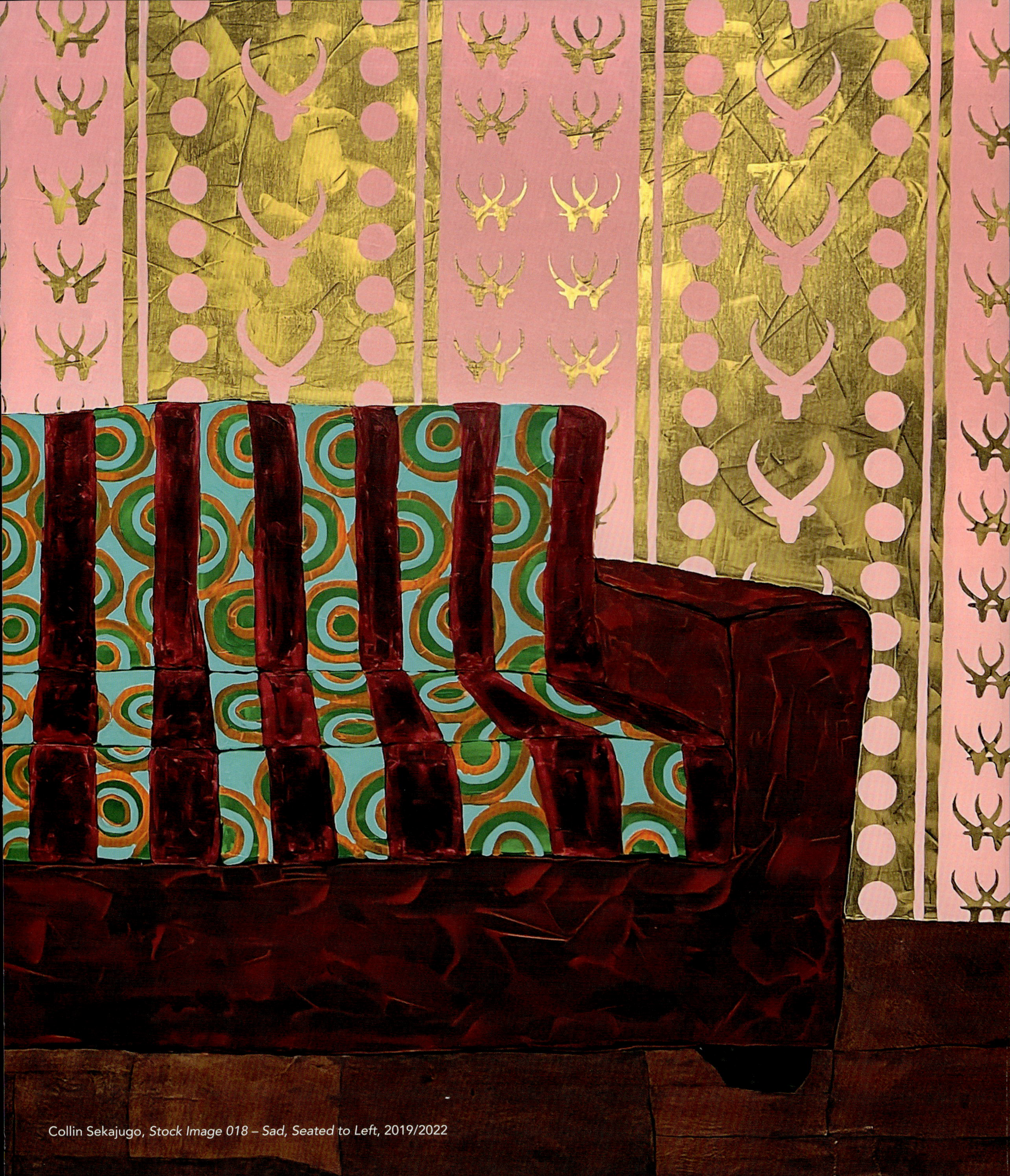

Collin Sekajugo, *Stock Image 018 – Sad, Seated to Left*, 2019/2022

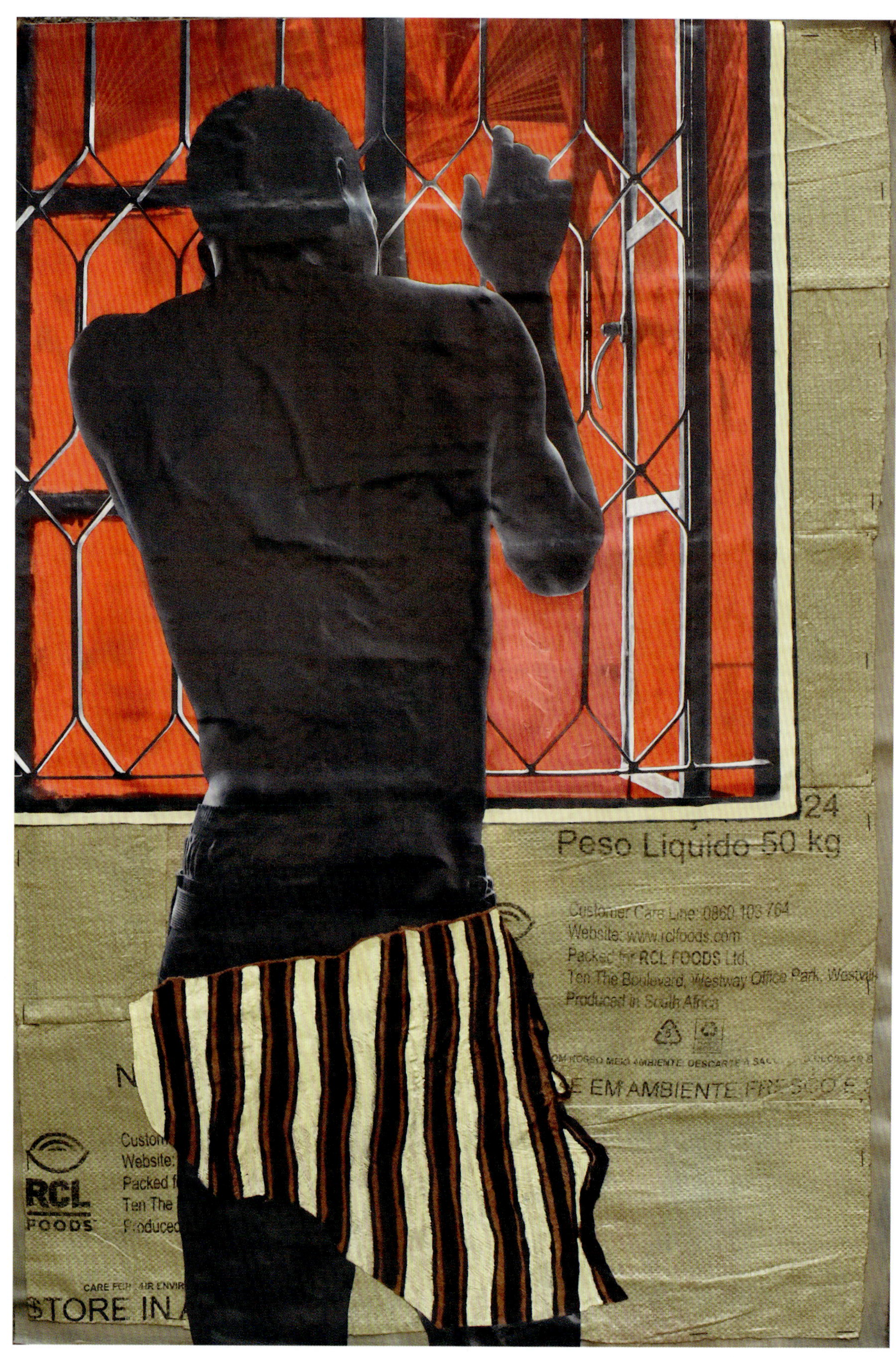

Collin Sekajugo, *Red Sky*, 2021, acrylic, barkcloth and mixed media on denim, 150 x 100 cm (59 ⅛ x 39 ⅜ in.)

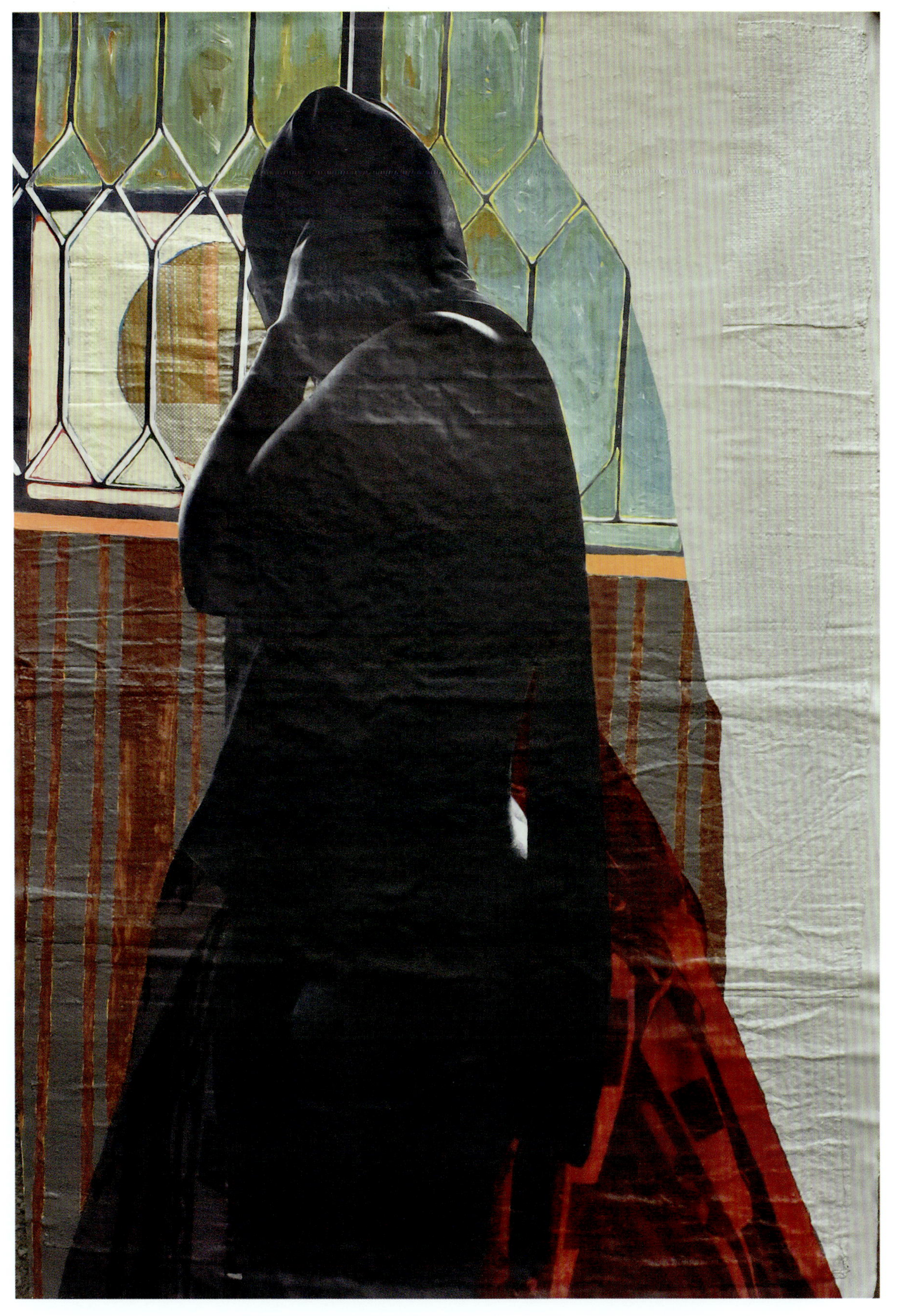

Collin Sekajugo, *Full Moon*, 2021, acrylic, barkcloth and mixed media on denim, 150 x 100 cm (59 ⅛ x 39 ⅜ in.)

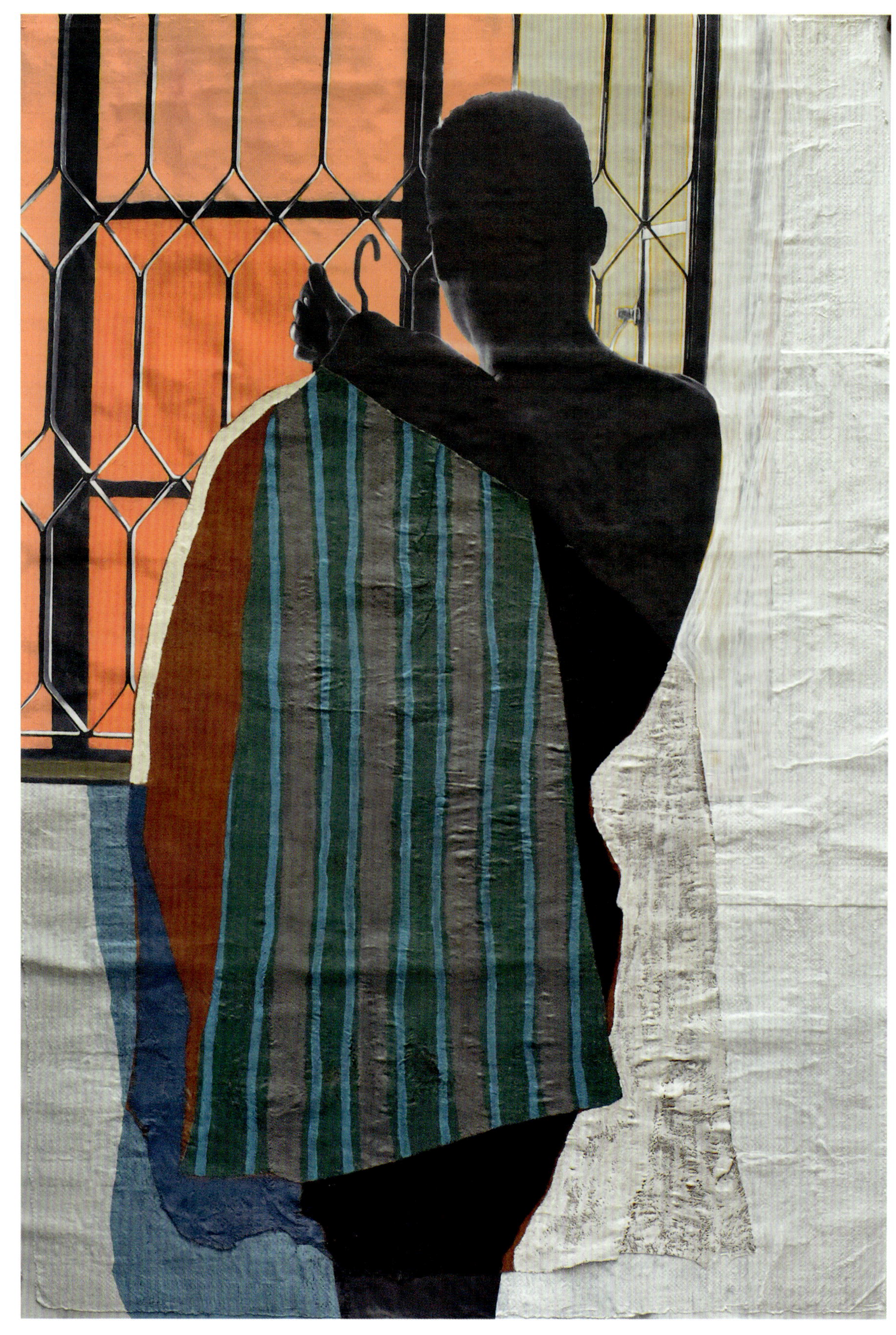

Collin Sekajugo, *The Patrician*, 2021, acrylic, barkcloth and mixed media on denim, 150 x 100 cm (59 ⅛ x 39 ⅜ in.)

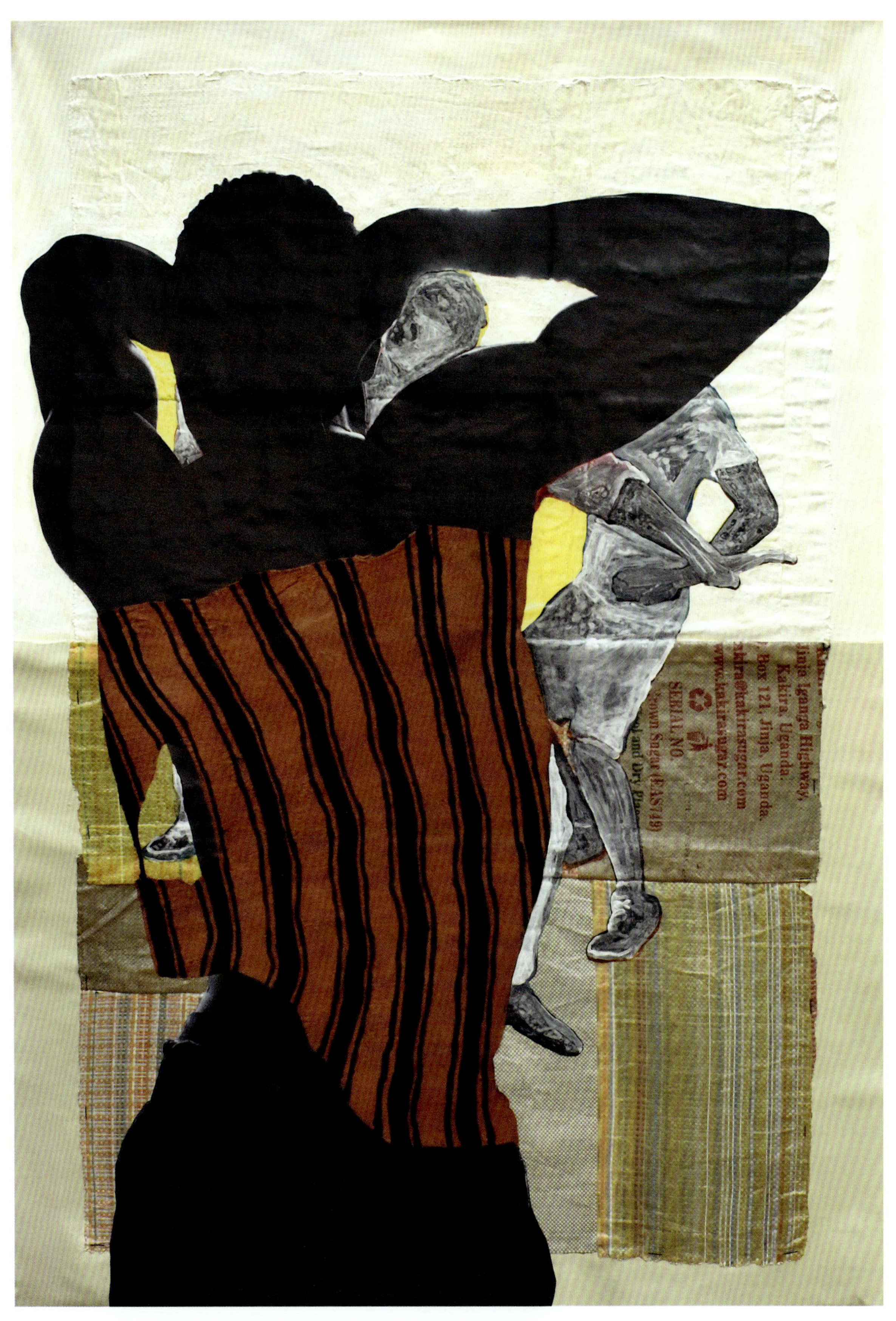

Collin Sekajugo, *Imitation*, 2021, acrylic, barkcloth and mixed media on denim, 150 x 100 cm (59 ⅛ x 39 ⅜ in.)

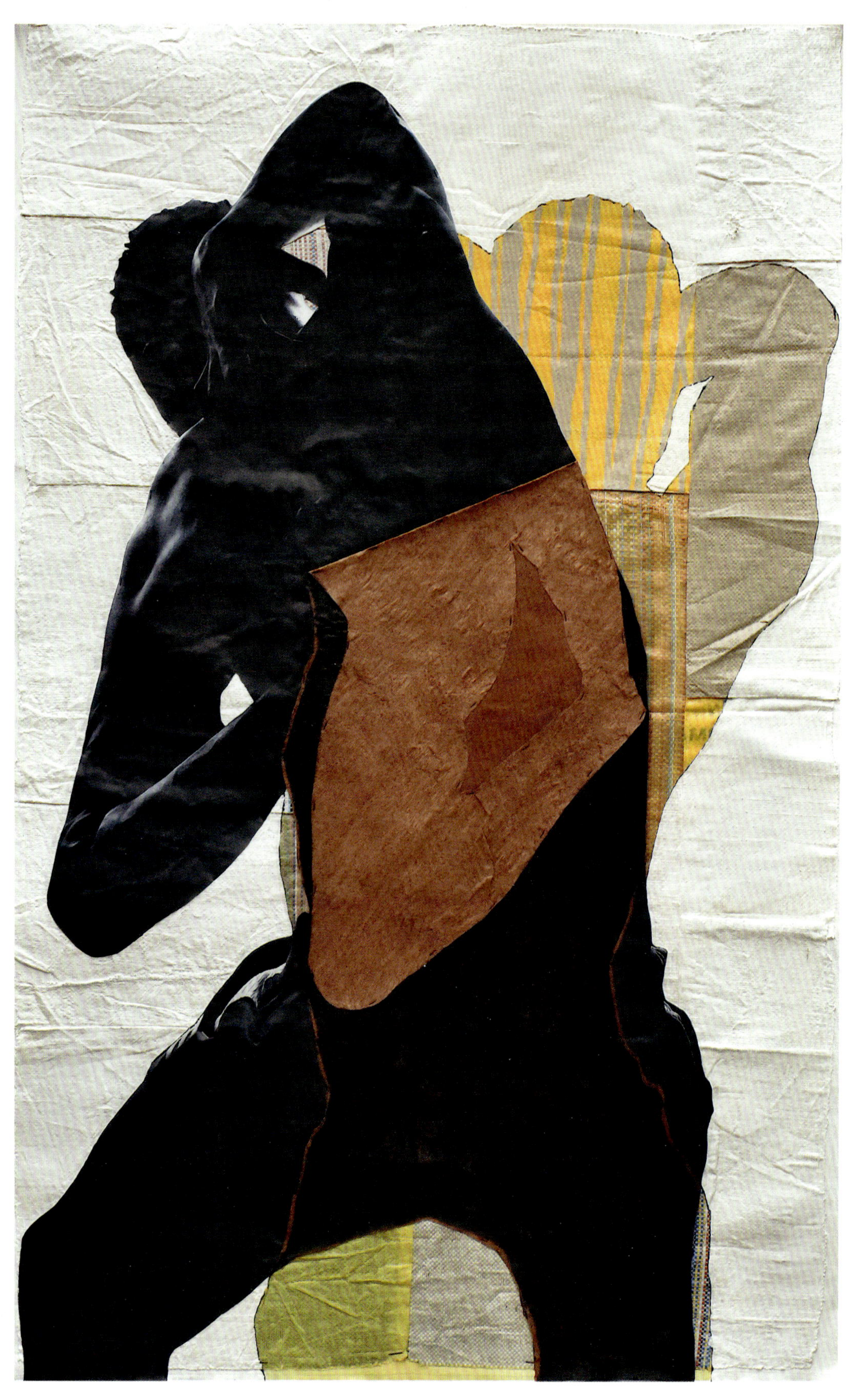

Collin Sekajugo, *Stung*, 2021, acrylic, barkcloth and mixed media on denim, 150 x 100 cm (59 ⅛ x 39 ⅜ in.)

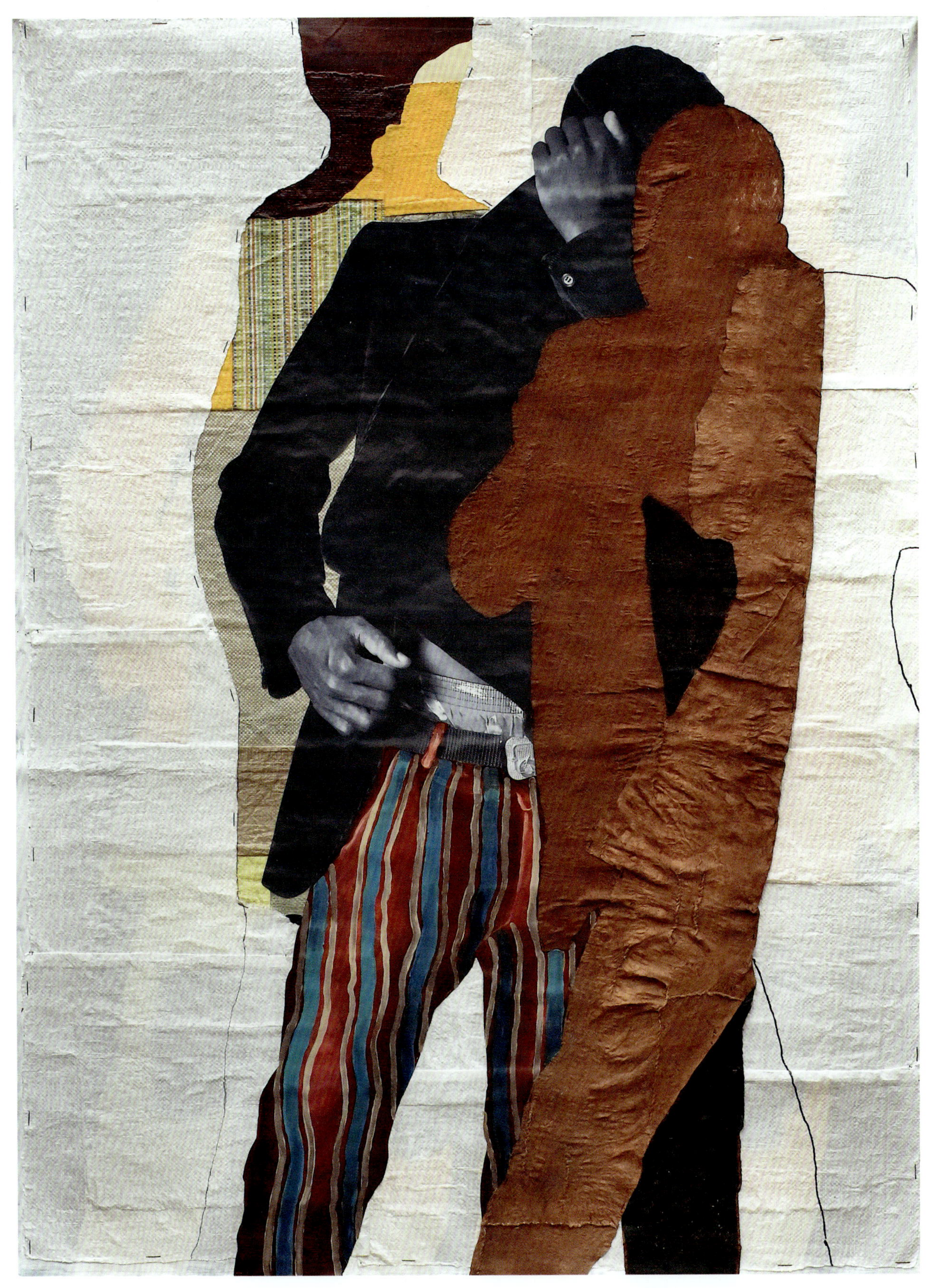

Collin Sekajugo, *Conversing with Self*, 2021, acrylic, barkcloth and mixed media on denim, 150 x 100 cm (59 ⅛ x 39 ⅜ in.)

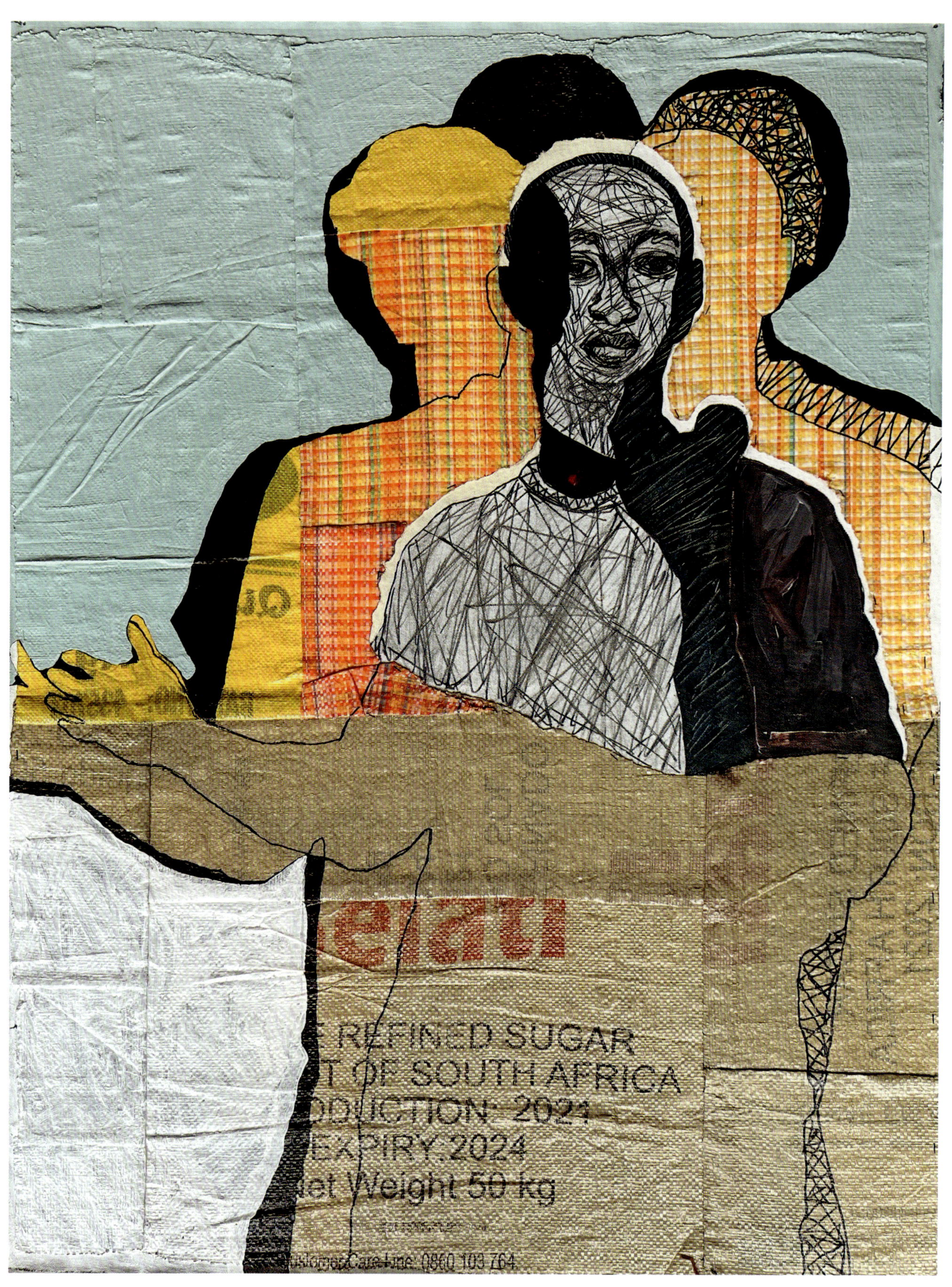

Collin Sekajugo, *Zuckerberg* (from the *Transition* series), 2021, acrylic and mixed media on denim, 120 x 90 cm (47 ¼ x 35 ⅜ in.)

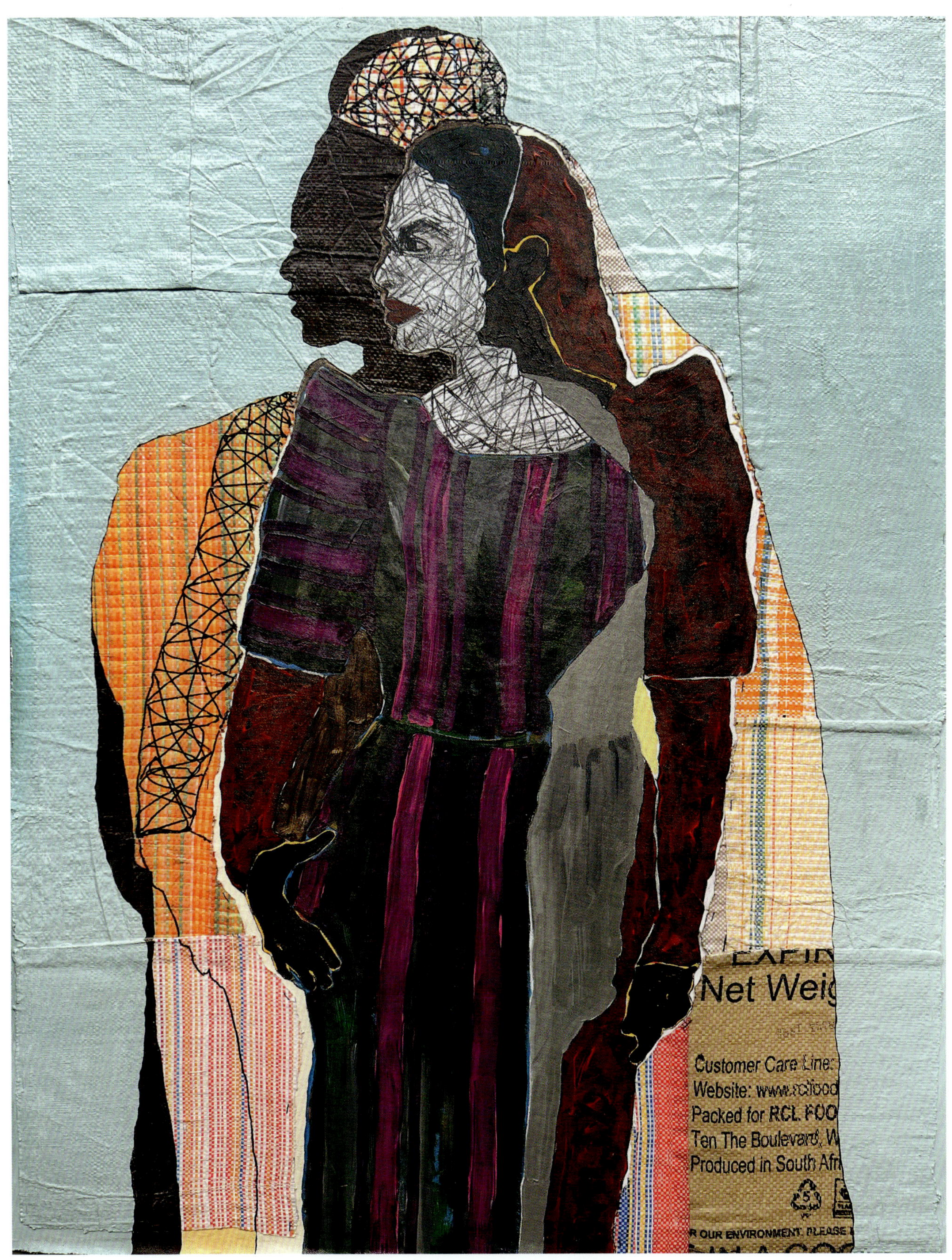

Collin Sekajugo, *Kardashian* (from the *Transition* series), 2021, acrylic and mixed media on denim, 120 x 90 cm (47 ¼ x 35 ⅜ in.)

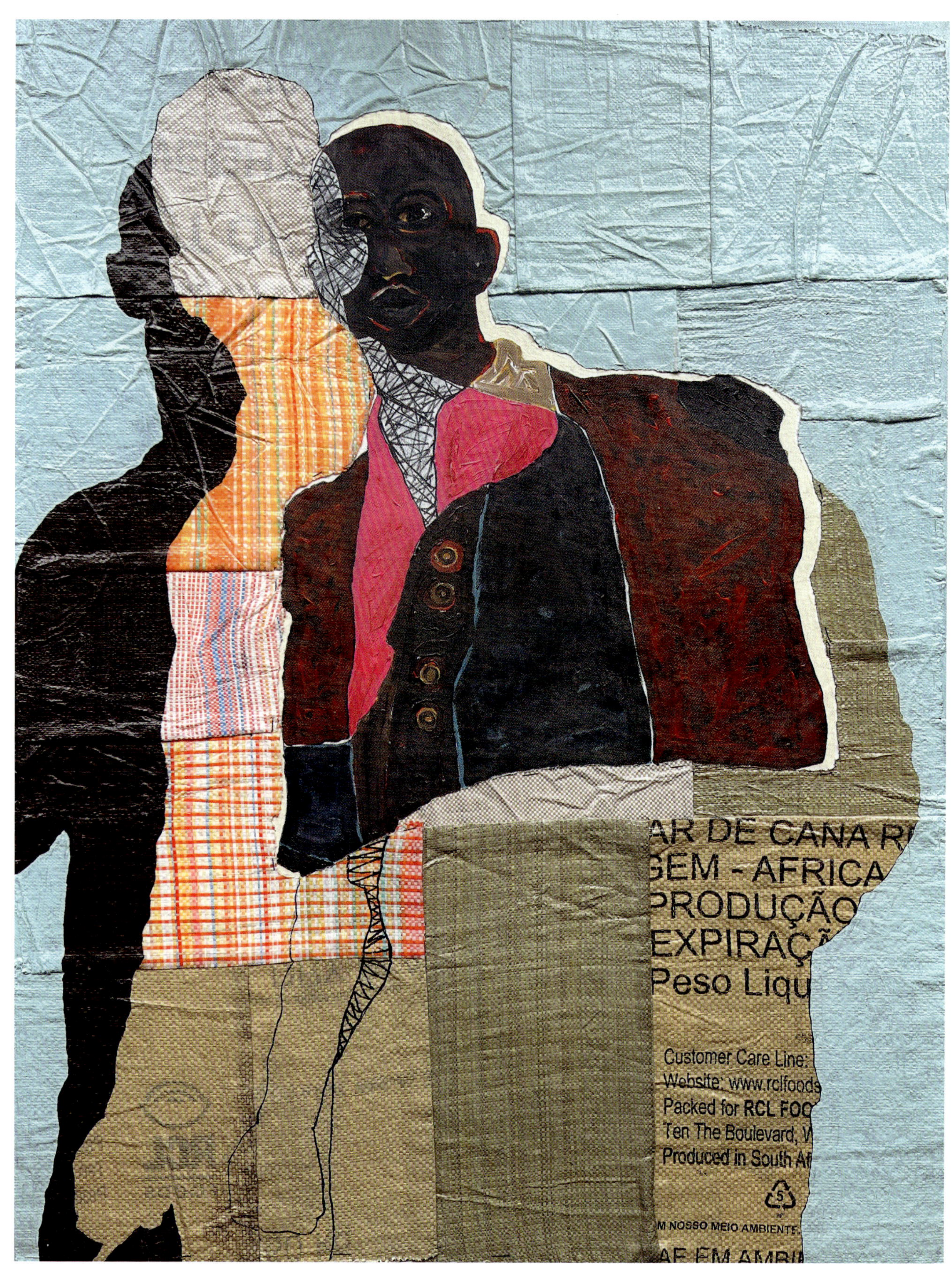

Collin Sekajugo, *Bezos* (from the *Transition* series), 2021, acrylic and mixed media on denim, 120 x 90 cm (47 ¼ x 35 ⅜ in.)

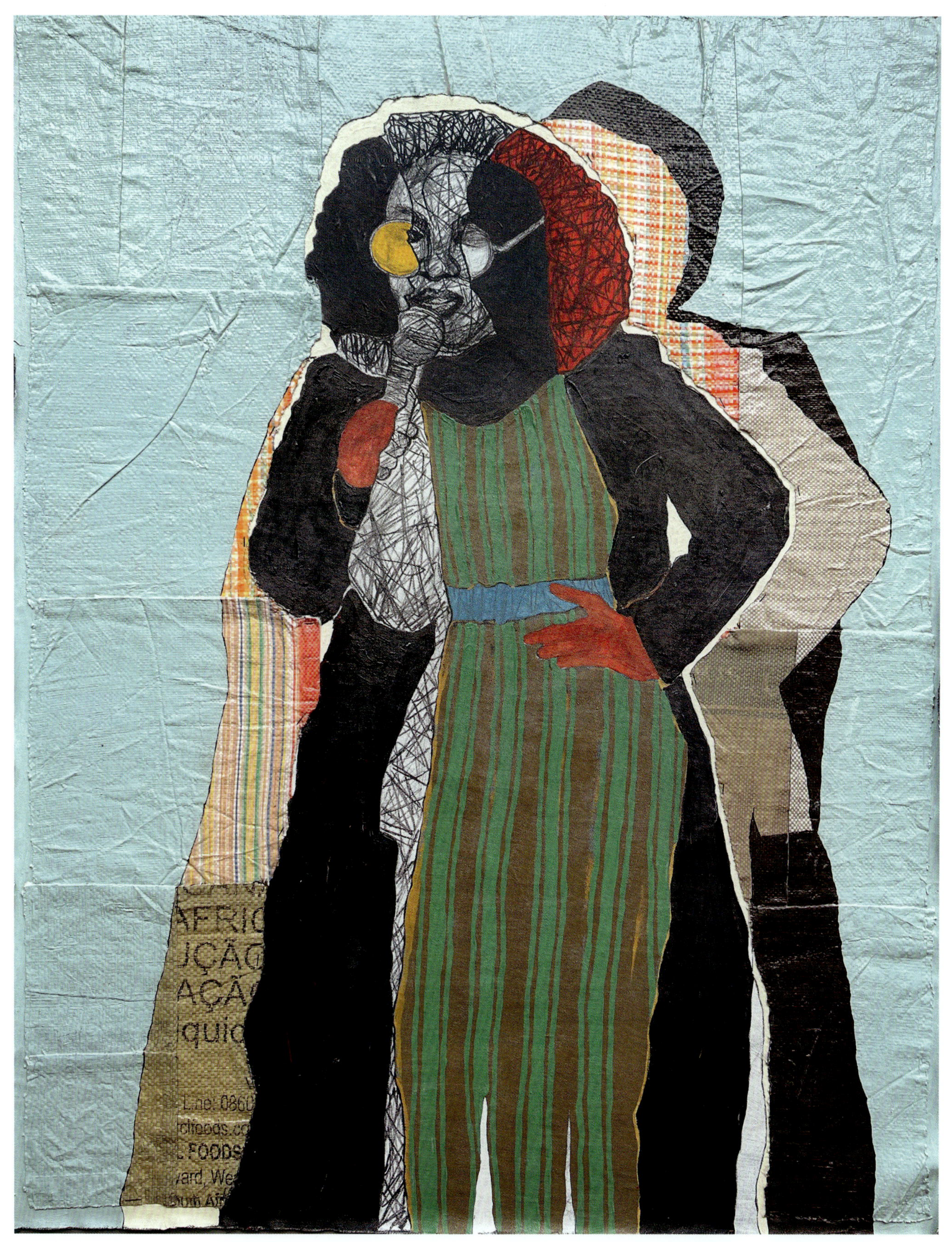

Collin Sekajugo, *Oprah* (from the *Transition* series), 2021, acrylic and mixed media on denim, 120 x 90 cm (47 ¼ x 35 ⅜ in.)

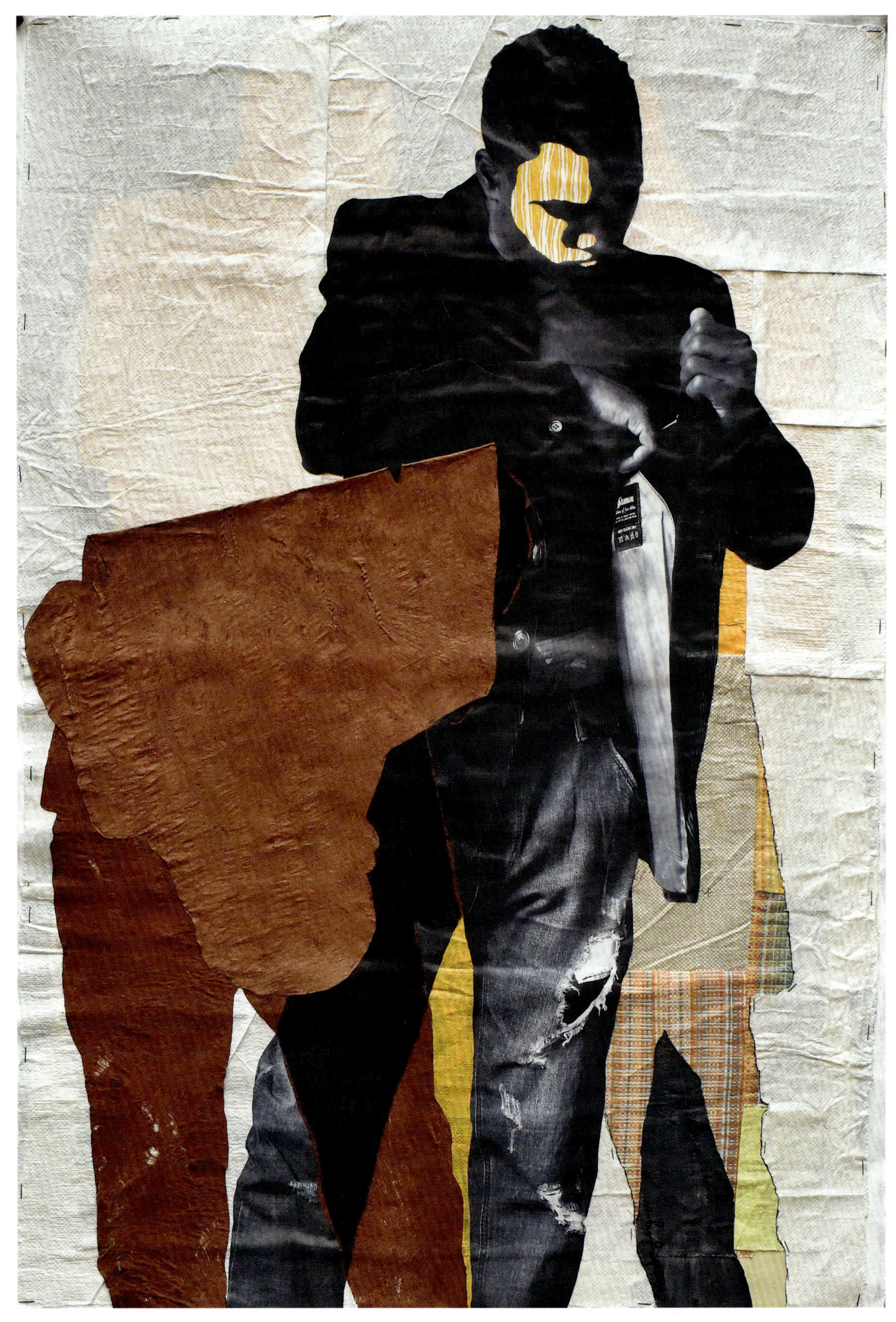

Collin Sekajugo, *Fifty Cent*, 2021, acrylic, barkcloth and mixed media on denim, 150 x 100 cm (59 ⅛ x 39 ⅜ in.)

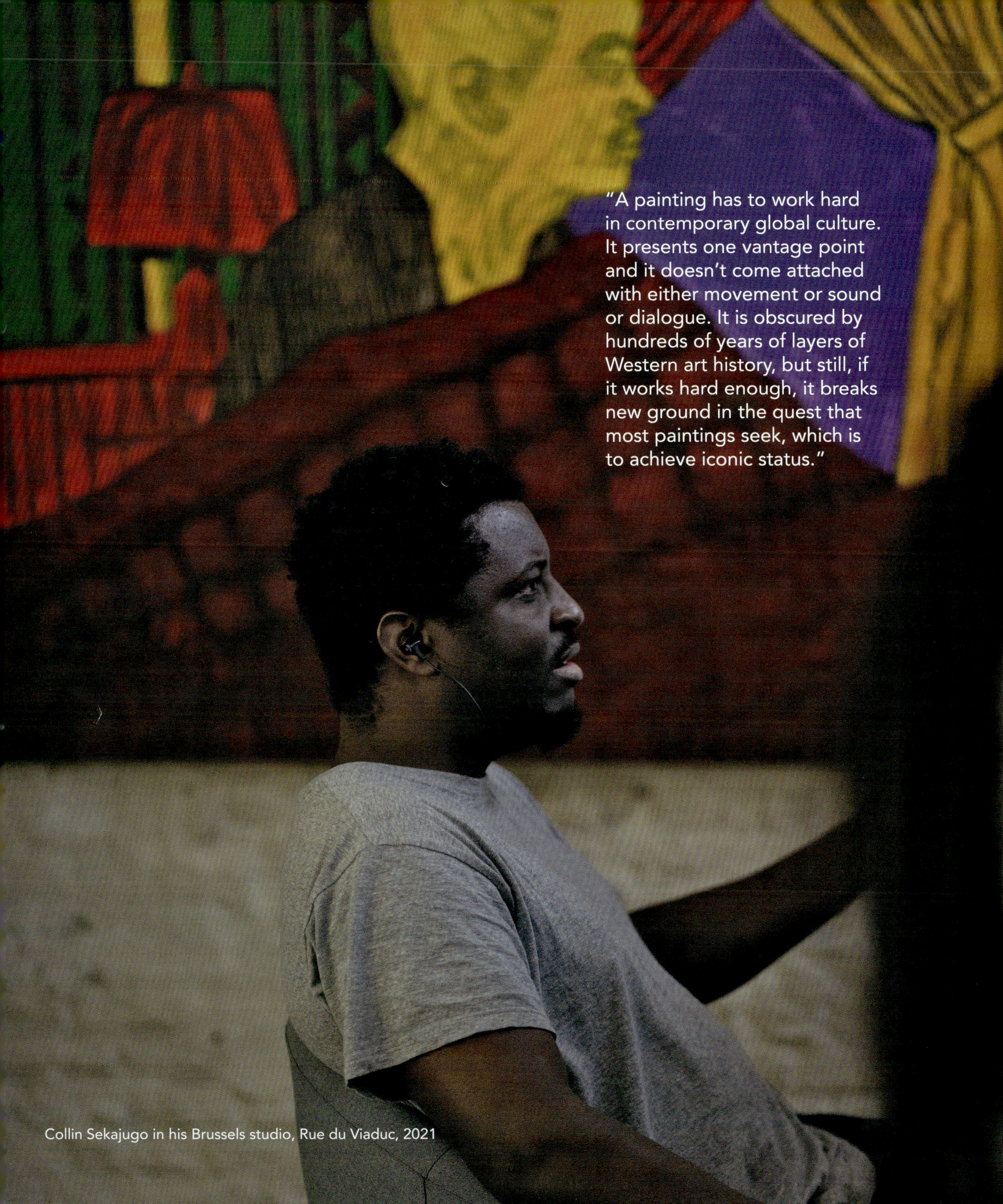

Collin Sekajugo in his Brussels studio, Rue du Viaduc, 2021

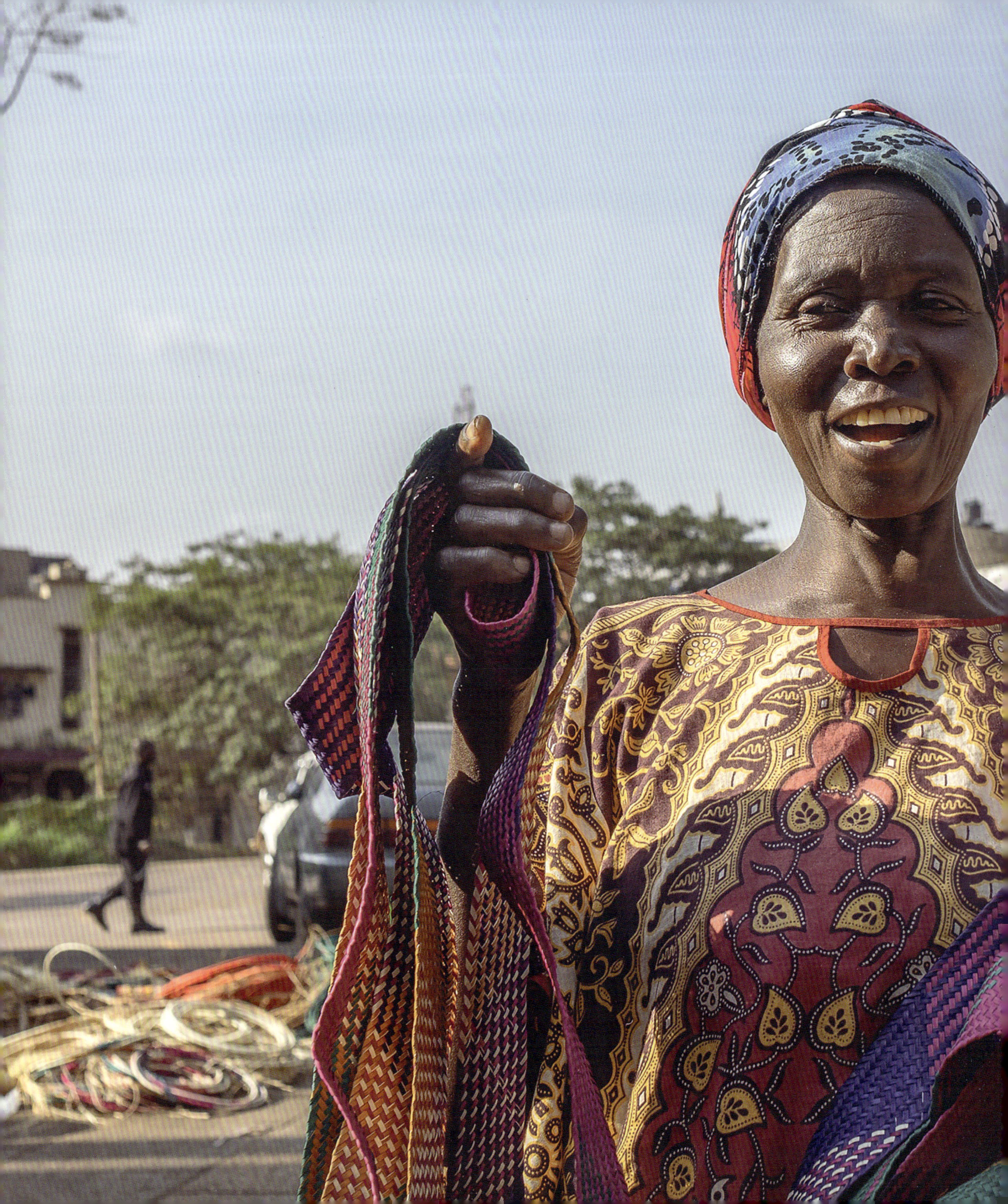

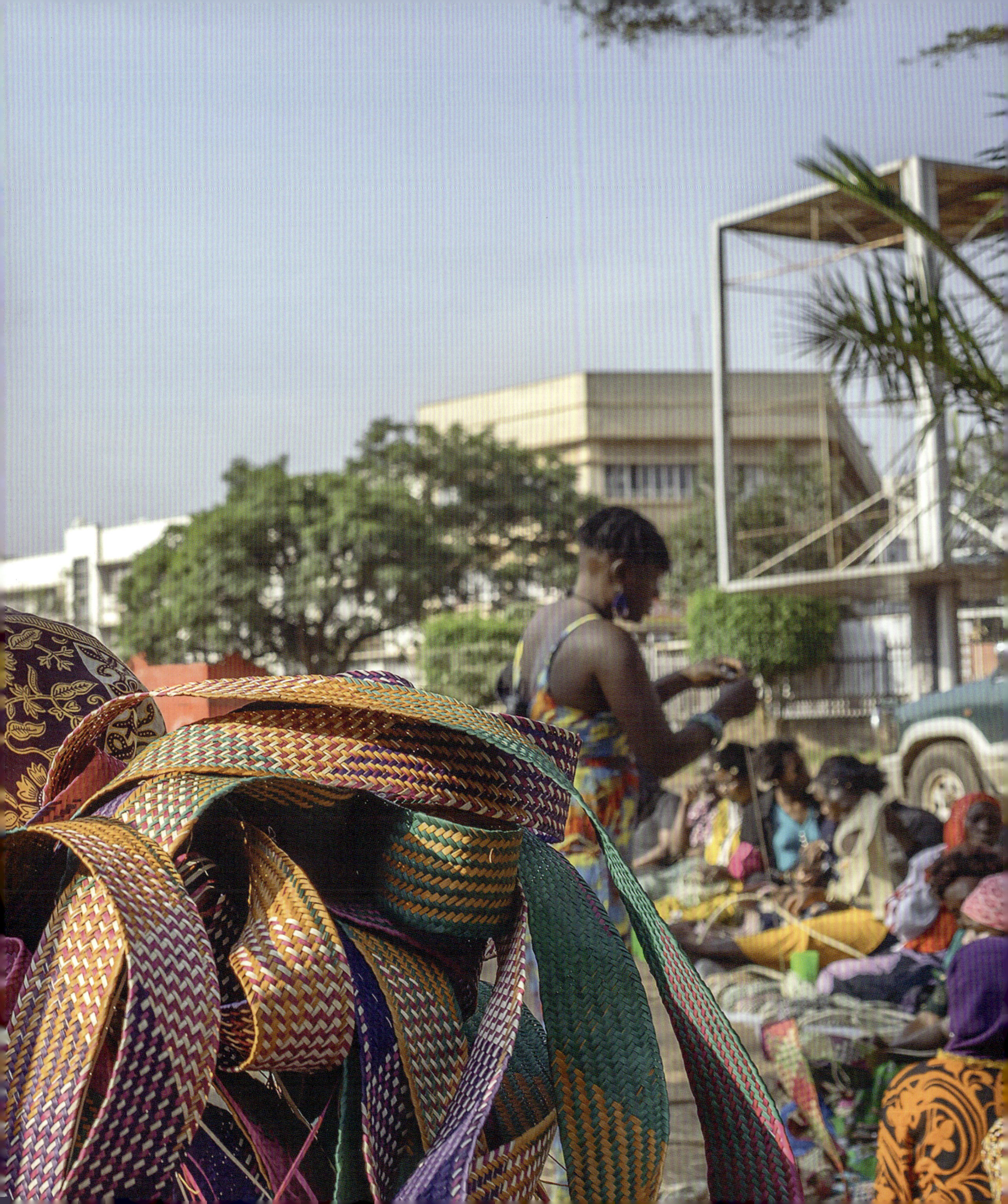

Radiance, They Dream in Time (Rearranged)

Shaheen Merali

Introduzione

Nel turbinio della Biennale di Venezia, due artisti ugandesi attivi a Kampala, Acaye Kerunen e Collin Sekajugo, espongono il loro lavoro in una mostra intitolata "Radiance, They Dream in Time" a Palazzo Palumbo Fossati. Per ogni nazione che partecipa per la prima volta a questa manifestazione internazionale, questa possibilità rappresenta un momento storico, e il padiglione inaugurale dell'Uganda alla Biennale di Venezia diventa il luogo ideale in cui presentare le idee degli artisti per comprendere meglio il significato delle tradizioni e la modernità dell'Uganda.

La molteplicità di mostre nelle varie sezioni della Biennale, che spesso hanno origine a partire dalle location principali ai Giardini e all'Arsenale, ramifica le sue finalità nelle celebri calli di Venezia e nei canali. Qui mostre, curatori e artisti evocano narrazioni che partecipano alla vita in continua evoluzione dei veneziani, la cui eredità va dalla Via della Seta al dramma umano della peste nera, fino ad arrivare all'Illuminismo europeo. La città che affonda offre il massimo, spesso in relazioni triangolari col passato e, in questo tempo sconcertante della storia umana, gli organizzatori della Biennale chiedono agli artisti e ai curatori di abbracciare la città e permettere ai visitatori di sperimentare le diverse forme artistiche del mondo come qualcosa che sta tra uno specchio, un documento e un ritorno all'incanto.

Il Padiglione dell'Uganda nella città sull'acqua

La celebre sezione collaterale della Biennale e i Padiglioni nazionali fuori dai Giardini e dall'Arsenale occupano autonomamente le vestigia dello spazio pubblico veneziano per tutta la durata della manifestazione. Questi eventi hanno il compito di presentare una posizione critica basata su precetti concettuali stabiliti da ciascun direttore artistico. Spesso questi eventi e mostre uniche combinano le influenze vertiginose della famosa città sull'acqua nel mappare e tracciare i confini della laguna adriatica. Essere fuori dalle alte mura e dagli ingressi recintati dei Giardini e dell'Arsenale permette ai curatori di ridefinire il modo di fare mostre. Spesso tutto si fonde in una prossimità irreale e offre una duplice attrazione, che arriva a definire "l'essere a Venezia" per mostrarsi al mondo come una parte importante della propria storia culturale.

La presentazione prosaica all'interno della città si confronta ulteriormente con la realtà e i ritmi dei sestieri, permettendo un'inflessione completamente diversa rispetto a quella di chi si esibisce nella coerenza strutturale e nella stabilità delle due sedi principali della Biennale. Il Padiglione nazionale dell'Uganda è presentato nel sobrio splendore di Palazzo Palumbo Fossati, un modesto edificio nell'itinerario dei milioni di turisti che vagano liberamente in un percorso postmoderno tra cultura e consumo. Sono proprio questa eterogeneità e questa molteplicità insite nella città che rendono il Padiglione dell'Uganda un luogo adatto alla prima celebrazione artistica globale del paese. La mostra "Radiance, They Dream in Time" segnerà il momento del "We are here" all'interno della città, come hanno fatto molti paesi africani e asiatici. Il curatore e direttore artistico della 56a Esposizione Internazionale d'Arte di Venezia, Okwui Enwezor, chiamò una delle sue sezioni il "Giardino del Disordine". Il Padiglione è rimasto fuori dal regno del disordine, i Giardini, l'area centrale contrassegnata dalle nazioni europee, e sempre più invasa dal privilegio eurocentrico, di una demografia legata all'espansione capitalista, o di coloro che godono della vicinanza a essa, compresi i colonialisti. Lontano dal centro veneziano, il Padiglione dell'Uganda è un altro testimone venuto a proseguire questo processo iterativo "globale" noto per la sua diffusione delle prospettive emisferiche che la 59a Esposizione sta ulteriormente abbracciando.

Venezia e le libertà oltre noi stessi

L'Uganda è un territorio la cui popolazione è stata segnata e governata dalle potenze tedesca (1885-1916) e

britannica (1916-1961); un dominio lungo otto decenni che ne ha compromesso la sua identità geopolitica. La fuga verso l'indipendenza implicava il ritorno alla dimensione umana, un percorso accessibile solo cancellando i precedenti vincoli ideologici e immaginando un movimento nazionale che avrebbe portato
alla liberazione.

Il sempre crescente capitale di risorse, analisi critiche, borse di studio, approcci variegati e risposte interpretative o creative ha dato benefici al mondo e agli ugandesi. I vari progetti umanitari, educativi e di "sviluppo" raggiungeranno il loro sessantesimo anniversario nel 2024, comprendendo un vero e proprio patrimonio di esperti e competenze le cui voci idiosincratiche permangono in un'assimilazione inconscia di idee e conoscenze. Ancora lo "sviluppo" si pone a metà strada tra un obiettivo e un'indagine, preso tra molte prospettive filosofiche, e tuttavia ogni cosa, inclusa la verità, rimane secondo Oscar Wilde "raramente pura e mai semplice". La tendenza a unificare la percepire di nazione e razza (Fanon, 1961)[1] ha effettivamente condizionato la sovranità indipendente di molti paesi del sud del mondo; il loro sforzo per una "palingenesi", una rinascita, una nuova comunità nazionale (dopo il colonialismo) è stato usurpato dall'identificazione esplicita di razza e nazione come biologica ed epistemologica – un'illegittimità che colpisce le relazioni con il cambiamento, il vero supporto degli alleati, le intenzioni.

Nella mostra "Radiance, They Dream in Time" è presente una serie di opere d'arte allestite in modo che venga mitigato il divario tra le tradizioni artigianali e le belle arti. Le opere di entrambi gli artisti si pongono come il raggiungimento della promessa di un linguaggio universale in grado di stimolare l'immaginazione di una cultura rigenerativa. I principi creativi di Kerunen e Sekajugo servono come uno strumento comune attraverso il quale vengono esplorati lo stato sociale individuale e comunitario.

In modo permeabile, tutti i sei spazi da visitare sono curati per contestualizzare il potenziale di comprensione intellettuale ed emotivo. Facendo appello alla capacità creativa dello spettatore di combinare e trovare la propria strada attraverso le simbiosi simboliche offerte dall'artista o dall'allestimento, il curatore enfatizza la valorizzazione culturale del patrimonio dell'Uganda. In molte delle opere sono presenti retaggi di simboli commerciali, concettualizzati rispetto alla gestione della terra, le affittanze agrarie che costituiscono la condizione coloniale della storia ugandese, cui si affianca una generazione di giovani imprenditori guidati da uno scopo, la cui esperienza traumatica della *flourishing youth*[2] è presentata al pubblico per essere esaminata nelle numerose stanze, e per contemplarne gli effetti.

Collin Sekajugo

The Call Centre Room di Sekajugo è un luogo per analizzare la doppia materialità del consumismo[3], una condizione che è stata resa necessaria dalla formazione dei servizi online; una stanza per eroi caduti, che si occupano delle lamentele ricorrenti su ciò che è apparentemente rotto. La disinformazione e il malfunzionamento fanno parte delle strategie per far passare gli utenti attraverso le linee di controllo dei call center. Si stipula e si guida, si convince, si rendono evidenti l'ignoranza e l'ansia dei consumatori. Sembra un centro di terapia in cui un credo giovanile abbraccia felicemente questioni di poco conto sempre sottolineate da una sorta di urgenza. Il cliente e le sue finanze personali vengono allontanati dai presunti disagi causati da un piccolo inconveniente o da un servizio fallito.
La straordinaria forza lavoro del call center viene educata a identificarsi con i contattati, a creare un ambiente accogliente e chiacchierone, per la facilità con cui si trovano conoscenze, competenze, idee e tecnologie, soluzioni che permettono agli scettici di tornare ai prodotti consigliati e di continuare poi la conversazione altrove.

I dipinti basati sul call center esplorano espressioni che diventano superfici significanti del controllo passivo che serpeggia sotto forma di informazioni fornite dall'industria dei servizi. È la strategia dei ritratti di Sekajugo, che parlano degli orribili retroscena essenziali per comprendere la ramificazione digitale, "definita come un macchinario piuttosto che una struttura"[4]. Sekajugo riesce a presentare gli infiniti e a volte fluidi modi in cui

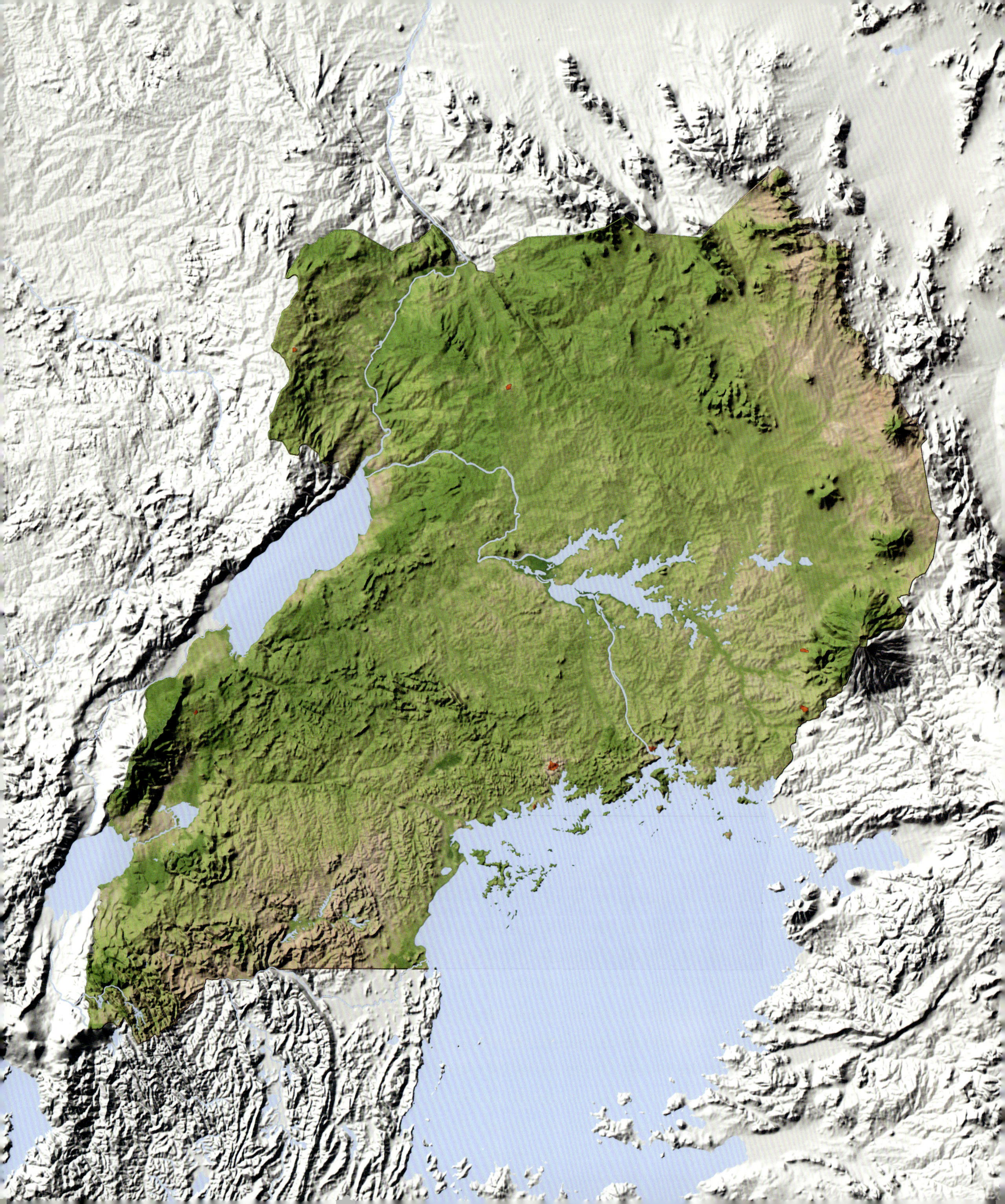

certe nozioni di soggettività sono asemblate per dirigere la megamacchina dell'era dell'informazione.

I bagliori delle luci che rendono i denti arancioni e le luci blu pulsanti all'interno dei cadaveri della tecnologia formano un *case study* per Sekajugo, narrazioni associative di spazi sommersi all'interno dei nostri incontri mondani. Questi tipi di avamposti online rivelano la tenacia della gioventù del sud del mondo alla ricerca di un'uguaglianza delle condizioni di vita. Incarnano l'accesso per coloro che hanno contratti e ordini da evadere, la cui urgenza è risolvere un problema tecnico. I ritratti dei call center, come i lavori di *stock image* e di *identity-hacking* di Sekajugo, sono liberi di mettere in discussione la sostenibilità operativa dell'ordine occidentalizzato, delle norme e del vantaggio del capitale.

Sekajugo suggerisce, per agire sull'osservazione, che laddove i confini estetici sono supportati dalla violenza dell'episteme coloniale è come quando appare il sole a mezzogiorno e si raggiunge un alto grado di chiarezza. Fabbricare complicate interconnessioni attraverso le variazioni di colore della tavolozza per rendere i diversi toni della pelle richiede un'ulteriore comprensione dei complessi esperimenti e delle esperienze degli artisti contemporanei dell'Africa occidentale e centrale, che stanno diventando centrali nell'ambito dell'arte globale e presso le case d'asta. I recenti ritratti dei call center sono sottili giochi mentali creati da Sekajugo in risposta all'interesse imprenditoriale per la cultura africana. La nuova propensione per l'arte contemporanea africana ha provocato sentimenti al di là delle valenze politiche, traboccanti dell'eccitazione delle opportunità che si creano quando nei luoghi dell'arte si superano le barriere della differenza.

L'esperienza dei soggetti di Sekajugo scivola in modo intrigante tra le relazionalità postcoloniali e gli incubi delle annesse tecnologie di asservimento. Molti dei soggetti immaginati per i ritratti di Sekajugo ricordano l'espressionismo tedesco, con i loro sguardi gotici da zombie che ci osservano da stanze con carta da parati su misura e illuminazione soffusa. Il call center fa parte del mondo occidentale per i nomadi digitali che viaggiano nel circo globale, tenendosi aggiornati sulle opportunità economiche nella loro onnipresente ricerca di manodopera a basso costo nel sud del pianeta. Sekajugo traduce la scuola di comportamento della società capitalista internazionale, che facilita le Q&A o FAQ ventiquattr'ore su ventiquattro.

I ritratti rappresentano l'eterno desiderio di giungere al termine del turno di notte (ossia povertà e prestiti studenteschi). Nello scenario da fine del mondo, operatori del sud del pianeta serviranno ancora i clienti come hanno fatto a partire dall'avvento dei fusi orari seven-eleven. Tra i luoghi globali di outsourcing IT/ITeS (Information Technology enabled services) ci sono la città di Bangalore nell'India meridionale e i call center ispanici bilingue in città come Puerto Vallarta, controparti di giovani laureati ed equipollenti, reclutati e formati con pseudo accenti del medio Atlantico, che guidano i clienti a installare con successo l'ultimo aggiornamento per le loro app o a consolare la perdita dei risparmi di una vita minimizzando il phishing (le truffe online).

I ritratti di Sekajugo mostrano l'angoscia mentale dei giovani speranzosi dei call center, al limite della pazienza dopo aver ripulito il disastro degli investimenti globali nella landa delle obbligazioni, delle azioni e dell'e-commerce attraverso l'eterna ragnatela digitale. Lontano dalla Silicon Valley, la domanda del cliente scontroso diventa un altro fardello per questa generazione, che cancella la paura di milioni di persone che sono collettivamente costrette a operare in una giungla digitale di distruzione ambientale nelle loro vite troppo complicate.

Acaye Kerunen

Gli spazi collettivi che permettono la possibile condivisione delle stesse preoccupazioni ci portano al gruppo di tessitori con cui lavora l'eclettica artista di Kampala, Acaye Kerunen. Il significato codificato nell'artigianato tradizionale si è evoluto in cesti, borse e altri oggetti domestici – tra cui stuoie per il pavimento, ceste per il cibo o tovagliette – che si trovano abitualmente nelle case. Kerunen tratta ogni oggetto presente nella quotidianità come un progetto per esaminare i richiami che sono incorporati da generazioni di donne che fanno artigianato.

La comprensione di Kerunen, attraverso la vasta gamma di schemi popolari, modelli sofisticati e combinazioni, attinge a regioni, spazi tribali e quartieri. Kerunen ha raccolto le differenze e le sfumature che le forniscono sempre più un ambito in cui sviluppare collaborazioni. Forme di decolonizzazione irrompono nello spazio della raffigurazione dove la normalizzazione della vita urbana e del sé, nella modernità in continua espansione delle forme occidentalizzate, entrano come rappresentazioni artistiche di pessima fattura, unicamente rivolte ai turisti.

Sconvolgendo lo scopo gerarchico fatto per un'altra classe, un'altra razza di donne, attraverso fibre e tinture naturali, Kerunen decostruisce gli oggetti accuratamente intessuti, visivamente complessi, per ricreare collage rassicuranti, sculture e installazioni a parete. Kerunen sfida la percezione del pubblico e rifiuta le aspettative producendo opere d'arte "attraverso il lavoro di tessitura di artigiani che sono donne, e le loro storie […] come i loro prodotti raccontano storie oltre gli oggetti utili che alla fine diventano […] una parte intricata della produzione (dell'Uganda)"[5].

L'attenta comprensione da parte di Kerunen di queste narrazioni si espande e sfida la natura, data per scontata, del luogo sia storico sia odierno di lavoro delle donne in Uganda. Kerunen rifiuta una visione discriminatoria razziale e di classe, consolidata dalle amare esperienze dell'opposizione binaria in cui l'artigianato esiste solo in antitesi alle belle arti. Il suo rapporto con le pratiche culturali è quello di creare, partendo da una cultura visiva, un settore indipendente e underground che detesta la categorizzazione.

Nel realizzare queste opere Kerunen rivisita il modo femminista di esplorare le narrazioni delle donne, spesso trascurate nella ridistribuzione dei privilegi riemersa dopo l'indipendenza. La ricostruzione dello stato sovrano ha negato il dolore delle madri e delle sorelle nella politica patriarcale, sostenendo salari diseguali e scarsi diritti sul lavoro. L'interesse dell'artista per certe tecniche e disegni, in particolare quelli sviluppati nella mostra, si genera quando le artigiane parlano tra loro o cantano insieme. Nella condivisione e nell'ascolto profondo, Kerunen si è resa conto di come le esperienze vissute da queste donne, inclusi i molteplici conflitti, abbiano definito ogni punto e ogni nodo. La collocazione stessa all'interno di pezzi essenziali, di materiali come i rotoli di Mikeka, il Biibo, gli anelli intrecciati e il bikapuà, ha assunto significati concettuali e ha attinto all'estetica della forma e della trama per coinvolgere il loro mondo.

Nella materialità della rafia o del sisal, Kerunen e la sua visione del femminismo classico sono state ridefinite al di là della perdita di autonomia. Se "il lavoro delle donne è un lavoro di diritto"[6], Kerunen sostiene che la giustizia è vista nella relazione più elementare con la terra, i suoi prodotti, la sua capacità di sostenere la crescita e la fertilità umana. La proprietà, nel suo caso, è un trampolino di lancio per comprendere il valore in relazione ai conflitti che l'indipendenza ha ereditato. Molti sistemi prevalenti di violenza fanno parte dello spettro dell'indipendenza e hanno bisogno di essere aboliti piuttosto che supportati dalla politica liberale. Tralasciando l'interesse conflittuale del femminismo classico nell'usurpare la leadership capitalista attraverso le donne emancipate, Kerunen sostiene la necessità di negare la violenza del capitalismo liberale. Per Kerunen lo sguardo del turista bianco si rivolge automaticamente alla crisi climatica a causa delle sue priorità, obiettivi storia e importanza.

Kerunen e Sekajugo

Alle molte domande che si stanno ponendo, entrambi gli artisti hanno fornito risposte diverse. Sia il desiderio di Kerunen sia quello di Sekajugo sono seguiti dalla creazione di un programma attraverso il quale la realtà ugandese può essere ri-catalizzata, per riorientarsi e allontanarsi dai giochi di potere e perseguire un'unità e una nuova mentalità con sistemi alternativi. Per entrambi, altri artisti e artigiani fanno parte della lobby che mira a oggettivizzare l'Uganda. Recentemente le relazioni e associazioni tra gruppi di artisti sono aumentate tanto quanto la loro preoccupazione di contribuire di nuovo al mondo delle arti, così come al mondo da cui le arti si sono evolute, le concezioni riparatrici della vita vissuta nel capitalismo liberale. L'uso crescente di Kerunen del sapere tradizionale, incluso il lavoro con le donne che raccolgono stagionalmente radici, foglie e bacche nella giungla secondo antiche conoscenze, permette possibili pratiche sostenibili. Sekajugo ha sempre lavorato con la tela di corteccia e con un concetto chiamato Kyambaro, che si basa sulla storia del design del Luganda o Uganda e del Kinyarwanda o Ruanda.

Entrambi gli artisti hanno colto l'opportunità di introdurre in questo padiglione inaugurale l'estetica ugandese, la consapevolezza primaria dello stimolo di un paese che collega l'Africa orientale a quella centrale. Entrambe le regioni sono cambiate enormemente; quanto e quanto poco siano state alterate può essere valutato attraverso il lavoro dei due artisti o nelle serie installate nelle sale. Gli eventi recenti e il dibattito internazionale degli ultimi due decenni hanno influenzato le idee di entrambi questi artisti e la dimensione e la velocità del consumismo sono evidenti nelle loro opere. Inoltre, il modo in cui gli artisti mostrano gli effetti della decolonizzazione permette al pubblico di comprendere le comuni esperienze coloniali e postcoloniali che influenzano l'estetica delle vite africane.

Il risultato è una materialità sempre più ibrida che permette a entrambi di ricercare e rendere più efficaci le loro tavolozze. Entrambi stanno creando testimonianze forti e complesse, memori dell'eredità ugandese. Sognano insieme in un momento in cui sia la tradizione pittorica sia quella scultorea propugnano un approccio olistico ai canoni globali del ventunesimo secolo.

Parte II

"Facilmente importato, ma malamente tradotto."[7]

Uno degli obiettivi chiave da affrontare a Venezia era quello di arrivare a una comprensione trasferibile al pubblico del lavoro degli artisti e della loro critica del mondo dell'arte. Allo stesso modo, è importante considerare il ruolo dell'artista e del curatore nell'alimentare le discussioni contemporanee sulla natura umana e sulla società ricostituita nelle sue dinamiche interne e nel ruolo della cultura. È stato spesso sostenuto che per mantenere un alto grado di connettività e circolazione in un mondo in via di globalizzazione, è importante considerare sia la circolazione delle forme che le forme della circolazione, e sviluppare una teoria che metta in relazione le due cose. In questo senso il Padiglione dell'Uganda fornisce agli artisti molteplici punti di partenza per affrontare le idee e le forme che circolano nell'arte a livello globale. Le considerazioni che seguono si basano su una domanda chiave che è sorta in occasione di un colloquio informale che ho avuto con Sana Gateja, in cui ha sollevato una domanda provocatoria che va valutata e cui va prestata la dovuta attenzione.

"Chi è un artista?"[8]

Kerunen aveva già scritto un trionfante post sui suoi social: "Il mio ingresso su questo palcoscenico mondiale è un fatto e un fattore di tempo; tempo che ho passato per anni lontano da molti occhi, imparando, disimparando, decostruendo, rifacendo […] Bene, ora sono qui. Sono qui per restare nella mia luce e per seguire la luce della mia stagione e dei miei tempi"[9].

Suggerirei che un artista passi il tempo a ripensare e a interrogare, così come a esaminare la sottile relazione con il soggetto, l'oggetto e i complessi intrecci storici esistenti. Kerunen e Sekajugo hanno racchiuso nel loro lavoro particolari aree di interesse che abbiamo parzialmente iniziato a discutere. Probabilmente entrambi gli artisti sono interessati al ruolo dell'arte così come è attualmente compresa o espressa da diversi esponenti della storia dell'arte, del design e dell'artigianato.

Entrambi gli artisti hanno una gamma variegata di interessi che includono la semplificazione dell'arte e del design/artigianato per accentuare le loro differenze nelle pratiche di progettazione e studio.

Kerunen e Sekajugo rivelano un interesse cruciale verso il settore del design dell'Uganda: entrambi hanno individuato, e di conseguenza mostrato, la sua rilevanza per le attuali condizioni di vita dei suoi abitanti. La loro risposta non è né monoculturale né monotradizionale. Invece, nel rimuovere il processo subordinato, ci spostiamo al di fuori dei confini dati verso l'inclusione nella cultura visiva efficace nel suo linguaggio. La loro semplice richiesta rimane la democratizzazione delle conversazioni tra la cultura visiva ugandese e l'allestimento di mostre come forma di attivismo culturale, in modo da influenzare il contesto per il recupero di idee all'interno di campi sensoriali sostenibili a livello tribale e regionale.

Nel mondo occidentale le arti sono generalmente svolte da personalità dalla mente singolare, mentre i designer seguono le linee guida e le tecnologie dei brief, dei progetti e della produzione. In entrambi i casi questi artisti stanno smantellando lo status subordinato delle tradizioni africane assegnato dai gruppi dominanti che includono musei, curatori, critici d'arte e istituzioni artistiche. Kerunen e Sekajugo provengono da una generazione che ha prodotto molteplici sperimentazioni condotte nella tradizione artistica del sud del mondo e che ha organizzato laboratori con artigiani, designer e artisti popolari per creare una disciplina artistica. Questi tentativi non sono percepiti come revivalismo o progressismo, ma piuttosto come la continuazione delle tradizioni in quanto conoscenza vivente, a volte giustamente intitolata "tradizione vivente". Per il padiglione inaugurale dell'Uganda, il lavoro di Kerunen e Sekajugo propone una mostra come esperienza in cui mediare le tradizioni viventi attraverso la complessa interazione di motivi e valori umani presentati come le realtà mutevoli di antiche divisioni. Il professor Mahmood Mamdani della Makerere University ha suggerito che la modernità coloniale può essere altrettanto efficace:

"Dopo l'insediamento, gli inglesi all'inizio del ventesimo secolo hanno politicizzato i confini etnici, ricostituendo la differenza culturale come differenza tribale. Gli eredi di questa mentalità coloniale governano come gli inglesi, non come i loro antenati"[10].

All'epoca della Biennale Architettura del 2014, in un colloquio con l'architetto Rem Koolhaas e il curatore Hans Ulrich Obrist, tenutosi fuori dal Padiglione svizzero presso i Giardini, Okwui Enwezor suggerì che la mostra potrebbe essere vista "come un oggetto"[11].
Il fatto che questa particolare enfasi sulla mostra come oggetto sia emersa alla Biennale, con i molteplici dibattiti e riflessioni tratti dal suo programma a rotazione, sottolinea l'importanza di Venezia come ambito di studi nel quale si attinge dalla diversità. Per smantellare gli stati conflittuali della differenza culturale come logica del dominio coloniale indiretto, gli artisti devono agire promuovendo la decolonizzazione, "caratterizzata da una relazione al reale (alla terra, al mondo e a noi stessi)"[12]. Inoltre, in un momento di molteplici crisi e di graduale scomparsa di una stabilità politica, entrambi gli artisti stanno avanzando propositive esperienze post-indipendentiste che riguardano la vita e l'estetica africane. Costruire e contribuire dall'Uganda, assemblando reti che annullano le divisioni che hanno forzato separazioni tra epistemologie, generi e impegno intellettuale. Questa condizione ne ha precedentemente ostacolato la tutela e il riconoscimento, confinando all'interno della modernità occidentale le esperienze che producono realtà globali. Nel periodo della Biennale di Venezia, approssimativamente sette mesi, le esposizioni conservano la sfera di influenza delle opere e degli archivi come momento per le molteplici domande che emergono nel corso dell'anno. La costante indagine sulla rappresentazione del cambiamento climatico, delle crisi dettate dalla disuguaglianza, delle storie legate alle estrazioni minerarie e della povertà di carburante sono parte dell'agenda di un pubblico internazionale risvegliato e stimolato dalla propria esperienza. L'archivio istituzionale di qualsiasi spazio pubblico, inclusa la Biennale di Venezia, è ora più che mai un fido strumento per orientare le proprie risorse verso l'esplorazione dei profondi cambiamenti di pensiero evocando (e provocando) ulteriori forme di approccio e di creatività così come distinte linee di indagine. Tuttavia "la sbalorditiva quantità di paesi partecipanti alla Biennale è sempre stata la rovina della maggior parte dei paesi africani, limitando la partecipazione attiva dell'Africa alla Biennale di Venezia. A parte qualche sporadica apparizione, i paesi africani sono stati in gran parte assenti alla Biennale di Venezia"[13].

Fin dalla prima Esposizione Internazionale d'Arte nel 1895, ogni edizione della Biennale di Venezia rimuove e smonta persistentemente le domande pregresse, così come porta attraverso la città un modello articolato di affascinanti indagini artistiche. La Biennale permette plurimi punti di accesso nella storia dell'arte; ogni edizione fornisce un focus contemporaneo attraverso un'affascinante esplorazione e un'invenzione curatoriale e artistica.

Per il pubblico che affolla la Biennale di Venezia (Cinema, Arte, Architettura e Danza), che cammina per chilometri, spesso circumnavigando la sede ufficiale, per entrare infine nell'esposizione, la performance, la proiezione, gli incontri per presentare gli artisti, la visione dell'opera d'arte o la partecipazione all'evento non possono mai essere sottovalutati. Dan Karlholm, professore e capo dipartimento di Storia dell'Arte alla Södertörn University di Stoccolma, definì *All the World's Futures*, il tema della 56a Biennale di Venezia (2015), curata da Okwui Enwezor, come "un'esposizione che si può riassumere in tre parole chiave: disordine, vitalità e capitale"[14]. Ovviamente, queste tre parole sono estratte dal testo del curatore che riassume gli intenti espositivi con il termine *All* del titolo:

"All the World's Futures è composto da tre filtri tra loro intersecanti, rispettivamente Garden of Disorder (Giardino del Disordine), Liveness: On Epic Duration (Vitalità: Sulla Durata Epica) e Reading Capital (Leggere il Capitale). I tre filtri, nella loro coreografia iterativa, attraverso l'esposizione, rappresentano una costellazione di para-metri, che verranno approcciati per immaginare e realizzare una diversità di pratiche"[15].

Filtri e preconcetti sono presenti in ogni processo realizzativo di una mostra, condizioni che soffocano il respiro delle intenzioni curatoriali. I para-metri cui fa riferimento Enwezor restano centrali nel diversificato palinsesto dei lavori di Kerunen e Sekajugo in "Radiance, They Dream in Time", un mondo ugandese che rinvia alla perdita del patrimonio e della fiducia allorché molti africani sono stati sottoposti a un "sistema internazionale (che) ha fornito differenti norme e razionalizzazioni, così come opportunità diversificate per gli attori africani nelle colonie, una continuità che, ciononostante, è più comunemente esperita e dominata dai movimenti sociali che dai cambi nella gestione politica"[16]. La Post-war Colonial Administration (Africa), introdotta tra il 1914 e il 1918, sembra appartenere al passato, tuttavia molti studiosi ancora negli anni sessanta e settanta hanno sottolineato come questo mandato abbia stabilito delle "regole indirette" e "la mise en valeur"[17] per la continuità imperialista dell'amministrazione internazionale. È sufficiente anche solo esaminare il ruolo della Francia verso le sue colonie come una morale osmotica per mantenere l'egemonica impronta francofona in Africa. Vista da questa prospettiva la Biennale di Venezia agisce come un sistema che da un lato difende un modello produttivo (di oggetti ed esposizioni) e dall'altro tenta di scongiurare la "costruzione di quei futuri emancipatori e/o creativi che giacciono dormienti all'interno delle diverse realtà conflittuali del mondo" (Karlholm 2015). È interessante notare come Enwezor usi il termine parametro nella versione sillabata para-metro. In italiano il termine "para" si riferisce al significato di preparazione, dal latino "parare", allestire, disporre, preparare. Lo si ritrova in paracadute, parasole, parapetto ecc., così come in parassita. "Para" può anche essere utilizzato come "difesa, protezione contro, quel qualcosa che ci protegge da", e parametro definisce un sistema o un insieme di condizioni della sua operatività. L'esposizione come oggetto assume sia valenze osmotiche sia, per gli artisti africani e delle ex colonie, anima il desiderio di considerare le contraddizioni intrinseche dei dialoghi intimi. Per considerare uno di questi dialoghi in corso, dobbiamo riprendere la 58a Biennale d'Arte dove il Padiglione della Nigeria presentò il lavoro di Victor Ehikhamenor che, da allora, è stato chiamato a partecipare a eventi organizzati in numerosi stati, inclusi diversi accesi dibattiti, uno dei quali si è tenuto al Jesus College all'Università di Cambridge, sul tema della connessione tra schiavitù e Tobia Rustat, un benefattore del college. La recente installazione di Ehikhamenor *Still Standing* alla cattedrale di Saint Paul a Londra (febbraio 2022) è un arazzo dell'*oba*, re, del Benin fatta con i grani di un rosario. *Still Standing* si pone come una confutazione dell'eredità di "Harry Holdsworth Rawson, il cui monumento in marmo e bronzo è stato installato nella cripta della cattedrale dal 1913. Rawson è stato determinante non solo nella spedizione punitiva a Benin City, ma anche in una quantità di altre campagne militari altamente controverse del diciannovesimo secolo, inclusa la seconda guerra dell'oppio in Cina"[18]. In un'intervista con Kabir Jhala pubblicata il 17 febbraio 2022 su "The Art Newspaper" l'artista afferma: "Non credere nella piena restituzione è per me come non credere nella piena giustizia", dice. "Ogni paese o regno o stato che chieda ciò che è stato depredato dalle sue terre ancestrali dovrebbe obbligatoriamente ricevere il maltolto senza troppi indugi. Noi dobbiamo ora passare dal 'tenere e spiegare' a ciò che io chiamo 'restituire e spiegare' […] aggiungendo artisti contemporanei all'interno di questo dialogo in modo che sia chiaro al mondo che gli artisti africani che hanno cominciato a realizzare opere postcoloniali non sono emersi dal nulla"[19].

Questo tipo di rivendicazioni ha fatto parte della ricerca degli artisti dell'Africa e di molte altre parti del sud del mondo. È una pratica comune usare verità spesso controverse e travisate, che includono la restituzione degli manufatti di una cultura, come si evidenzia dall'uso di immagini di repertorio da parte di Sekajugo, per crocifiggere l'eredità fondamentale dei bianchi. La fotografia ha un ruolo preciso con la sua peculiare capacità di capovolgere lo sguardo coinvolgendo sia lo spettatore sia l'autore. La particolarità delle tecnologie del "vedere senza guardare" fa parte della scatola dei trucchi del canone estetico imperialista occidentale. Nel dispiegare la critica come parte della revisione del canone, gli artisti della diaspora hanno spesso presentato i migliori esempi di come l'arte nera politicizzata possa essere creata attraverso le fasi della storia dell'imperialismo occidentale in quanto punto di rottura del suo stesso modello. Lo strano rapporto con i bronzi del Benin ha le sue radici nell'estetica occidentale perché presenta "una sensazione peculiare, questa doppia-coscienza, questo senso di guardare sempre se stessi attraverso gli occhi di un altro, di misurare la propria anima con il metro di un mondo che guarda con divertito disprezzo e pietà"[20].
Questi bronzi sono opere spettacolari create, in questo caso, da artisti del popolo Edo del Benin a partire dal tredicesimo secolo. La loro realizzazione in forma di ritratto e la tecnica con cui sono stati prodotti sono insuperabili. La sottrazione di opere dal paese di origine fa parte dei meccanismi del dominio coloniale che spesso trasferisce l'intera documentazione storica di regni e civiltà nei propri musei e nelle collezioni reali. Ciò che mi interessa come artista-curatore è il ruolo dell'artista rispetto alla sua possibilità d'azione. L'ottuagenario poeta e artista sudafricano, Pitika Ntuli, associa l'atto creativo, in relazione all'esperienza culturale, a un impulso che è provocato dalla distruzione. La cultura e il paesaggio africani sono ancora promossi attraverso lo sfruttamento coloniale e i saccheggi, il che sollecita l'artista in quanto "l'atto creativo è una battaglia titanica tra carne e spirito. Ogni opera d'arte è una diversione della carne, del corpo. Ogni volta che l'artista muore, nasce una nuova opera, o piuttosto il contrario: ogni volta che nasce un'opera d'arte l'artista muore un po'. Una piccola morte invoca un maggior desiderio di vivere e quindi crea un'altra opera d'arte. Quando alla fine l'artista muore, continua a vivere attraverso la sua prole – i suoi figli e le sue opere d'arte"[21].

Sekajugo e Kerunen ci hanno permesso di contemplare la trasformazione del sistema ricollocando i dubbi storici e il luogo dei "fatti" attraverso l'indipendenza artistica avvolta e guidata dalla relazione personale e impersonale, "in sintonia con le crepe e le disgiunzioni che percepiamo ma che potremmo non essere ancora in grado di articolare in relazione alle cose che pensiamo di conoscere bene"[22].

Per quanto riguarda i 2000 oggetti in bronzo e in legno recentemente rimpatriati dopo più di un secolo, Cosme Houegbe Lo Behanzin, pronipote del re Behazin, ha commentato: "Non avevamo libri, ma avevamo questi oggetti, questi sono gli oggetti che raccontavano la nostra storia prima che ci venissero portati via"[23]. Un'ulteriore finalità per i beninesi era quello di invitarli "a scoprire la seconda parte della mostra, dove 34 artisti contemporanei beninesi presentano un centinaio di opere". Collettivamente, le recenti esposizioni degli artisti contemporanei del continente africano stanno accelerando la ripresa, muovendo verso il cambiamento e traendo benefici dalla risoluzione dei problemi relativi alla considerevole eredità africana grazie gli sforzi degli artisti.

Gli intenti del padiglione inaugurale dell'Uganda alla 59a Esposizione d'Arte della Biennale di Venezia 2022 sono stati resi possibili dal lavoro del primo curatore africano Okwui Enwezor e dalla rilettura delle sue preoccupazioni da parte del direttore artistico di questa edizione, Cecilia Alemani, il cui consapevole interesse per questo periodo trasformativo suggerisce un ulteriore parametro nella ridefinizione di "soggettività, gerarchie e anatomie"[24].

Alemani ha collocato i testimoni, centrando le dichiarazioni di precedenti soggetti il cui inserimento in questa convergenza planetaria è diventato una necessità. Questi soggetti erano rimasti assenti nelle gerarchie cosmopolite delle élite che trascuravano le prospettive del sud del mondo. Le comunità indigene del nord del pianeta erano considerate poco rilevanti e faticavano a intervenire nell'assalto occidentale alle risorse globali.

Nella riunificazione di un pianeta avviato verso l'estinzione di molteplici specie e popolazioni, uno spazio di mediazione per superare la pandemia del coronavirus e l'ascesa della giustizia razziale sono diventati una sfida esistenziale sul piano storico. C'è un movimento che mira a una salvezza almeno parziale dai sogni di conquista e di gloria dei bianchi, intesi come colonizzazione che ha prodotto lo sfruttamento di massa e la preoccupazione nei confronti del potere. Il primo Primo Ministro della Repubblica Democratica del Congo indipendente (in precedenza denominata Repubblica del Congo) fu Patrice Hemery Lumumba, che giocò un ruolo significativo nella trasformazione della struttura ideologica del panafricanismo e del nazionalismo africano, guidando il Movimento Nazionalista Congolese (CNM) dal 1958 fino al suo assassinio avvenuto nel 1962 dopo l'indipendenza dal Belgio. L'ultima lettera di Lumumba a sua moglie Pauline conteneva molti dei temi che rimangono attuali per tutti gli africani in lotta per l'indipendenza e il pensiero indipendente del continente:

"Né le aggressioni brutali, né i maltrattamenti crudeli, né le torture mi hanno mai portato a chiedere pietà, perché preferisco morire a testa alta, con una fede incrollabile e la massima fiducia nel destino del mio paese piuttosto che vivere in schiavitù e nel disprezzo dei sacri principi. La storia un giorno dirà la sua; tuttavia non sarà la storia insegnata nelle Nazioni Unite, a Washington, Parigi o Bruxelles, ma la storia insegnata nei paesi che si sono liberati del colonialismo e dei suoi burattini. L'Africa scriverà la propria storia e sia a nord che a sud del Sahara sarà una storia piena di gloria e dignità"[25].

Il direttore artistico della 59a Biennale d'Arte ha sottolineato l'attuale sforzo a livello planetario di comprendere e contemplare "soggettività, gerarchie e anatomie"[26]. Kerunen offre un'unica e complessa risposta. Le sue esperienze africane nel trasporre gli ambienti naturali in contesti artistici aiutano il pubblico a esplorare nuovi frangenti in cui le tradizioni artigianali si mantengono in equilibrio con l'ambiente naturale, piuttosto che aumentare la sofferenza di una pandemia scatenata a livello ambientale. Sekajugo allarga il terreno del discorso esprimendo il suo punto di vista, basato sulle proprie esperienze, sulle forme occidentali di consumismo e si rivolge a nuovi sistemi di pensiero e di percezione per presentare la povertà e la crisi dettata dalle disuguaglianze legate al capitalismo. Entrambi gli artisti stanno estendendo i confini delle soggettività e delle gerarchie sviluppando questi temi all'interno delle nuove "ecologie" dell'estetica e della solidarietà. Così, contribuiscono alla nostra comprensione dell'emergere della decolonizzazione in Uganda come aspirazione nazionalista. C'è un po' di Kerunen e Sekajugo in ognuno di noi, un impegno all'azione in ognuno di noi, mentre cerchiamo modi per legittimare insieme il valore di un futuro più sostenibile.

[1] https://www.marxists.org/subject/africa/fanon/pitfalls-national.html (accesso 24 marzo 2022).

[2] H. Sabiiti, *Young and Flourishing. A Rising Fearless Cop of a Purpose Driven Generation*, Xlibris, Kampala 2020, p. 33.

[3] Il concetto di doppia materialità riconosce che un'azienda dovrebbe rendere conto simultaneamente su questioni di sostenibilità che siano 1) finanziariamente rilevanti nell'influenzare il valore di mercato; 2) rilevanti per il mercato, l'ambiente e le persone. https://www.greenstoneplus.com/blog/what-is-double-materiality-and-why-should-you-consider-it (accesso 26 febbario 2022).

[4] M. Lazzarato, *Signs and Machines: Capitalism and the Production of Subjectivity*. Translated by J.D. Jordan, Semiotext(e), Los Angeles 2014, p. 33.

[5] Conversazioni inedite con l'artista, 3 febbraio 2022.

[6] L. Olufemi, *Feminism, Interrupted. Disrupting Power*, Pluto Press, London 2020, p. 5.

[7] "La mostra sfida il modo in cui l'arte è tradizionalmente curata. Mette in discussione come l'arte è contestualizzata e alza l'asticella non solo per quanto concerne il modo in cui l'arte moderna africana deve essere capita e discussa, non solo per come tutta l'arte postcoloniale deve essere esposta, ma per come tutta l'arte è contestualizzata e dunque capita. Tutta l'arte esiste nella storia, non solo in un certo momento e non solo nella storia dell'arte. L'ispirazione per l'arte e per la cultura popolare, in qualsiasi momento, è infinitamente complessa", C. Becker, *Interview with Okwui Enwezor*, "Art Journal", 57, n. 2, 1998, pp. 101-107.

[8] Conversazioni inedite con Sana Gateja in data 10 febbraio 22.

[9] Acaye Kerunen sul suo profilo Facebook in data 13 febbraio 2022.

[10] https://www.thebritishacademy.ac.uk/blog/book-prize-2021-neither-settler-nor-native-mahmood-mamdani/ (accesso 26 febbraio 2022)

[11] O. Enwezor, *The Exhibition as an Object*, conversazione con Rem Koolhas e Hans Ulrich Obrist al Padiglione della Svizzera, Biennale Architettura, Venezia 2014, https://youtu.be/z8uyl0eenDk (accesso 1° gennaio 2022).

[12] https://time-issues.org/vazquez-the-question-of-precedence/.... Vázquez,R., 2022… (accesso 26 febbraio 2022).

[13] Rikki Wemega-Kwamu sui padiglioni africani su Facebook in data 27 gennaio 2022

[14] D. Karlholm, *Filtering Futures La Biennale di Venezia. 56th International Art Exhibition, 2015. All the World's Futures. Artistic director and curator: Okwui Enwezor*, Konsthistorisk tidskrift/Journal of Art History, 84, n. 4, 2015, pp. 248-251.

[15] O. Enwezor, "Introduction", in *All the World's Futures*, guida breve, 2015, p. 18.

[16] https://encyclopedia.1914-1918-online.net/article/post-war_colonial_administration_africa (ultimo accesso 26 febbraio 2022).

[17] F. Lugard, *The Dual Mandate in Tropical Africa*, online: http://archive.org/details/cu31924028741175, e A. Sarraut, *La Mise en Valeurs des Colonies Françaises*, online: http://archive.org/details/lamiseenvaleurde00sarr (accesso 26 febbraio 2022).

[18] https://www.theartnewspaper.com/2022/02/17/nigerian-installation-in-londons-st-pauls-cathedral-provokes-debate-around-restitution-and-colonial-monuments (accesso 20 febbraio 2022).

[19] *Ibidem*.

[20] Il concetto di doppia-coscienza fu proposto da W. E. B. Du Bois in *The Souls of Black Folk* del 1903, online: https://bombmagazine.org/articles/double-consciousness-collages-frida-orupabo-interviewed/.

[21] https://themelrosegallery.com/artists/30-pitika-ntuli/biography/ (accesso 28 febbraio 2022).

[22] A. Hammar, "The Concept and Paradoxes of Displacement", in *Framing African Development*, cap. 6, p. 111, Africa-Europe Group for Interdisciplinary Studies, vol. 16, 2015; https://brill.com/view/book/edcoll/9789004305465/B9789004305465-s007.xml (accesso 26 febbraio 2022).

[23] *Ibidem*.

[24] Dichiarazione di Cecilia Alemani, https://www.labiennale.org/en/art/2022/statement-cecilia-alemani (accesso 20 settembre 2021).

[25] https://www.blackpast.org/global-african-history/primary-documents-global-african-history/patrice-lumumbas-letter-pauline-lumumba-1960/ (accesso 1° gennaio 2022).

[26] Dichiarazione di Cecilia Alemani, https://www.labiennale.org/en/art/2022/statement-cecilia-alemani (ultimo accesso 20 settembre 2021).

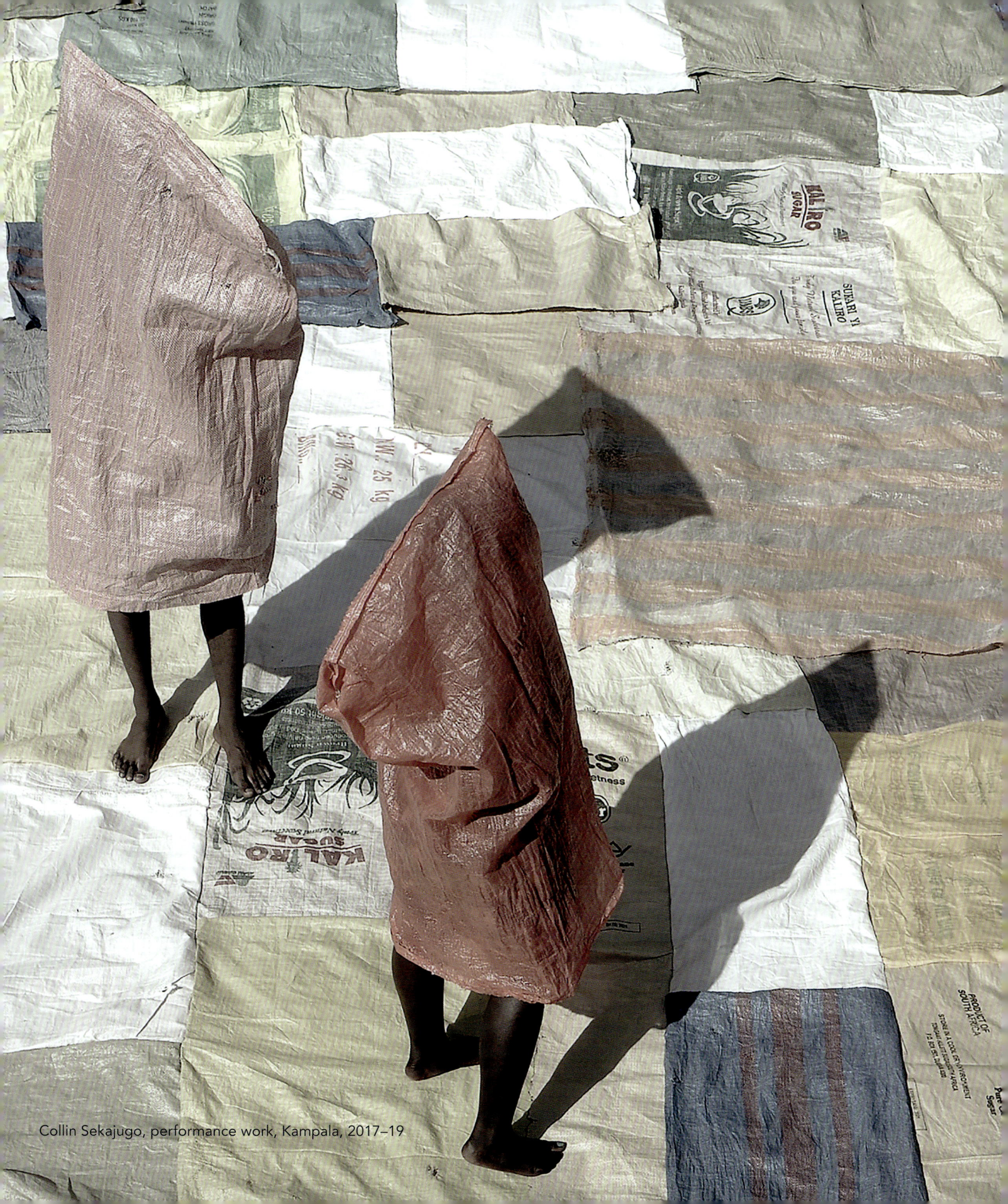

Collin Sekajugo, performance work, Kampala, 2017–19

Acaye Kerunen nell'occhio del tempo

Domenica 31 ottobre 2021 ho ricevuto un messaggio dall'Uganda. Diceva: "Salve. Sono Acaye Kerunen dall'Uganda. Sono un'artista/curatrice che esplora le fibre tessili naturali attraverso le installazioni"[1].

Questo è stato l'inizio di una serie di meravigliose conversazioni fatte via Zoom, Gmail, WhatsApp, ogni possibile modo che ha permesso di incontrarsi virtualmente e organizzare la sua partecipazione a questa mostra in continua evoluzione, "Radiance, They Dream in Time". Ovviamente il pronome "They" è adatto sia per Kerunen sia per Sekajugo, dal momento che le conversazioni fatte si sono sviluppate con molti altri che hanno rivendicato il loro potere sui fronti culturali di Kampala, Bruxelles, Londra, New York ecc.
Domenica 31 ottobre 2021 è stato come entrare sotto la sfera di controllo di Kerunen, un "ciclone" che lei stava osservando e che ha detto "sto costruendo". Costantemente dirompente, Kerunen sembrava costruire secondo le forme a spirale della vita contemporanea, con una base al centro che si estende verso l'esterno. Spirali resistenti alla gravità e a tutte le altre forze naturali da lei descritte come "una vera e propria tempesta".

Kerunen, nota anche come Acaye. E. Pamela, è un'artista poliedrica, ben inserita nel contesto pubblico ugandese; è performer, scrittrice, compositrice e, più recentemente, ha lavorato a stretto contatto con l'artigianato tessile per interpretare concettualmente il lavoro delle donne. Per la sua prima personale, dal titolo in swahili "Iwang Sawa" (Negli occhi del tempo), svoltasi presso la Afriart Gallery di Kampala, Kerunen ha presentato una reinterpretazione degli oggetti quotidiani come tovagliette e cestini, realizzati in materiali naturali. Il risultato è stata una sorprendente serie di opere a muro e installazioni. Attirando l'attenzione locale, ha ispirato molte altre persone a riflettere sul suo forte simbolismo. I temi legati alla mercificazione e alla cultura artigianale racchiusi in una serie di assemblages creati a partire da fibre naturali hanno portato a un'analisi che ha stimolato simboli del lavoro femminile. Nel suo lavoro si possono riconoscere relazioni tra regioni dove le condizioni in gioco sono basate sulle trasformazioni della storia della figura femminile moderna. Ebisu (rafia), sisal, byayi (fibra di banano), canne, steli di sorgo sfogliati ed ensansa (foglie di palma) hanno assunto tutti significati concettuali attingendo a un'estetica formale fatta di figure e *texture*. Un'estetica come consapevolezza elementare, e non ben delineata, di stimoli si trovava già nelle sue dichiarazioni di indipendenza dall'eredità coloniale. Questa prospettiva ha ignorato confini e ha liberato la superficie di questi oggetti artigianali dal loro autentico e caratteristico lignaggio dell'Africa orientale, per creare una produzione ibrida da lei denominata *Iwang Sawa: In The eye of time*.
Kerunen assume così il ruolo di artista/curatrice, ricollocando le fibre naturali intrecciate, da lei commissionate a una comunità di tessitrici. Attraverso il suo processo di reinterpretazione di oggetti quotidiani come tovagliette, vassoi e cesti per il raccolto, ricrea parti di un prodotto. L'autrice Lola Olufemi sostiene che "L'arte è utilizzata al meglio come un'arma, una riscrittura, come prova che siamo stati qui".
Per Kerunen, arte e artigianato coesistono per fornire un modo strategico in cui mappare la presenza dell'Uganda, una replica come ugandesi, e le prove che vanno a definire i suoi confini e la sua relazione con la regione dei Grandi Laghi. Kerunen libera gli oggetti artigianali fornendo una ricca superficie di scambio in cui riesce a discutere differenze dense di significati politici, includendo la storia dell'Uganda, le sue vicende di confini e di donne, le sue risposte al cambiamento climatico e il suo ruolo nelle culture e nei linguaggi dell'Africa orientale tribale. Ciò permette ai visitatori di re-interpretare non solo la lunga esperienza artigianale delle tessitrici ugandesi ma anche il significato del lavoro all'interno della tradizione artigianale.

L'installazione *Ouganda* è in parte improntata alle logiche del colonialismo europeo, per cui le case commissionate dai coloni venivano arredate secondo lo stile di vita e il gusto occidentali. Il tavolo e la sala da pranzo così disposti nell'opera d'arte ne sono un perfetto esempio: i mobili e le stoviglie sono un insieme che Kerunen esplora alla luce delle tradizioni europee e della grande abilità delle donne che hanno contribuito all'ospitalità attraverso il loro lavoro e la loro impressionante bravura come creatrici. Nella logica femminista liberale, tutte le donne nere rimangono più in ombra. Kerunen ci rimanda a una critica femminista nera che è esistita ed è stata documentata da molte donne che, impavide, hanno esplorato il ruolo della politica attraverso molteplici risposte che includono l'artigianato, al di fuori dei limiti della *whiteness*.

Kerunen ha incorporato molteplici meccanismi oltre il controllo dell'arte o la sorveglianza patriarcale dello stato, concentrandosi sull'ambiguità costitutiva dei concetti e delle emozioni occidentali. L'obiettivo di Kerunen, ispirato al destino della terra, è di ricercare sfumature di colori e forme nelle foreste e nei Grandi Laghi. Il *flâneur* che è in lei è stato fortemente influenzato dalla capacità e dall'intuizione del suo popolo provato dal colonialismo che ancora narra, attraverso vari interventi, la storia della centenaria indipendenza africana.

Recentemente ha riunito donne che producono tinture naturali, con foglie e cortecce raccolte ai piedi delle colline e oltre i limiti della coltivazione selvaggia, facendo coesistere le violente tempeste con i cavi di fibra ottica plastificati che corrono sotto l'Oceano Indiano, portando la tecnologia in Africa. Scolpisce lungo i meridiani dell'entroterra dell'Africa orientale per rintracciare i messaggeri di fede, i processi di pensiero in transizione, e per trovare la rivoluzione nella dualità. "Questo è ciò che sto cercando di rappresentare con la connettività."

I meridiani

Al di là dell'attuale sistema *mainstream*, la spiritualità di Kerunen trova il suo destino nelle divinità, dee gemelle, che si fondono in una crescente dualità, sognando nel tempo. Queste divinità guidano coloro che cercano un riparo, attraverso case a prezzi accessibili, per i senzatetto, preparando cibo fresco e garantendo sicurezza a coloro che vivono per strada. Queste realtà e filosofie esistenziali rimangono relazionate sia alla connettività Wi-Fi sia alla tintura fatta da una donna di Kisoro come colorante per la rafia, nella nuova era.

Kerunen mette in scena i suoi lavori come un router per la psiche del sud del mondo, i ritratti degli antenati e dei mentori appesi agli angoli, lontani dalle pareti, rivolti verso il basso, verso la terra e verso se stessi in cammino durante ogni Giorno dell'Indipendenza. Questa è una vera e propria tempesta.

Shaheen Merali, febbraio 2022

[1] Conversazione inedita tra l'artista e il curatore.

Sekajugo e le Stalking Images

Ciò che abbiamo esperito in questi ritratti moderni è puro teatro; su uno sfondo di carte da parati radiali, disegnate con uno schema a strisce, si stagliano figure, che hanno goffamente ri-sognato i dubbi e le incertezze della metropoli.

Una di queste figure si sporge verso lo spettatore, con un grande sorriso e i pollici alzati: un'immagine confusa e annerita di Richard Branson al posto di un qualche predicatore rivoluzionario nero del ventesimo secolo, che serviva come muro del pianto.

I dipinti di Sekajugo si pongono in una distanza intermedia dall'aver sognato la radiosità nera, emersa (con la brillantezza della tradizione black) nel ventesimo secolo e che è tornata recentemente alla ricerca di giustizia razziale con una profusione di pubblicazioni e di discorsi, che incoraggiano visioni di afrofutursimi e dibattiti su afropessimismi.

La preoccupazione di Sekajugo à la verità al di là dei fatti e delle cospirazioni; la falsa rappresentazione è senza dubbio una realtà collettiva, in questo sconcertante periodo della storia dell'umanità. Gli artisti più attenti stanno cominciando a offrire un'arte che ci aiuti a modellare la nostra esperienza, rispetto agli antagonismi del tardo capitalismo: non è più praticabile la sua geometria di scambio, dove la maggioranza esisteva genericamente come tribù, setta ed etnia.

Dal 2012 i dipinti di Sekajugo si sono evoluti radicalmente, come strumenti di de-canonizzazione, e la sua tavolozza viene usata in modo da esaminare uno specifico filone culturale, abitato da corpi di diversa natura, creati da errori involontari negli studi fotografici e nei laboratori, fortemente influenzati dal pensiero di matrice bianca. I suoi dipinti sono una risposta a questo archivio di immagini di repertorio, che hanno proliferato come un'infestazione deteriorante su ogni modalità di comunicazione umana. Dai giornali, alle riviste, ai volantini, ai manifesti, le fotografie di ragazzi bianchi e giovani ragazze alla moda, la progenie della fascinazione delle eroine, sono state rifiutate dal suo campo.

Invece, un cast black sta performando una versione ugandese del ribaltamento parodistico di ruoli alla Spike Lee. Nelle tele di Sekajugo questi individui, per lo più giovani e sapientemente vestiti, sono entrati passeggiando e si sono posizionati nello stesso punto, con uno sguardo semi-rilassato, eseguendo un cambio di guardia. In alcuni casi, stanno re-esistendo in un ambiente nostalgico; ricordano le fotografie inglesi e tedesche dell'Africa orientale prima dell'indipendenza. Spesso gli sguardi di questi eccezionali dipinti lavorano al posto di oggetti di tendenza in un mercato del tipo di Etsy, ipnotizzato da un sistema che ricicla continuamente, per istituire il suo dominio di valore nel mercato secondario e terziario. In un modo o nell'altro stiamo assistendo a una convergenza planetaria, stiamo creando un periodo di trasformazione, in cui c'è una rimappatura senza precedenti di "soggettività, gerarchie e anatomie"[1].

Come può tutto ciò affinare la nostra abilità nel capire le pratiche di artisti spesso poco conosciuti, senza ridurre sempre il loro lavoro a conclusioni vacillanti, basate sul "breve termine"? Nell'apprezzare l'intrigante desiderio di Sekajugo "di creare cosmologie alternative"[2], ci stiamo preparando a diverse "conoscenze e nuove politiche di identità"[3], nell'impegno civile e nei significati mutevoli della razza. Un immaginario con un forte linguaggio vernacolare, che crea motivi di desiderio, commenti trattenuti delle aspirazioni dell'Anglosfera.

La mentalità materialista si trova nelle vite della maggior parte della popolazione globale, che è stata paradossalmente esclusa dalla partecipazione alle strutture occupazionali, invisibili nei nostri schermi, escluse dal mondo accademico o, come notato con tanto fervore da Sekajugo, escluse dalla fotografia di repertorio. Mentre i giovani professionisti black stanno cominciando a prendere il loro giusto posto rispetto agli stereotipi dei bianchi, allo stesso tempo non si allontanano da una concezione fisionomica occidentalizzata di occhi da cerbiatto, denti perfetti e look patinato. Infatti, come Barbara Kruger suggerisce "alla fine, la storia accade"[4].

La mostra prenderà in considerazione questo discorso fallocentrico sulla storia del privilegio nel femminismo bianco, per arrivare a una comprensione generale del concetto espresso da Baldwin di "rovine di talento […] in quanto disciplina, amore, fortuna, ma più di tutto, la resistenza" aiutano lo stato di crescita verso "un'accuratezza e una completezza della nostra conoscenza del mondo"[5].

Shaheen Merali, marzo 2022

[1] Dichiarazione di Cecilia Alemani, https://www.labiennale.org/en/art/2022/statement-cecilia-alemani (accesso 20 settembre 2021).
[2] *Ibidem.*
[3] *Ibidem.*
[4] Barbara Kruger, *Urban Museum Amsterdam*, 2021.
[5] https://www.universityworldnews.com/post-mobile.php?story=2021090713235631&fbclid=IwAR2XY38UfFqprpTS0K-J0chLgoEnHfEz5kw2w5hCAtdlAkwSw3EYw36AKLag

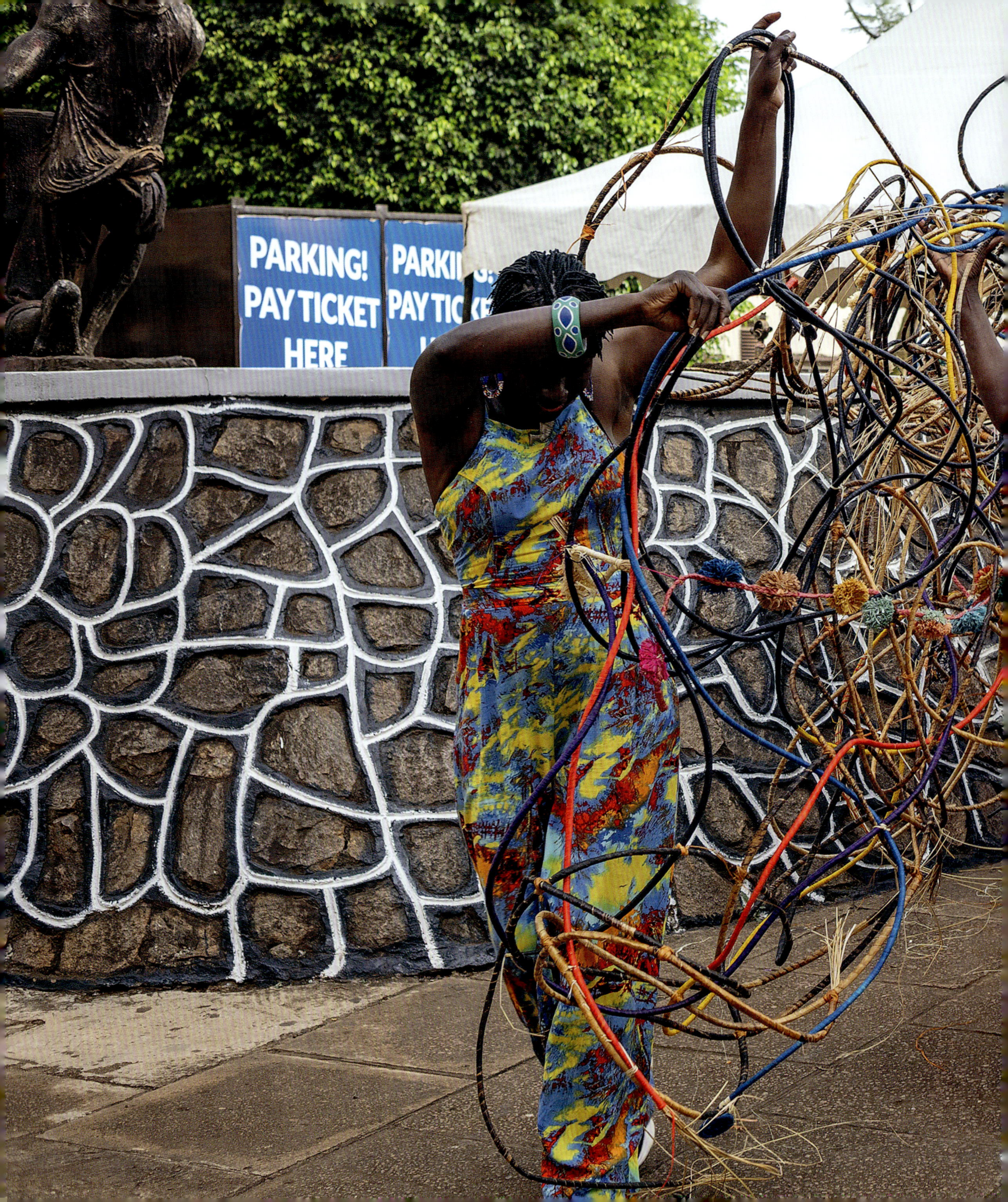
PARKING!
PAY TICKET
HERE
PARKING;
PAY TICKET

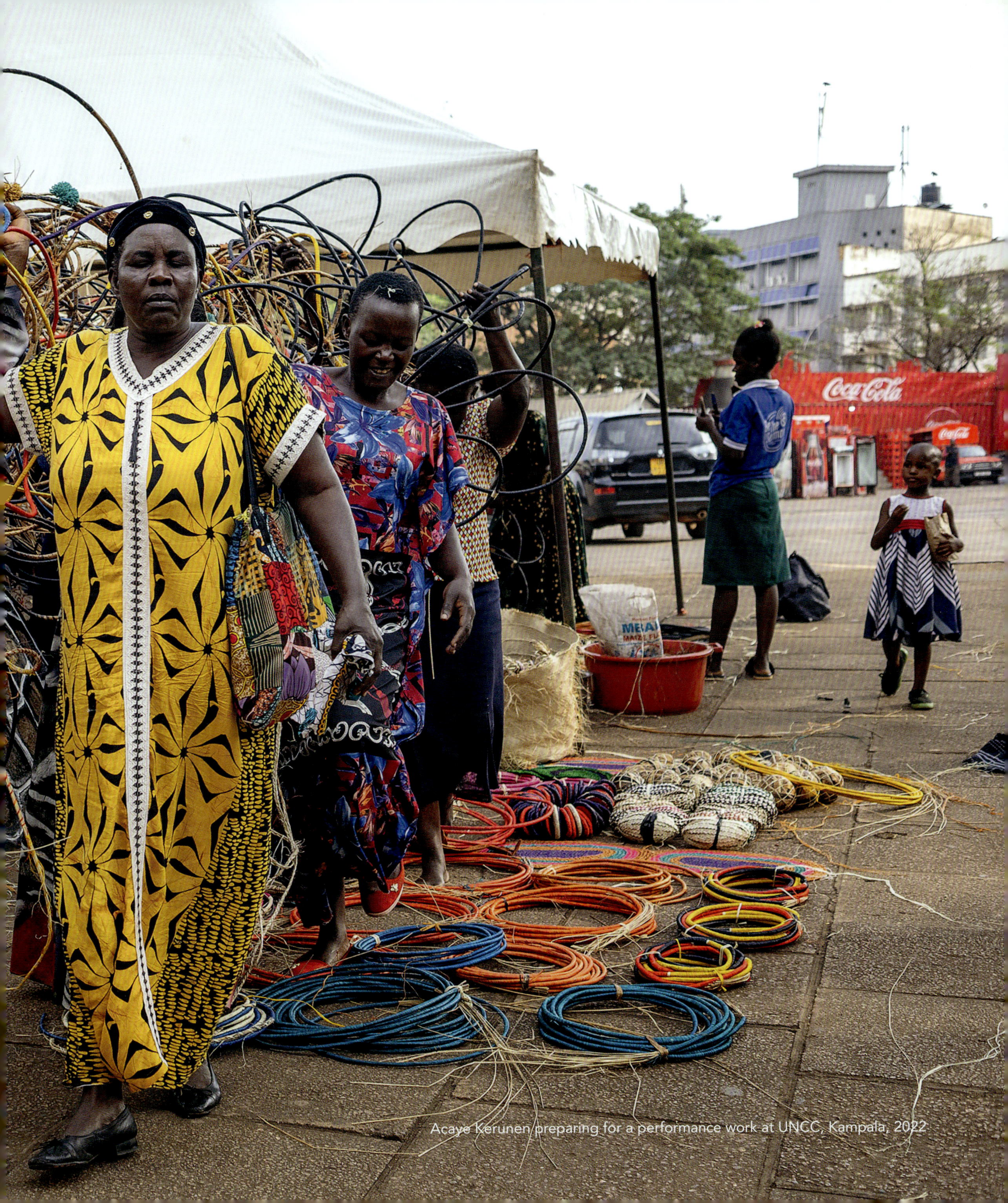

Acaye Kerunen preparing for a performance work at UNCC, Kampala, 2022

Works specifically produced by the artists for the exhibition after the publication of this catalogue can be accessed by scanning this QR code.

Shaheen Merali is an artist, independent curator and writer of Asian descent. Born in Tanzania, he lives and works in London. Merali has held positions at Central Saint Martin's School of Art (1995–2003) and was a visiting lecturer and researcher at University of Westminster (1997–2003). Currently, he is a PhD candidate at Coventry University.

In 1988, Merali founded the One Spirit Gallery and Workshop, which he later merged and co-founded Panchayat Arts Education Resource Unit (1988–2003), an organisation that combined research of the historical condition and philosophical inquiry of contemporary art concentrating on the political Black arts. The Panchayat collection is characteristic of its time representing contemporary artists who produced issue-based work, with a particular focus on cultural identity. In 2015, the collection was donated to the Tate Library, Tate Britain, where it is held as a Special Collection. In 2021, Merali was appointed as the curatorial consultant by Tate Research for the Provisional Semantics Case Study funded by the AHRC on the Panchayat Collection; his findings will be published on the Tate Publishing in spring 2022.

Merali was the head of the department of Exhibitions, Film and New Media at Haus der Kulturen der Welt (HKW), Berlin (2003–08), one of the first Asian/POC to hold such a position in Germany's history, a milestone appointment where he curated several exhibitions accompanied by publications that he edited/contributed, including *The Black Atlantic: Modernity and Double Consciousness* (commissioning artists including Isaac Julien, Keith Piper, Lisl Ponger and Tim Sharp); *Dreams and Trauma: Moving Images and the Promised Lands (Palestine and Israel); New York States of Mind* (toured to Queens Museum, NY), as well as leading the curation and global research for five years of programming. At the HKW he co-curated with Professor Wu Hung, *Re-Imagining Asia, One Thousand Years of Separation* (toured to the New Art Gallery, Walsall) and the 6th Gwangju Biennale, Korea (2006). Between 2008–09 he was the artistic director of Bodhi Art (Berlin, Mumbai, New York and Singapore). In 2014, he co-curated *Berlin Heist: The Enduring Fascination with Walled Cities*, the leading exhibition for the Mediations Biennale, Poznan, Poland.

During the last decade Merali co-initiated, authored and organised several exhibitions, publications, screenings and performances in India, China, Iran, Japan, the USA and throughout Europe. His discursive activities have included organising conferences, editing publications, webinars as well as engaging artists in reflecting on contemporary cultural responses to globalisation, colonialism and anti-imperialism histories in Western Europe, North America, East Africa and South Asia. He has contributed to numerous exhibition catalogues, including Michael Wutz (Galerie Klaus Gerrit Friese), Probir Gupta (Anant Art) and Rita Keegan (Goldsmith Press) as well as editing a series of monographs, including *Tavares Strachan, I AM* for Desert X (Isolated Labs) and *JJ XI* (Carrots Publishing).

He was on the board of trustees of the Live Art Development Agency (London) and a member of the British Art Network. He is the curator for the first Uganda National Pavilion at the 59th International Art Exhibition La Biennale di Venezia.

Collin Sekajugo was born in Masaka, Uganda. He is a multimedia art practitioner whose art is rooted in his deep sense of empathy for the human condition.

In 2006, Sekajugo undertook a study tour around East and Southern African countries exploring diverse perspectives on the making of art. Travelling extensively shaped Sekajugo's communal conscience, assisting him to explore issues of social, cultural, economic and political identity. Within the local and, increasingly in a global context, his art provides a reflection of the society he lives and allows him to change the lives of the people in his community.

In 2007, Sekajugo opened the Ivuka project using the moniker "Using Art to Change Lives". The Ivuka project was the first visual arts space in Kigali, and in 2010, Sekajugo initiated Weaver Residency, a community based arts organisation that aims to foster creative development in the Masaka area. The initiative runs art workshops and residencies at Camp Ndegeya, a retreat centre in Masaka that brings together the public and the creative sector to interact beyond the hectic metropole of Kampala, the capital city of Uganda.

Sekajugo's art work examines and questions the notion of personal identity in a self-absorbed contemporaneity - re-imagining subjects from visual, oral and digital culture, shifting and evolving into a new subject/ citizen. Sekajugo refers to his community by using found elements that he combines in his collage and superimposes into the photographic record. Often his mix-media work exists as a critique of the mainstream image employed in painting styles, including the hyperreal and postmodern tropes of portraiture. The found elements are mostly locally sourced and recycled; these include bark-cloth, polypropylene bags, denim fabrics and waste paper.

The inclusion of contemporary consumer materials in his technique proposes a conversation between drawing, collage, photography and overprinted surfaces, all in painterly formats that allow the multiple cultural sources to be both relatable, and yet, to portray puzzling realities.

Collin Sekajugo is internationally recognised and his work is to be found in many permanent collections including the Smithsonian National Museum of African Art in Washington, DC, as well as notable private and corporate collections in the US, Europe, Africa and Asia.

Acaye Elizabeth Pamela Kerunen / Acaye Kerunen is a multidisciplinary performance and installation artist, storyteller, writer, actress and activist based in Kampala, Uganda. She graduated with a BSc in Mass Communication from the Islamic University in Uganda, Kampala and obtained a Diploma in Information Systems Management from Aptech.

Acaye was the Assistant Director on the Volcano Theatre production of Goodness in Canada in 2012 and is the founding Director of KEBU Theatre. In 2012, *Vogue Italia* featured her as one of the social activists Africa should watch closely. Since a young age Acaye has also been an actress and has performed in productions such as *Silent Voice* by Judith Adong. Her poetry and musical theatre, which was published under the same title in 2006, *DAWN OF THE PEARL*, have received public performances at the National Theatre in Uganda and the Phoenix theatre in Kenya, launching her career as a director/producer/composer. Acaye has written stories for publications including the Ministry of Education, Bayimba Productions and FEMRITE Uganda. She also writes for various online and print media, both locally and internationally.

Raised by her single mother who was also an artist, shaped her world view to become woman-conscious. The maternal values transferred from her mother are evident in Acaye's work ethic, which involves multitude collaborations with women, some in transition from domestic violence, poverty or internal displacement to women who are struggling to find outlets for their inherent creativity.

Acaye Kerunen's installation and multimedia works speak of a strong conviction in Ugandan women's empowerment through the indexical collaborative work made with community artisan women, which are orchestrated by Kerunen into installations that question the scaffolding of fine art versus craft as predicated by Western art traditions. She does so in order to illuminate the centre of creative gravity that emanate from her sense of place and context, which is not rooted in Western doctrines of creativity.

In addition, her works are the result of performance, collaboration, social work, environmental consciousness and addressing authentic creation as lived experience. Her overall artistic practice also brings into question the sympathetic views of Western liberal feminism formed from laissez-faire capitalism and consumerism which she finds challenging to translate into versions of African feminism that are applicable to other values and different outcomes close to the realities of African women.

Acaye's installation work employs hand stitching, appending, knotting and weaving with natural fibre. These are all tasks Acaye watched her mother employ in her work – from embroidery, to needle work to hand stitching garments. She grew up at a time when the landscape of Kampala was fast changing from lush and green into a concrete land. Earth-consciousness is at the core of Acaye's work, especially with regards to how the land can continue to feed and sustain a populous, both holistically and practically.

In 2018, Acaye installed an interactive installation titled *Kendu*, a womb-like structure made from locally sourced barkcloth at the Nyege Nyege Ugandan Culture and Music Festival. The installation prompted people to reflect on their relationship to regeneration and origin whilst being nurtured with locally sourced refreshments prepared by the artist. More recently, in 2021, Acaye participated in a self-led online dance fellowship with the Saisan Foundation of Japan. Under a curatorial fellowship with Newcastle University, Acaye also debuted her first solo exhibition *Iwang Sawa* in Kampala at the AfriArt gallery to much acclaim and in collaboration of 32 Degrees East Ugandan Arts Trust, which focused on repurposing artisan craft made by women of the local and regional Ugandan communities as contemporary art.

Bibliography

Art & Culture

Bossan, E., 2014. *Uganda/Rwanda/Burundi: Traces of the Past, Signs of the Future*. Ponzano Veneto: Fabrica.

Brandel, R., 1961. *The Music of Central Africa: An Ethnomusicological Study*. The Hague : Martinus Nijhoff.

Clarke, I., 2021. *Uganda: The Essential Guide to Customs & Culture*. London: Kuperard.

Deliss, C. and Havell, J., 1995. *Seven Stories about Modern Art in Africa*. London: Whitechapel Art Gallery.

Gross, Y., 2010. *Kitin-tale*. Bussigny: Centre d'impression Edipress. Translated by Schneiter, Y.

Kizza, I., 2011. T*he Oral Tradition of the Baganda of Uganda*. Jefferson, NC: McFarland & Co.

Kruger, M., 2010. *Women's Literature in Kenya and Uganda*. N.p. [United Kingdom]: Palgrave Macmillan.

Mabingo, A., 2021. *Ubuntu as Dance Pedagogy in Uganda*. London: Palgrave Pivot.

Middleton, J., 1965. *The Lugbara of Uganda (Case Studies in Cultural Anthropology)*. Belmont, CA: Wadsworth/Thomson Learning.

Morton, C. and Newbury, D., 2016. *The African Photographic Archive*. London–New York: Bloomsbury Academic.

Otiso, K., 2006. *Culture and Customs of Uganda*. Westport, CT: Greenwood Press.

Picton, J., Loder, R. and Court, E., 2002. *Action and Vision: Painting and Sculpture in Ethiopia, Kenya and Uganda from 1980*. [London]: Triangle Arts Trust.

Stultiens, A., 2010. *Pose*. Rotterdam: Post Editions.

Stultiens, A., Kisitu, A. and Kaddu Wasswa, J., 2010. *The Kaddu Wasswa Archive: A Visual Biography*. Rotterdam : Post Editions.

Stultiens, A., 2013. *Crafted*. San Francisco: Blurb.

History

Atkinson, R., n.d. *Roots of Ethnicity: The Origins of the Acholi of Uganda Before 1800*. Philadelphia, PA: University of Pennsylvania Press.

Byrnes, R., 1990. *Uganda*. Washington, DC: Federal Research Division.

Eichstaedt, P., 2009. *First Kill Your Family: Child Soldiers OF Uganda and the Lord's Resistance Army*. Chicago, IL: Lawrence Hill Books.

Mamdani, M., 1983. *Imperialism and Fascism in Uganda*. Trenton, NJ: Africa World.

Nabudere, D., 1980. *Imperialism and Revolution in Uganda*. London: Onyx Press.

Okuku, J. A., 2002. *Ethnicity, State Power and the Democratisation Process in Uganda*. Uppsala: Nordiska Afrikainstitutet.

Peers, C. and Health, I., 2004. *East Africa: Tribal and Imperial Armies in Uganda, Kenya, Tanzania and Zanzibar, 1800 to 1900*. Nottingham: Foundry Books.

Reid, R. J., 2017. *A History of Modern Uganda*. Cambridge: Cambridge University Press.

Rice, A., 2019. *The Teeth May Smile but the Heart Does Not Forget: Murder and Memory in Uganda*. New York: Picador.

Suhrke, A. and Adelman, H., 1999. *The Path of a Genocide: The Rwanda Crisis from Uganda to Zaire*. New Brunswick, NJ: Transaction Publishers.

Vanzwanenberg, R. and King, A., 1977. *An Economic History Of Kenya And Uganda: 1800–1970*. London–Basingstoke: Macmillan.

Zayyan, H., 2021. *We Are All Birds of Uganda*. London: Random House.

Politics & Media

Decker, A. C., 2014. *In Idi Amin's Shadow: Women, Gender, and Militarism in Uganda*. Athens, OH: Ohio University Press.

Mamdani, M., 1976. *Politics and Class Formation in Uganda*. Kampala: Fountain Publishers.

Omara-Otunnu, A., 1987. *Politics and the Military in Uganda, 1890–1985*. Oxford: Macmillan Press.

Otunnu, O., 2017. *Crisis of Legitimacy and Political Violence in Uganda, 1979 to 2016*. Cham: Palgrave Macmillan.

Rubongoya, J., 2016. *Regime Hegemony in Museveni's Uganda*. N.p.: Palgrave Macmillan.

Tamale, S., 2020. *WHEN HENS BEGIN TO CROW: Gender and Parliamentary Politics in Uganda*. N.p.: Routledge.

Tripp, A., 2000. *Women & Politics in Uganda*. Madison, WI: University of Wisconsin Press.

Tutu, R. and Busingye, J., 2020. *Migration, Social Capital, and Health*. New York: Springer International Publishing.

Photographic books

Bacigalupo, M., 2013. *Gulu Real Art Studio*. Göttingen: Steidl.

Mondedeu, D., 2014. *Further South Than Planned*. Algeria.

Olden, B. and Vennemann, W., 1933. *Mdisi, Bibi, Safari*. Berlin: Gebr. Mann.

Rwakoma, E., Stultiens, A. and Rumanzi, C., 2014. *Ebishushani 3 – All the Tricks*. Edam: YdocPublishing.

Stultiens, A. and Canon, R., 2014. *EBIFANANYI 6 – Duc in Altun / Dive into the Deep*. Edam: YdocPublishing.

Stultiens, A. and Mukasa, H., 2015. *EBIFANANYI 4 – Simuda Nyuma – Forward Ever, Backward Never*. Edam: YdocPublishing.

Stultiens, A., 2014. *EBIFANANYI 1 – The Photographer*. Edam: YdocPublishing.

Stultiens, A., 2014. *Ebishushani 2 – People poses places*. [Rotterdam]: HIPUganda.

Stultiens, A., 2017. *EBIFANANYI 7 – Staying Alive*. Edam: YdocPublishing.

Stultiens, A., 2017. *EKIFANANYI 8 – The King Pictured*. [Kampala]: HIPUganda.

Wambwa, M. and Stultiens, A., n.d. *PICHA 5 – Uhuru (Minor Accidents)*. Edam: YdocPublishing.

Wasswa, J. and Stultiens, A., 2019. *The Ttabo: If You Are Not in Here, No One Will Know You're Out There*. Stichting In/druk.

Other materials

Kingdon, Z. (director), 2006. *Founding a Dream: The Ruwenzori Sculpture Foundation. A Story About Cultural and Educational Exchange Between Artists in Africa and the UK*. DVD.

Acknowledgements

The organisers would like to extend sincere thanks to Luca Berta and his team at Venice Art factory. Lainya Magana and the A&O Public team, Elena Casadoro and Francesca Fungher, John Dodelande, Edoardo Ghizzoni, Alex Possati, Jeppe Curth, Michael Short, Patrick Saletta, Sam Okelo Kello from UNCC and a special light is sent to Acaye Pamela Elizabeth Kerunen for her extraordinary cultural diplomacy.

Shaheen Merali

We thank many artists, curators and colleagues for access to research and are deeply grateful to the subjects and their departments for their generous assistance. Katie Blackford, Senior Liaison Librarian -Tate Britain and St Ives, Sana Gateja, Serubiri Moses, Carolina Rito, Marianne Simon-Wagner, Femi Dawkins, Nathalie Melikian, Peter Putz of Studio Putz, Pamela Merali for proofreading and Brunna da Silva for architectural renderings.

Acaye Kerunen

I am because of so many contributors, big and small. First, my gratitude is due to Newcastle University. Through your timely curatorial fellowship, my first solo exhibition was birthed in collaboration with 32 Degrees, Afriart Gallery and Makere University. Thank you to Professor Andrew Burton, Teesa Bahana, Wanja Kimani, Professor Lilian Nabulime. 32 Degrees East team namely: Teesa Bahana, Nikissi Serumaga, Sandra Suubi for embracing me as an artist/creative, for seeing me, for showing me, for celebrating me. Daudi Karungi for mentoring me through my first solo exhibition. To Agnes Kizito and Mr.Kizito and Family, your support to me as my extended family in childcare support allowed me the grace and time to create and excel. To all the press and media: Edgar Batte, Matt Kayem, Bamuturaki Musinguzi, Katumba Badru, Natasha Khadijja Sebunya who take the time to celebrate my work through reviews, conversations and referrals. African Women In Art: Linda Mutesi and Ola Reina. To Ethel Anyu my very spirited Assistant, colleague and friend. Thank you for not needing a lot of words to understand my process. Afropocene : Martin Kharumwa , Odur Ronald, Ministry of Gender Labour and social Development for supporting myself and the pavilion, Uganda National Cultural Center (UNCC) and team, Charles Batambuze for giving me master Classes in effective lobbying, Taga Nuwagaba, for the bamboo, advice and encouragement. To all my family and meaningful friends, thank you for your part in my story.

Collin Sekajugo

When I first learned of the possibility for showcasing my work at the Venice Biennale, my mind was thrown into an array of thoughts. Not knowing exactly how to react, I was inclined to think it was too good to be true. This is the world's oldest and biggest art exhibition and participating in such a prestigious arts event was far-fetched for me especially during these times when the global art scene is caught up in a mix of unstoppable creativity and competition emerging from all corners of the world. Everyone can become an artist overnight and everything can be art. Having been recognized as one of the outstanding African creatives over the recent past and then later selected to participate in the 59 th Venice Biennale, I am overly proud of the hard work, zealousness and sacrifices that have gone into my art practice ever since I started more than a decade ago. I would like to extend my sincere gratitude to STJARNA especially Mr Bjorn Stern for the trust that you have invested in me plus the impeccable work you have done by turning what most of us thought was a mystery into a reality. Thank you Brunna da Silva and Mattie Wang for refilling my gas whenever it ran low. I can't thank you enough Ms. Acaye Kerunen for always keeping me in check and reminding me of deadlines – smiles. Your devout professionalism in ensuring that this show came fruition is so inspirational. Everyone else that has been a part of this unique journey, thank you always for believing in me.

Photo Credits

If not otherwise mentioned,
photo credits:
Maximilien de Dycker
Acaye Kerunen Studio
Collin Sekajugo Studio

Page 53 (from left):

Boy in wheelchair
Photo: Rich Legg, #157329227
Getty Images, 2008

Sir Richard Branson, Chairman of Virgin Group,
poses at a private party in Shanghai, 9 January 2008
Photo: ChinaImages

Rich woman drinking tea
Photo: Andrea Piacquadio, licensed by
Shutterstock #80317417

Works generously on loan from the collections of

Ford Phillips, New York
Victoria Golembiovskaya, London
Nicholas Collection, Herefordshire, UK
Irena Hochman Fine Art, New York
Laurie Ziegler Collection, Los Angeles
John Jonas Collection, New York
Vincent Matthu, Brussels
Boghossian Family Collection, Brussels

as well as others who wish to remain anonymous.

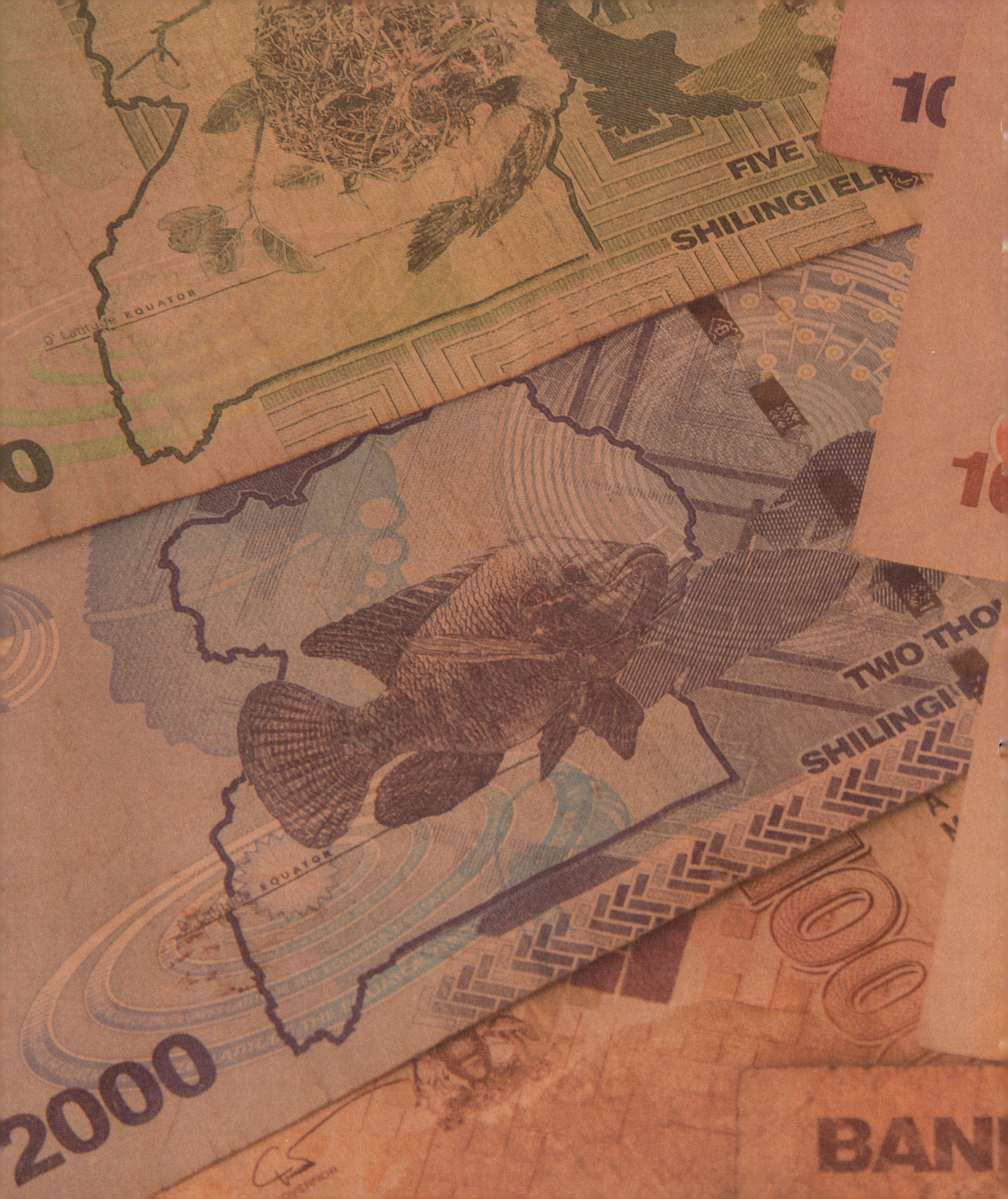

0° Latitude EQUATOR
FIVE T
SHILINGI EL
1
10
18
TWO THO
SHILINGI
0° Latitude EQUATOR
2000
100
BAN